ed ... or b...

ENSEMBLE
WORKS

ENSEMBLE WORKS

WORKS

AN ANTHOLOGY

EDITED BY

Ferdinand Lewis

THEATRE COMMUNICATIONS GROUP
NEW YORK
2005

Ensemble Works: An Anthology is published by Theatre Communications Group, Inc., 520 Eighth Avenue, 24th Floor, New York, NY 10018-4156.

This publication is made possible in part with public funds from the New York State Council on the Arts, a State Agency.

TCG books are exclusively distributed to the book trade by Consortium Book Sales and Distribution, 1045 Westgate Dr., St. Paul, MN 55114.

Library of Congress Cataloging-in-Publication Data

Ensemble works : an anthology / edited by Ferdinand Lewis
p. cm.
ISBN-13: 978-1-55936-262-7
ISBN-10: 1-55936-262-6
(alk. paper)
1. American drama—21st century. 2. Drama—Authorship—Collaboration.
I. Lewis, Ferdinand.
PS 634.2.E57 2005
812'.608—dc22
2005012827

Text and cover design by Lisa Govan

Cover collage by John Evans, from the book *John Evans: Collages*, published by The Quantuck Lane Press. Reprinted by permission of the artist

First Edition, June 2005

This book is dedicated to my son, Caleb Lewis

CONTENTS

ACKNOWLEDGMENTS

This book was made possible by the generous support of the Flintridge Foundation and Theatre Communications Group. I must also acknowledge all the ensemble theater artists and associates around the country who kindly took me into their work and into their homes and hearts. I have gained immeasurably from knowing this extraordinary group of people.

INTRODUCTION

By Ferdinand Lewis

This is an anthology of performance texts by ensemble theaters. Generally speaking, the term "ensemble theater" refers to professional theater companies that work with the same core artistic personnel over an extended period of time, creating productions in a collaborative fashion.

THE ENSEMBLE MODEL

The history of ensemble theater is in a sense the history of the theater itself, since historically the traditional theater of every continent has adhered to the ensemble production model. In America today, however, the ensemble genre exists in contrast to the dominant "Broadway" or "specialist" model of play development and production. The specialist model describes a pyramid-style organizational approach to which most American mid-size to large not-for-profit theaters currently adhere, where most of the authority in the organization resides at the top (or in the smallest part) of the pyramid. In this model, authority over the artistic process is divided among many categories of specialization, such as playwright, director, actor, producer, designer or stage manager. There is collaboration between the specialists, of course, but it is particular and specialized. Although the specialist model may streamline the administration of theater and encourage a high level of specific craft technique, it reduces the amount of artistic control that any one specialist has over the final product, and also reduces the amount of influence one craft tends to have on the others during the development process. It makes collaboration in its truest sense impossible.

In contrast, ensemble theaters tend to be composed of *generalists* who create work in full collaboration, with each contributor directly responsible for a number of production and organizational elements, if not the entire production. The artists have their specialties of training and inclination, but they are generalists where the overall product is concerned.

In this model, oversight is distributed in ways that serve an artistic process rather than an administrative hierarchy. Therefore, all elements of an ensemble production tend to have the imprint of the hands of all the artists involved. The ensemble model thus offers great flexibility. Each company can shape its production process according to artistic, rather than administrative, needs. That process can change as often as new artistic processes demand. Unique administrative and management systems can be developed for an individual ensemble production, in which a wide variety of artistic decisions, including casting, design, direction, even publicity, can be generated directly out of the artistic process rather than a prescribed organizational flowchart.

The most significant dimension of ensemble theater, though, is its relationship to the community. The stories of the theaters included in this book suggest that over time an ensemble will tend to become at some points a nexus for its community, a crossroads at which social elements can come together. To begin with, each ensemble is itself a community, whose members come to know and rely upon each other through their years of close collaboration, and the theater can naturally extend that spirit into the larger community. Because ensemble artists work collectively, it is easier for them to relate to collective enterprises in their neighborhoods, towns and cities.

Ensembles and the Mainstream Audience

Although American ensemble theater has at times been highly visible, at present the genre operates well below the mainstream cultural radar, at least since the latter half of the twentieth century. In the 1930s, the Works Progress Administration's Federal Theatre Project created and supported ensemble theaters across America, enabling them to make a high-profile, almost legendary, contribution to mainstream national culture. The sudden demise of the WPA/FTP in 1939 withdrew the national limelight from ensemble theater. No longer driven by national vision and funding, the genre retrenched into its local and regional identities. Today, most ensembles are well outside the notice of the mainstream media. Ensemble theaters that are well known and even pivotal in their own communities can be almost unknown in other regions.

Although there are a handful of ensemble theaters with national profiles in the arts community (a current sampling includes Cornerstone Theater Company, The Wooster Group and SITI Company, for example), such groups are exceptions. For decades the ensemble form has largely gone unnoticed. Ironically, there may be as many ensembles in this country as there are any other kinds of professional theater, but a significant percentage of them are based in small towns and tucked into city neighborhoods that aren't likely to show up on tourist itineraries.

Yet the ensembles represented in this anthology have a fairly steady base of audience support, which has translated into an ability to survive in an otherwise difficult funding environment. In interviews with audiences of ensemble theater around the country, I repeatedly heard great enthusiasm for the form, for a professional art made by artists who share in the local economic, political and social realities: "People we know, telling our story." Audience members who did not attend other types of theater told me that they always attend productions by their local ensembles. This struck me as particularly significant.

The Craft of Ensemble Theater

Because ensembles tend to be directly engaged with the communities that are often their subjects, the genre implies a unique and powerful partnership between artist and audience. The ensemble form allows artists and audiences to develop a deep rapport over time, and in time a community may come to include the ensemble among its cultural representatives. Within the cultural realm, ensembles can truly represent the *e pluribus unum* ideal of one voice drawn from many.

In addition, this genre also represents a desire by theater artists to develop a deep rapport with a group of fellow artists that is not generally supported in the wider culture. It is ironic that while the impulse for collaboration is prevalent among young people in college and university theater departments, most American college theater programs train students according to the specialist model, not the ensemble one. In discussions and workshops with theater instructors from around the country, it has become clear to me that a significant number of theater school graduating classes contain at least one group of young artists that wants to work collaboratively. (It was drama school chums, in fact, who founded many of the ensembles that I visited in gathering material for this book.) Unfortunately, while American higher education may have enthusiasm for ensemble work, only a few schools have been able to adapt their administrative and pedagogical structures to collaborative creation. This trend may be changing, as ensemble-created, non-Aristotelian structure. The Carpetbag Theatre's commitment to human rights is as likely to be expressed in dance or poetry as it is in the straightforward narrative form of *Nothin' Nice*. Further confounding expectations, consider that the three premier American grassroots companies that collaborated on *Promise of a Love Song*—a play about love—each feels this play to be among its most socially engaged works. Although the work of the postmodern Goat Island can be claimed as ensemble theater, there is no accounting for the artistic and intellectual ardor with which the "Goats" challenge the very meanings of performance, authorship and ensemble.

The important thing to emphasize here is the *diversity* of approaches, traditions and strategies that represent the ensemble form. Stylistically, the plays in this anthology are diverse and even disparate, like the diversifying society in which they operate. However, all of these companies have in common some combination of the ideals of collaboration, community and originality, which are the means by which a community—and a theater—can come to better know itself, and be known. A constellation of these conscious, interrelated artistic communities may describe a new hope for civil society in the twenty-first century.

Calhoun, C. J., ed. *Social Theory and the Politics of Identity*. Cambridge, MA: Blackwell Publishers (1994).

Castells, M. *End of Millennium*. Malden, MA: Blackwell Publishers (2000).

Castells, M. *The Rise of the Network Society*. Malden, Mass: Blackwell Publishers (2000).

Castells, M. *The Power of Identity*. Malden, MA: Blackwell Publishers (2003).

Held, D. *et al. Global Transformations: Politics, Economics and Culture*. Stanford, CA: Stanford University Press (1999).

Held, D. and A. McGrew, eds. *The Global Transformations Reader: An Introduction to the Globalization Debate*. Cambridge, U.K.: Polity Press in association with Blackwell Publishers, distributed in the U.S. by Blackwell Publishers (2003).

Hutton, W. and A. Giddens, eds. *Global Capitalism*. New York: New Press, Distributed by W.W. Norton (2001).

PROMISE OF A LOVE SONG

Pregones Theater

Roadside Theater

Junebug Productions

From left to right: Kim Neal Cole and Ron Short of Roadside Theater; Desmar Guevara, Ricky Sebastian, Soldanela Rivera and Jorge Merced of Pregones Theater; Waldo Chávez (on bass), Donald Harrison, Jr., John O'Neal and Adella Gautier of Junebug Productions.

JOSE J. GARCIA II

Introduction

Promise of a Love Song is a collaboration between three of America's premier grassroots ensembles, whose histories collectively represent not only a tradition of imaginative and entertaining theater, but also a heritage of engagement with cultural and human rights. I caught up with the two-year nationwide tour of *Promise* in Cincinnati, Ohio, in April of 2001. This was just a week after police there shot and killed a young man, sparking three days of riots. By the time the *Promise* cast had arrived to conduct pre-show workshops in the community, a citywide curfew was imposed and black leaders were organizing a boycott of the city. Cincinnati's municipal dirty laundry was national news, and frustration and anger were as obvious as the boarded-up storefronts in the neighborhoods near the theater.

I interviewed a "conflict management consultant" that the city had hired in the wake of the riots. When the subject of *Promise* came up, he assumed that because the theaters involved were grassroots-oriented, they would be focusing on the riots in their work. Community members and some media assumed the same. Frankly, so did I, and in so doing nearly overlooked the project's most important dimension.

Because it is known for focusing on specific cultural and community issues, the grassroots genre is often assumed to be more medicine than art. That view is far too spare, however, as collaborator/cast member Ron Short explained to me in an interview:

> People want a quick fix, but you can't say that this play is going to come and solve the problems of this community, or "Here's the formula." It's too much weight to put on anybody. The question isn't how do you deal with the riots, but how do you keep going 365 days a year, year-in and year-out, over and over. It shouldn't always be about repairing stuff that's broken, or wait until somebody dies until they say that there's a problem.

Short believes that artists—especially grassroots artists who work in a particular place and on particular issues—should commit their work to timeless themes *while* working practically, in workshops, music jams, story circles and other forms of community contact. The bottom line on which Short adds up both the timely and the timeless is this: "An artist's job is to make work that allows people to see themselves in a larger way."

After performances, I spoke with audience members who had convinced themselves that the play was specifically addressing the riots. "I'm so glad to see something like this, something about us and our situation," one woman told me. When I suggested that the play is about love, not riots, she responded, "What do you think the problem *is* out there, honey?"

In the weeks after the 1992 riots in my hometown, Los Angeles, I recall people everywhere I went—even complete strangers—finding excuses to talk to each other: in stores, at the post office, in the street. None of us quite knew what to talk about, but in our trauma we instinctively reached out for community and, looking back, I think we were all a bit ashamed that we hadn't done it before. *Promise of a Love Song* is a reminder that community, like love, need only be as far away as the next person we encounter.

—F.L.

Promise of a Love Song
is dedicated to the next generation
of ensemble artists working to create theater
that builds community and
serves the cause of social justice.

Acknowledgments

Collaborators: Dudley Cocke (Roadside Theater), Alvan Colón Lespier (Pregones Theater), Theresa Holden (Holden and Arts Associates), Arnaldo López (Documenter).

In New Orleans: Ashé Cultural Center and the Contemporary Arts Center. In Whitesburg, Kentucky, and Norton, Virginia: Appalshop and the University of Virginia's College at Wise. In New York: Hostos Center for the Arts and Culture.

Management: Holden and Arts Associates, Austin, Texas.

Co-commissioners: Lied Center for the Performing Arts (Lincoln, Nebraska), Flynn Center for the Performing Arts (Burlington, Vermont), Cincinnati Arts Association—Aronoff Center for the Arts.

Funding: Association of Performing Arts Presenters Arts Partners Program, National Endowment for the Arts, the Knight Foundation, National Performance Network, New York State Council for the Arts, New York City Department of Cultural Affairs, Arts Council of New Orleans.

Promise of a Love Song is a production of The Exchange Project, an ongoing artistic exchange among Junebug Productions, Pregones Theater and Roadside Theater.

Production Information

Promise of a Love Song was written by John O'Neal and Ron Short, with adapted text by Rosalba Rolón from "Silent Dancing" and "El Olvido," from *Silent Dancing: A Partial Remembrance of a Puerto Rican Childhood* by Judith Ortiz Cofer (Arte Público Press, Houston, 1990); and composed by Desmar Guevara; Donald Harrison, Jr.; Ricardo Pons and Ron Short. It was directed by Steve Kent and Rosalba Rolón; and the musical direction was by Ricardo Pons. The set and lighting were designed by Douglas D. Smith, the costumes were designed by Theresa Holden, the dramaturg was Rosalba Rolón, the company manager was Nicole McClendon and the executive producer was Theresa Holden. The original cast was Kim Neal Cole, Adella Gautier, Donald Harrison, Jorge Merced, John O'Neal, Soldanela Rivera and Ron Short. The original musicians were Waldo Chávez; Desmar Guevara; Donald Harrison, Jr.; Ricardo Pons; Ricky Sebastian and Ron Short.

Lyrics: "Toda una Vida," by Oswaldo Farres, 1950s, Bourne Co, c/o Ms. Beebe Bourne, 5 West 37th Street, New York, NY 10018 (page 12); "La Ultima Copa," by Juan Andrés Caruso, music by Francisco Canaro, 1926 (pages 39–40).

Setting/Set

There are three distinct playing areas: a rural Appalachian house, a New York tenement and a New Orleans shotgun house. Each area has a scrim and full curtain in front of it, which can be opened and closed as needed. The scrim depicts the locale for each playing area. Both the scrim and the curtain create various effects, such as silhouettes and lighting patterns.

There is a fourth playing area for the band, which is set upstage of the rest. There is a scrim, which can be opened or closed (but no curtain). The band area is as significant as the other three, as characters emerge from there to take on roles, and as characters from the other three playing areas engage the band throughout the piece.

Once the actors and musicians enter the stage, they remain for the entirety of the play, as the action moves seamlessly from one playing area to another. Lights, music and other effects determine the focus of the action.

ACT ONE

SCENE 1

All performers enter. A soft spot comes up on the bandstand. The musicians go to the bandstand and tune their instruments. Each male actor moves to his respective playing area: a rural Appalachian house, a New York tenement and a New Orleans shotgun house. As the banjo plays "Greenwood Sidee'o" softly, the actors in New York and New Orleans open their curtains. The rural Appalachia curtain remains closed.
    Lights fade.

SCENE 2

The soft sound of cymbals fills the stage. The cast whispers:

CAST *(In a whisper)*: Mother . . . madre . . .

    (An actor puts on an apron, slowly turning into Mother.
      Lights fade.)

SCENE 3

Lights come up on Mother in the Appalachian house. Two other women, one in the New York house and one in the New Orleans house, look on and listen to Mother. She sings a verse of "Greenwood Sidee'o":

MOTHER *(Singing to the audience)*:

> There was a lady lived in York
> All alee and lonely.
> Fell in love with her father's clerk
> Down by the Greenwood sidee'o.
> She loved him up, she loved him down
> All alee and lonely.
> Loved him till he filled her arms
> Down by the Greenwood sidee'o.

Aunt Mary Holyfield, who was my doctor that brought me into this world, taught me that song. She brought many a youngin into this world, so I reckon somehow or other that song 'bout them poor little babies that never had a chance stuck with her. It stuck with me. I thought it was the saddest, most tragic story ever. *(Sings:)*

> She bent her back against an oak
> All alee and lonely.
> First it bent and then it broke
> Down by the Greenwood sidee'o.

When I was a young girl, I'd sing it and cry for her. Mommy didn't like me singin' it, said it wasn't proper in the first place and it caused me to be too melancholy in the second. And she said that come from having too much time to think.

(Lights fade.)

SCENE 4

We hear "Donna's Paris Theme." Lights come up on the New Orleans shotgun house as Donna puts on a stole, swirls around and sings.

DONNA:

> The nighttime seemed as bright as day
> With all the lights on old Broadway
> I was overwhelmed the first time that I went there
> But New York's charms were swept away.
> When first I went to Paris
> The elegant way
> The Champs-Elysées
> Embraced the small café that lived there.

In '64 I won a scholarship to study law at the Sorbonne. Oh, what a time to be a student in Paris! I met many of the great black artists and intellectuals in exile—Richard Wright, Josephine Baker, Louis Armstrong *(Pause for trumpet's arpeggio)* and lots of others. *(Sits)* One evening, I was invited to participate in a salon that James Baldwin, "Jimmy," was hosting in his home. He was even more eloquent in real life than he was in print. He spoke of how "The Movement" had changed his life. He needed the relative freedom from American racism that he found in Europe in order to write. At the same time, as a "native son," he had to take part in the struggle for justice in America.

He also spoke of the passion of a young Movement leader in Louisiana named Nelson Hardiman. Like Baldwin, Hardiman was a brilliant high school dropout who Jimmy thought was cut from the same cloth as Malcolm X and Nelson Mandela.

("Donna's Paris Theme" ends. Background kalimba music begins as lights come up on Nelson. He is behind the New Orleans scrim, standing on a platform. The audience sees through the scrim and into the past. Donna is sitting in front of the scrim, in the present.)

NELSON *(Over background music; alive in his memory)*: When I was a kid, every time the circus came to town, me and my best buddy would be the first ones there to help set up. If they paid us fifty cents, they'd pay the white kids a dollar but we didn't care. We'd have been there if they hadn't paid a penny. We wasn't just chasing a dream, we were learning things.

They'd use the elephants to do the heavy lifting. They'd hitch the elephant to the big poles that hold the tents up, then tell him to, "Pull!" A single elephant could raise a whole tent by himself. When they didn't need that elephant anymore they'd take him off to the side and tie him up to a little stake in the ground with a little rope. And the elephant would stay there! That elephant, who could lift a whole huge tent by himself, wouldn't pull a little stake up from the ground because he was afraid to be free!

DONNA: Baldwin's stories of the passionate young hero were magnetic to me.

(Following a rhythmic beat, Nelson's voice fades as he delivers the following lines, emphasizing the word "fear" and fading the rest of the line, retreating, while Donna speaks over his fading voice.)

NELSON: *Fear!* . . . keeps us from calling a spade a spade . . .
DONNA: He was so bold.
NELSON: *Fear!* . . . keeps us riding on the back of the bus!
DONNA: Fearless!

NELSON: If these white people were truly committed to the struggle for justice, they'd be fighting against racism in the white community. I tell them to take on the Klan, the White Citizens Councils, hell, let them take on their own mamas.

DONNA: He was willing to talk about white people out loud in public the way most of us would only whisper in private. It was so liberating.

(Lights fade on Nelson. The kalimba music ends. "Donna's Paris Theme" resumes, bringing her back to the present.)

I admit, I'd been tempted by the romantic challenge of living the lush life on the Left Bank of Paris among the *Afro literati*. But after that evening at Jimmy's house I knew. A seed had been planted in me that would become my life's work. I knew I had to go back home.

("Donna's Paris Theme" ends. Lights fade.)

SCENE 5

Musicians play "Toda una Vida." Lights come up on the New York tenement house. Father sings two verses of "Toda una Vida" behind the scrim while Angela opens a trunk in front of it. She finds some letters. These letters are represented by several yards of paper rolled and tied with a red ribbon. (He sings:)

FATHER:
>Toda una vida
>Estaría contigo
>No me importa en qué forma
>Ni cómo ni dónde
>Pero junto a ti.
>
>Toda una vida
>Te estaría esperando
>Te estaría adorando
>Como vivo mi vida
>Que la vivo por ti.

(A spotlight comes up on Angela.)

ANGELA *(Reading letters)*: Dear Granma, I don't know what Mami has told you about our new life in the States. Has she told you about our apartment? It is tiny, in a huge apartment building that had once housed Jewish families, they tell me. It has just been turned into a tenement by us. *(Pause)* Hey, it is almost 1960, Puerto Ricans have arrived! So here we are in el building. Papi's doing well, with his job in the Brooklyn Navy Shipyard and all.

(To the audience) My father. My father died a long time ago. *(We can see Father's shadow behind the scrim as Angela continues reading)* He says that with myself and my brother, the military was the only option away from the sugarcane fields in the island.

(She chooses another letter.)

FATHER AND ANGELA: Querido Hermano, Las cosas por acá están bien.

(Father's voice fades as Angela continues to read:)

ANGELA: Sé que que no querías que me enlistara en el Navy, pero no había otra opción fuera de las centrales de caña, y con una esposa y dos niños. Todavía estoy asignado al Brooklyn Shipyard. *(She chooses another letter)* I like it here I guess. But everything is gray, the streets, the building, even the coat that Papi bought for me. Anyway, I'll write again soon. —Your favorite granddaughter, Angela.

(The band plays "El Recuerdo," which means remembrance, a bolero. Father comes in front of scrim and faces Angela. They move together as if dancing, looking sideways, at the outside world. Father stands on the trunk, and from his pocket he pulls out a very long strand of rolled red ribbon. He throws it over Angela's shoulder. She catches it and ties up her hair with one end of the ribbon as Father makes a tie from the other end. Then he throws the strand of letters over her shoulder, which she also catches. She reads them silently, as Father reads them out loud:)

FATHER: I continue to look for a larger apartment. Not that we are uncomfortable or anything, but I do want what's best for my family. The children are small for now, but they will need more space eventually. In the meantime, I have given strict orders to my wife to keep the doors locked, *(The bolero ends abruptly. Father looks sideways, as if looking out a window)* the noise down. Ourselves to ourselves.

("Greenwood Sidee'o" plays as the lights fade on the New York tenement and come up on the rural Appalachian house.)

SCENE 6

Billy appears behind the Appalachian scrim. We hear banjo music, while the band plays an overlapping Latin rhythm. The Latin rhythm drops out as Billy takes his place by Mother, who is sitting.

A follow spot comes up on Billy, shyly playing the notes to "Greenwood Sidee'o" on his banjo.

Father sits in the New York tenement house, writing letters; Nelson sits in the New Orleans shotgun house, reading.

MOTHER: Mommy was fifteen when she married my daddy. He was eighteen or nineteen. Had eight children all told. I was the fourth. Started out on a piece of land belonged to Daddy's daddy. I remember Mommy telling how she got water out of the head of the Pound River. It starts as a spring and gets bigger as it goes along.

(Pause. Billy and Mother's hands move together in a gesture that follows the flow of the water. Father and Nelson make subtle sounds of breathing, turning pages and handling paper.)

I was born on Big Branch in 1910. Growed up down there. Went to school at Osborne's Gap, finished up the seventh grade. *(Sings:)*

> She bent her back against a thorn
> All alee and lonely.
> There she had two wee babes born
> Down by the Greenwood sidee'o.

I married Wesley Mullins in 1926. I was sixteen years old. I had my first baby in 1927. We named him Henry. In 1929 I had a baby girl. We named her Hetty. In 1931 I had another little boy, and his name was Lewis James. In 1933 Billy was born. *(Lights up on Angela; she stares out from the New York tenement. "Greenwood Sidee'o" ends)* Then I had a daughter in 1935, and her name was Lilly. In 1937 I had another little boy, and his name was Clovis.

BILLY: Bud. *(The light on Angela fades)*

MOTHER: Bud—we called him Bud. I don't know what got into us. In 1940 I had another girl. Her name was April. We ran out of names and began using months. In 1944 we had another baby. We named him Dwight David. *(Billy sits near Mother)* Mommy had eight and I had eight. Ever' household had about that many. Some had more. They didn't pay no 'tention to it, you just raised 'em and that was it. When we first married, we lived all over the place. Last sixty years though

I've settled down some. My husband's gone now these past thirty years and the children all married off and left me, except Billy.

BILLY *(Sings)*:
> Can she bake a cherry pie,
> Billy Boy, Billy Boy?
> Can she bake a cherry pie,
> Charming Billy?

(He continues singing softly as Mother speaks:)

MOTHER: Billy was eleven when he started takin' fits. Then he started in on that singin', the same thing over and over, sometimes it didn't make any sense at all . . .

BILLY *(Sings)*:
> St. Luke, Mark and John
> Hold ole Pete while I get on.

MOTHER: Over and over till he'd jist freeze and fall over and start shakin' all over. They got worse and worse . . .

BILLY *(Sings, louder and louder)*:
> Billy Boy, Billy Boy.
> I'm a wise boy, but some boys
> Are silly.

MOTHER: Then he'd jist set fer a long time and stare out.

BILLY *(Getting up)*: This'n here don't remember. That'n says she does, so I guess she does. When it comes to it, if you can believe one, that's good. Them ain't got nothin' to do with it. Us ain't got nothin' to do with it. This'n and that'n, that's all they is.

MOTHER: He went to school till the seventh grade. He was always smart. But, the seizures got so bad and he got to where he hurt people. Pinch and hit, not cruel, I don't think, just like that singing, *(Billy sings softly)* not able to help it. And they said he couldn't go no more.

BILLY *(Overlapping slightly)*:
> Home, home on the range
> Where the deer and the antelope play
> Where seldom is heard a discouragin' word,
> A discouragin' word, discouragin' word.

Why, I asked that'n? Why?! The rest of 'em goes. That'n says this'n is goin' to a special school. So, we go.

(Lights fade on Mother and Billy and the rural Appalachian house.)

Scene 7

The band plays "Sincerely Yours/Funkily Yours." Lights come up on Donna in the New Orleans shotgun house.

DONNA *(Takes briefcase and walks from behind the scrim to downstage)*: I had to fight against smile-in-your-face racists every step of the way, but I finished Yale Law with honors in 1968 and took a job with the NAACP Legal Defense Fund.

(Lights come up on Nelson behind the scrim.)

NELSON: I stand with Mrs. Fannie Lou Hamer, who was kicked off her job as a timekeeper on a Mississippi plantation because she had the gall to go register to vote. Her byword was, "I'm sick and tired of being sick and tired!"

DONNA: The papers always showed him in some angry pose, fist clenched above his head with his mouth stretched wide. Distorted. But the more the media tried to make us hate him, the more the people loved him.

NELSON: Brother Kwame Torre's right: "The black man's got no business going to fight the yellow man to defend a country that the white man stole from the red man in the first place." *("Sincerely Yours/Funkily Yours" ends)*

DONNA: But when he came out *for* armed struggle in South Africa and the PLO, and *against* Israel and the war in Vietnam, the white power structure decided he'd gone too far. Though he hadn't even been charged with anything, Hardiman was dragged from his bed in the dead of night, beaten and held for weeks at the notorious Angola State Prison. Reluctantly, the NAACP national office agreed that we should take the case.

NELSON: They put this headstrong young woman, fresh out of law school on my case. They said that's the best they could do.

DONNA: I did all my legal homework, but I couldn't get a judge to hear the case until I got national network news to cover James Baldwin speaking about the Hardiman affair at a rally in New York.

NELSON: As it turned out, it was the best they could do.

DONNA: The very next day they let Hardiman out on bond. The road was muddy and rough but we got there.

NELSON: When the guards came to get me out of my cell I didn't know if they intended to lynch me or cut me loose.

DONNA: I knew what he looked like. I'd seen him on TV and in the papers. But I was not prepared for what happened when he stepped into the room.

(Nelson comes downstage from behind the scrim. The band plays a soft arrangement of "Sincerely Yours.")

NELSON *(Avoiding Donna's gaze)*: I felt the woman before I saw her.

DONNA: My heart began to pound. I felt faint. I wondered if the others noticed.

NELSON: What was this I was feeling?

DONNA: He acknowledged the group, then slowly he turned and he took me into a private place deep inside himself.

(They face each other.)

NELSON: When we looked at each other, I felt like she had seen me, I mean, really seen me. It was like she knew things about me before I had to say a word.

DONNA: On the backseat of the car, we sat together silently all the way back to New Orleans.

(They sit.)

NELSON: We went to my office. Worked late into the night.

DONNA: He went to the place where he'd been staying.

NELSON: I packed a few clean clothes.

DONNA: We went to my new apartment.

NELSON AND DONNA: We've been together ever since.

(They look at each other. They kiss. Lights fade on the New Orleans shotgun house as Donna hugs Nelson. She delivers a verse of "If I Could Promise You a Love Song":)

DONNA:

> If I could promise you a love song
> I'd take a meter soft and sweet and curve the words
> Until they meet the place your smile leaves off.
> I'd make a song that smiles the way you do . . .
> If I could promise you a love song.

("If I Could Promise You a Love Song" ends. Lights down on the New Orleans shotgun house.

Lights up on the New York tenement. A young Angela, with pony-tails, lovingly teases Father, who is seated on the trunk, writing letters.

In Appalachia, Mother playfully tries a new vest on Billy.

All three playing areas are now illuminated by bright pools of light.)

SCENE 8

We hear the sound of a keyboard and congas. A young Angela dances while she speaks. She is writing to her grandmother. Billy sits, cleaning his banjo; Nelson writes.

ANGELA *(Reciting her letter)*: Dear Granma, Mark today's date as my first spanking in the United States as a result of playing tunes on the pipes in my room to see if there would be an answer. *(Billy cleans the banjo and Nelson taps on his trunk, both creating heat pipe sounds)* There are these pipes, you see, they are called heater pipes. They bang and rattle, even as we sleep. I'm kind of getting used to it, so when they bang we just speak louder. *(The music builds as Angela dances. Then she sits on the floor)* The hiss from the valve makes you feel like some-one else is in the room. I say that's the dragon sleeping next to me. You know, it is curious to know that strangers live under our floor and above our heads, and that our own heater pipe goes through everyone's apart-ments. *(Music stops)* I miss our house in Puerto Rico. —Your Angela.

(The band plays a bolero. Father walks downstage from behind the scrim. Mother fixes Billy's vest. Behind the scrim, Angela caresses her father's Navy uniform while he speaks downstage, in front of the scrim.)

FATHER: Dear Brother, I have learned some painful lessons about prejudice while searching for the apartment. But I don't want to tell anybody. Maybe someday. So many of us coming over . . . things are changing in these neighborhoods and people are panicking over here. I went to look for an apartment, put on my Navy uniform to look my best. *(Nelson and Billy enter from behind the scrims and walk downstage, joining Father)* This man looks at my name tag, points his finger at it and asks, "You Cuban?" "No," I answered, looking past the finger and into his angry eyes. "I'm Puerto Rican." *(Pause. Billy and Nelson react, each in their own world)* And the door closed. *(Billy and Nelson begin to retreat. Father looks at Angela)* I wonder what will happen in this neighborhood if more Puerto Ricans continue to come here. For now, we are keeping busy with a New Year's Eve party, since we can't go to Puerto Rico. We'll have a good crowd of friends, Uncle Germán, our cousins and the kids. Our nephew will introduce his eighteen-year-old girlfriend to the family. I'll let you know how that goes. She just arrived from Puerto Rico.

(Lights fade.)

SCENE 9

The band plays "Greenwood Sidee'o." Lights with Appalachian patterns are projected over all three scrims. Mother and Billy venture out of their Appalachian world and into the other playing areas: looking, discovering and wondering. He wears the vest; she is dressed up, in a hat and blazer. They stop upstage center, in front of the band for a moment.

MOTHER *(Walking downstage center)*: Tell you the truth, this world is a big ball to me. I don't know how people ever got anywhere. I'd never been nowhere much less to a place like that university hospital, but from the time Billy was eleven till he was eighteen we went ever' three months. He had whooping cough and it affected his brain. They said they found a black streak in his brain from coughin' so hard, but they said they couldn't operate or he'd be in worser shape. If that was now, they'd do somethin', but it's too late. *(Angrily, Billy rushes off to his Appalachian home)* If he lives till fall, he'll be sixty-five.

(She observes Billy. Lights come up on Billy. He sings:)

BILLY:

To market, to market to buy a fat hog
Jiggety, jiggety, jiggety jog.

One of them said, "What's wrong with this'n?" Other'n said, "I don't know, some kind of fits. You know them hillbillies, probably married her uncle." I asked that'n if he was my pa or my uncle. She said, "Don't ask foolish questions!" At first it was fun to go, but I was glad when we quit.

MOTHER: They said there was nothin' more they could do. We could get his medicine from any doctor and I could give it to him.

(Mother takes off her hat and crosses behind the Appalachian scrim, forming a silhouette. Then lights rise on Mother. She sings a verse of "Greenwood Sidee'o":)

Then she drew out her wee penknife
All alee and lonely.
There she took those wee babes' lives
Down by the Greenwood sidee'o.

BILLY: I tried to go back to school, but that'n said no. She just wanted me to stay home and work.

MOTHER *(Enters and gives him a pot and spoon to batter)*: He'd slip off and they'd send one of the other children after me to come get him. *(Lights fade on her)*

BILLY *(Has been waiting for her to leave, then puts down the pot and spoon)*: At recess they played a game, the boys and girls together . . . housekeeping. I wanted to play housekeeping with my danged ole sweetheart Serecea . . . but she didn't want to.

(Lights up on Mother; she gives Billy back the pot and spoon, indicating that he should continue to batter.)

MOTHER: He like to wore me out. Ever' day was a rasslin' match. Tryin' to raise seven others: cook, farm, can. One day, I'd been up 'fore daylight canning beans outside in a tub. Well, this woman from the health department come by to see about Billy, and I just didn't have time to talk to her. She said, "My God. You work like a brute!"

Lord, that flew all over me. I ain't no brute. A brute is a dumb animal that has to be drove to work. Nobody drove me. I worked hard for a reason, my own reasons. Me and Billy we ain't no mindless brutes. But one day, later on up in early winter, I was feeding the livestock, and I was plumb wore out. I was cold and so tired I like to have cried. All the sheep was laying down in a stall. They looked so warm and restful all laying there together, and I real careful laid down, curled up next to 'em and they let me. I slept for 'bout an hour. When I woke up I thought, Lord that woman was right, I've become a brute. When I went back up to the house, my husband said, "Where in the world have you been? You stink like sheep."

(Mother teases Billy. The light on her fades. Billy sings:)

BILLY:
Baa, baa black sheep
Have you any wool?
Yes sir, yes sir
Don't be cruel
To a heart that's true.

(Angela is in the New York tenement, in silhouette, brushing her hair. The band plays "Bus Ride.")

Serecea started goin' to that town school and they wouldn't let me ride the bus. All them other'ns rode the bus, why couldn't I? I told that'n I wanted to marry Serecea. That'n said, "I reckon not." So I decided to ask Serecea. I went down to where them Vanover children lived. They was a whole mess of them, and I got on the bus with 'em, and I found Serecea and I set next to her all the way to town, but I couldn't git up the nerve to ask her. So we set, not sayin' nothin' and ever'body starin' at us. And when we got to town she got off and I stayed to save her seat, so's I could ask her goin' home. But some of them come an said, "Git off!" "This'n'll jist set right here, thank ye." "Fine, just set there all day then." And I did. It was hard but I did. Then come time to go home and the policeman come and said, "Git off!" And I locked hold on the seat rail in front of me, and I held on and they beat my knuckles till they bled and I held on, and one of them said, "They'll raise a fuss 'bout us beatin' up a dummy. Let's jist take the seats out." And they did, and they carried me out. All of the others was lined up outside . . . and there was Serecea in front . . . and I said . . . "Well, hello danged ole sweetheart . . ." *(The music turns discordant. Mother and Donna appear behind their scrims)* . . . and she slapped me . . . *("Bus Ride" ends. All three women stand in silhouette, as if staring out a window)* . . . hard in the face. Everybody laughed. This'n did, too.

(Billy fades from view. The women release the curtains—they close sharply.

Lights change. New York patterns appear over the scrims. Silence. All curtains open.)

SCENE 10

A teenage Angela peeks out from behind the scrim.

ANGELA: Dear Granma, You wouldn't recognize this neighborhood. *(A musician plays the congas. She enters from behind the scrim and walks downstage center)* Remember when we first moved here and you came to visit? Well, now it is mainly a Puerto Rican neighborhood. It is as if the heart of the city map was being gradually colored in brown. Papi's obsession with getting us out of here is getting to me. He doesn't want us to have friends because "we'll be moving out soon." But it is heaven for Mami.

(The band plays "Dear Granma." Angela dances all over the stage, in awe of her city's tall buildings and crowds of people. She sings:)

> Granma, let me tell you
> What it's like to live in New York.

Papi always wants us to do our grocery shopping at the supermarket when he comes home on weekend leaves, but Mami insists that she can cook only with products whose labels she can read, and so during the week I go with her to la bodega across the street from el building. Ah, and have I told you that the final "e" is not pronounced for Palmolive and Colgate the way we do it in Spanish? For years I believed that they were Puerto Rican products. Imagine my surprise at first hearing a commercial on television for Col*gate* and Palmol*ive*. I have to run. Bye. —Your favorite, Angela.

(She sings. The rest of the cast sings the chorus and dances behind the scrims.)

> Granma, let me tell you
> What it's like to live in New York.

CAST:

> Granma, let me tell you
> What it's like to live in New York.

(The cast continues to sing this refrain. Father comes from behind the scrim, wearing his Navy uniform. He stands downstage center.)

> Granma, let me tell you
> What it's like to live in New York.

("Dear Granma" ends.
Father speaks while a now adult Angela observes him, as if looking back into a memory.)

FATHER: I have devised a system of back-and-forth travel. Every time I am sent to Europe, you will go back to Puerto Rico with your grandmother. Upon my return to Brooklyn Shipyard, I will wire you, and you will come back.

(The band plays "Strangers," an Appalachian ballad, on the violin. As Angela speaks, she stares at this uniformed "image" of her Father. Then he turns around with military precision.)

ANGELA: My father was a man who rarely looked into mirrors. What was he afraid of seeing? My mother prefers to remember him as the golden boy she married. He was a sensitive man whose energies had to be entirely devoted to survival. And that is how many minds are wasted in the travails of immigrant life.

(Lights fade. The curtain is drawn.)

SCENE 11

The band plays "Sincerely Yours" with an African flair. Lights come up on Nelson and Donna behind the New Orleans shotgun house scrim. They are facing each other in silhouette. Nelson sings:

NELSON:

If I could promise you a love song
I'd cup my hands to catch the sound of clear running water
Bubbling through a bed of stone and pebble
And bring it to the sunny place that you make laughing.
I'd make a song that lights up the air the way your laughter does,
If I could promise you a love song . . .

(It's African Liberation Day, 1971. There is a musical transition into the "African Liberation Day Theme." Donna opens the curtain on the New York tenement scrim. Nelson is concluding a speech in Shakespeare Park. A crowd behind the scrims cheers him on, fists up. Shadows of the crowd are reflected on the walls.)

We've got a right to be proud of what we've done on this African Liberation Day. We're over two thousand strong here today. Next year we need to double our numbers if we want "South Africa Free by '73." 1971 is not the end. 1971 is a new beginning. But the best way we can help our brothers and sisters in Africa is to win the fight for justice here at home.

So what if it's true that white folk are guilty of making slaves of us back in the day, and ripping off the riches of Africa with colonialism. We need to understand all that, but let's not get bogged down in bitterness and anger because the future is in our hands. We're the only ones who can make ourselves free. "South Africa Free by '73."

(Lights go out on the crowd behind the scrims. Lights come up on Nelson, now in the New Orleans shotgun house. Donna enters carrying two coats and hats.)

Look at that crowd, Didi! This is the best African Liberation Day ever.

DONNA: Come on in the church office over here. Here, you need to put this on. *(Gives him a trench coat, hat and sunglasses)*

NELSON *(Makes believe he is putting them on, joking)*: What's this stuff? This ain't no Mardi Gras.

DONNA *(Putting on her coat)*: Just put it on, please. The federal court rejected our appeal. They refused to set aside your conviction. If you stay here these "crackers" will throw the book at you. So as your legal counsel I say you better get the hell out of here.

NELSON: We got people out there from every major black organization inside of two hundred miles . . . if I leave now the whole thing could fall apart.

DONNA: Any movement that depends on one man is no better than a one-man army.

NELSON: Where do you think I ought to go?

DONNA: We've got options. First stop is in Mexico. Then Cuba, Algeria, China. Here are passports, money, everything we'll need's in the car.

NELSON: They'd know you were involved. You'd lose your license to practice law.

DONNA: Attorney-client privilege, not to mention that they'd have to prove that I did something illegal. But that's all moot anyway. I'm going with you.

NELSON: Is this still my lawyer talking?

DONNA: No. It's the mother of your unborn child.

NELSON: The mother of my . . . Didi. You *gros com sa?* You don't mean I'm pregnant?

DONNA: No, fool. *I'm* pregnant.

NELSON: I'm gonna—hey, Rev! Somebody! I'm—we're going to have a baby! Come here, woman. We definitely got something to celebrate now.

DONNA: We'll have plenty of time to celebrate when we get to Mexico. Hurry up. Get changed.

NELSON: Didi . . . I can't do that. *(Takes off the sunglasses and hat)*

DONNA: You don't understand the urgency of the problem here.

NELSON: Don't ever tell me what I don't understand! Do you hear me? *(Pause)* What would I do in Cuba or Algeria or China? Or Africa far as that's concerned?

DONNA: What will you do in jail for the next thirty years?

NELSON: The same thing that Mandela's doing on Robbins Island, standing on principle.

DONNA: And what about me?

NELSON: You would not want a man who compromises on principle.

DONNA: What about our child?

NELSON: We'll love the child, Didi. That's what we'll do. And we'll teach the kid to love our people and to love the struggle for justice.

DONNA: You'll be in jail at best. What kind of father can you be sitting in jail?

NELSON *(Embracing her)*: I've got the best lawyer in the world. If they get me in jail, she won't let me stay in jail any longer than I have to, will you, baby? Come on, baby, let's go tell the people we going to have a new soldier for the revolution!

(The "African Liberation Day Theme" ends. Lights fade.)

SCENE 12

Lights come up on the rural Appalachian house. Mother is dusting the furniture with a rag. Donna is sitting in front of the New Orleans shotgun house scrim, rocking a baby, with a dim glow of light.

MOTHER: 'Bout the time Billy thought he was growed up, he wanted to go out on his own. Whenever he'd see his brothers and sisters goin' off, it was hard on him. He never saw the difference between him and them. I tried my best to explain it, but I don't understand either. *(She sits. Pause)* There are some things in this life we are not meant to understand. You don't have to understand ever'thing for it to be so and have a place in this world. Maybe that's what God is . . . understanding. *(She comes from behind the scrim and walks downstage)* One of my daughter-in-laws was here one time and I had 'bout a six-foot black snakeskin layin' out on the walk. I told her I found it under the house where I keep my taters. "Lord, have mercy, you mean there's a six-foot black snake living under your house? I would not stay here one minute. How can you live knowing that?" Ever'thing don't exist for my use and purpose. Some things have meaning beyond my knowing 'bout it. That snake's one of 'em. But I admit, if I run up on him, he's liable end up dead, 'cause I reckon they's things about me that snake don't understand either. *(She returns to behind the scrim. Lights fade on her and Donna)*

(Lights up on Billy singing:)

BILLY:

> Dim lights, thick smoke
> And loud, loud music.

You'll never make a wife
To a home-lovin' man.

There was one of them women in town and she had big breasts that she showed half of 'em and I was there one day gettin' a hot dog and a Grapette and she bent over and I pinched her on the breast and she screamed real loud and a man run up and this'n hit him in the pit of the stomach with my balled-up fist and he got this funny look on his face, and fell over. And this'n started laughing and the woman was screaming and this'n pinched the other'n and she slapped me and I grabbed her an squeezed her real tight till her breasts popped out . . . *(Lights up on Mother, who stares at him)* . . . and everybody was hollerin' and this'n felt so good . . .

(The band plays an instrumental bolero. Billy picks up his banjo and hugs it as though he is dancing with it. As he swings around he sees Mother, who has continued to watch him. He realizes she has heard him and he moves to the background shyly.)

MOTHER: They told me if he come back, they had no course but to put him in jail. The doctor said his body was changin' and all they could do was change his medicine and maybe it would help, but ever'body but me was afraid of him. *(She sings:)*

She rubbed the knife against her shoe
All alee and lonely.
The more she rubbed the redder it grew
Down by the Greenwood sidee'o.

(She sits.)

The longest I've ever been away from him was three weeks when my oldest girl got real sick and I had to go stay with her. He whipped all his brothers. The girls left and stayed with family. Rocked my husband for half a day, kept him penned up in the barn. When I come home Wes said, "Next time we're jist gonna burn the place down and come with you."

(Lights come up on Billy, standing, clutching his banjo, singing softly:)

BILLY:
Yes, I've been around the world,
But I never found no girl.
I'm a wise boy, but some boys are silly.

MOTHER: Some boys are just silly.

(Lights fade on them. Lights rise on Donna, who is seated in front of the New Orleans shotgun house scrim, holding the baby. A jail pattern is projected over the scrim. Nelson is behind the scrim, in "jail," reading a book.)

DONNA: Some boys are just silly. *(Sings:)*

> Hush little baby
> Don't you cry
> You know your daddy's bound to die
> All our trials will soon be over.

(Lights fade. Lights rise on Father behind the New York tenement scrim. Angela walks from behind the scrim to downstage. She watches her father, as if into a memory.)

FATHER: Estoy tratando de que nos asimilemos lo mejor posible. Acabo de comprar y cargar un arbol de Navidad cinco pisos hasta nuestro apartamento y ustedes son los únicos en el building que reciben regalos de Navidad y de Día de Reyes. Además tenemos el mayor de los lujos . . . nuestro propio televisor. Hey, ya estamos en los '60s. *(A Musician plays the chords of "Middle America" from behind the rural Appalachian house scrim)* We are one of the first families in the barrio to have a television set. And it keeps you kids inside the house. Compared to our neighbors in el building, we are rich. The Navy check is better than a factory check. The only thing is . . . I still can't buy a place away from the barrio. My greatest wish.

(A Musician enters, playing the guitar.)

ANGELA: His greatest wish was Mami's greatest fear . . . to live away from the barrio! The TV did help to keep us quiet inside the apartment. I loved the family series. My favorite was *Bachelor Father*, where the father treats his adopted teenage daughter like a princess because he is rich and has a Chinese houseboy to do everything for him. Then there was *Father Knows Best* and *Leave It to Beaver*. It was like a map of Middle America. *(Walks to trunk and stands on it)*

(Lights fade.)

Scene 13

Spotlight on a Musician. He sings:

MUSICIAN:
> The lives we live
> Are paid for by our children.
> The dreams we dream
> Slowly fade away.
> Still, we dance each dance
> Like it was the first time,
> But the fiddler's waiting
> And he has to be paid.
> Deep in the heart
> Of Middle America
> There's a two-for-one sale,
> A midnight madness jubilee.
> You can get it all here,
> Love, hope and happiness.
> It's all for sale,
> Satisfaction not guaranteed.

(Lights come up on the New Orleans house. The Musician walks over to Donna, who sits holding the baby as she sings:)

DONNA:
> There are some things
> We can never understand,
> How a man loves a woman
> And a woman loves a man.
> Are angels real?
> Does God really have a plan?
> How can some people live
> And never seem to give a damn?

DONNA AND MUSICIAN:
> Deep in the heart
> Of Middle America
> There's a two-for-one sale,
> A midnight madness jubilee.
> You can get it all here,
> Love, hope and happiness.

It's all for sale,
Satisfaction not guaranteed.

(Lights come up on the New York tenement. Father is singing. The Musician walks over and joins him.)

FATHER AND MUSICIAN:
This is not my home,
I'm a stranger here.
Wherever I travel,
I carry my home there.
This is not my voice,
No one listens anymore.
Deep in my heart I hear
A song from the other shore.

CAST:
Deep in the heart
Of Middle America
There's a two-for-one sale,
A midnight madness jubilee.
You can get it all here,
Love, hope and happiness.
It's all for sale,
Satisfaction not guaranteed.

(Blackout.)

ACT TWO

Scene 1

The playing area curtains are closed. There is a banjo placed on the trunk in front of the rural Appalachian house scrim. There are folded letters placed on the trunk in front of the New York tenement house scrim. And there is an open horn case placed on the trunk in front of the New Orleans shotgun house scrim. A spotlight rises on an Appalachian musician. He plays an Irish drum. He freezes. Spotlight fades. A spotlight rises on a Puerto Rican musician as he plays the congas in front of the New York tenement scrim. He freezes. Spotlight fades. A spotlight rises on an African American musician as he plays a tambourine in front of the New Orleans shotgun house scrim. He freezes. Spotlight fades. A spotlight rises on a drummer in the band as he plays a trap set. A keyboardist and bass player join in and play the "Act Two Overture." As the musical number reaches its peak, the cast members enter and take their places behind their respective scrims. The band plays "Mardi Grasly Yours." Donna sings over the music:

DONNA *(In silhouette behind the scrim)*:
    If I could promise you a love song
    I'd take the time to count the ways that love makes music,
    I'd take the days and stretch them out before your very feet,
    I'd take the nights' soft velvet sheets

Scene 2

Lights rise on the New York tenement. Father looks through the letters. He begins to read one:

FATHER: My Dearest Brother, You are going to miss a great New Year's Eve party. On Saturday the whole family will walk downtown to shop at the big department stores on Broadway. I admit that it's easier to go shopping in el barrio, where your face does not turn a clerk to stone. Where our money is as green as anyone else's. I'll buy a dark suit for the occasion. It's going to be a big celebration, and everyone is excited because my wife's brother has bought a movie camera, which he will be trying out that night. I wish you were here with us. Better yet, I wish we were in Puerto Rico, with you. —Your dearest brother.

(The band plays "Toda una Vida" as Father and Angela dress up for the party. Father wears a suit with a vest and a hat. Angela, her hair tied into a ponytail with a red ribbon, wears a scarf around her hips and a white, faux fur stole. "Toda una Vida" ends. They both sit on the trunk.)

ANGELA: We have a home movie of this party. Several times my mother and I have watched it together. It is grainy and short. And it is in color. The only complete scene in color I can recall from those years. The movie opens with a sweep of the living room.

(Movie music. Spotlights flicker, creating a "movie effect."
As Angela continues, Mother becomes visible behind the rural Appalachian scrim, rocking in silhouette. Angela comes from behind the scrim and walks downstage. Father stands on the trunk and pulls out a roll of red ribbons. He throws the ribbon toward Angela. She catches the ribbon and then lets it drop to the floor. Then he throws a second one, and so on . . .)

It is typical immigrant Puerto Rican decor for the time: the sofa and chairs are upholstered in bright colors, covered in transparent plastic. The linoleum on the floor is light blue. There are dime-sized indentations all over it, victim of the spike heels.

(Caught up in her story, she describes the flickering silent movie and lives it all at once. Father stands in front of the trunk, with gestures of handshakes and smiles.)

The room is full of people dressed in mainly two colors: dark suits for the men, red dresses for the women. We were dressed up like child models in the Sears catalog. My brother in a miniature man's suit and bow tie, and I in black patent leather shoes and a frilly dress with several layers of crinolines underneath. The women in red sitting on the couch are my mother and my eighteen-year-old cousin. My cousin has grown up in Paterson and is in her last year of high school. She doesn't have a trace of "la mancha," the mark of the new immigrant. She is wearing a tight, red-sequined cocktail dress. *(She and Father sit on the trunk)* Her brown hair has been lightened with peroxide around the bangs and she is holding a cigarette very expertly between her fingers.

(Silhouette of Mother fades.)

FATHER *(Walking downstage)*: She can pass for an American anywhere—at least for Italian, anyway. Her life is going to be different. She has an American boyfriend. He is older and has a car. If she marries him, even her name will be American. *(Returns to the trunk and sits next to Angela)*

ANGELA: For years I've had dreams and nightmares in the form of this home movie. Familiar faces pushing themselves forward into my mind. Like this old woman whose mouth becomes a cavernous black hole I fall into. And as I fall I can feel her laughter.

(The band plays "Old Woman" as Angela becomes the old woman of her nightmares. They walk downstage close together, in the same rhythm, speaking simultaneously:)

FATHER AND ANGELA:

> Your cousin is pregnant by that man
> She's been sneaking around with.
> Would I lie to you?
> I was not invited to this party,
> But I came anyway.
> Your cousin was growing a *gringuito* in her belly
> She put something long and
> Pointy into her pretty self.
> Hmmm?
> And they probably flushed it down
> The toilet.
> The father does not want that baby.
> He is growing real children,
> With a wife who is
> A natural blond.
> And guess where your cousin will end?
> Hmmm?

She'll be sent to a small town
In Puerto Rico.
A real change in scenery.
La Gringa, they'll call her over there.
Ha, ha, ha.
La Gringa is what she always wanted to be!

(The nightmare ends. Lights fade.)

Scene 3

A soft light comes up on the band. Donald, now a successful musician, steps downstage playing "Serenade." A spotlight comes up on him.

He crosses to the Appalachian house where a soft glow illuminates Mother and Billy exchanging gifts. She gives him an orange. He gives her a red ribbon for her hair.

Lights fade as Donald crosses to the New York tenement, where lights come up on Father and Angela. She is sitting on the trunk, where Father places a small package of old letters tied with red ribbon. He leaves. Donald continues to play for Angela.

Lights fade, then come up on the New Orleans shotgun house, where Donald now plays. Nelson and Donna sit together. "Serenade" ends. The spotlight on Donald fades.

It is Christmas 1998.

DONNA: Donald! This makes my holiday complete! You're supposed to be on tour with the band.

DONALD: I am, but I arranged a layover so I could see you guys for a couple of hours. Where've you been? I thought I was going to miss you.

DONNA: We were with Cousin Maudine and her family, celebrating Kwanzaa. She's got the sweetest little grandchild.

NELSON: Hey, it's great that you're here. I'm doing a fundraiser on "Creativity Night." You can be our guest star.

DONALD: I'm really sorry, Pops. I've got to split tonight. I'm headlining a benefit on New Year's Eve for the South African Children's Fund.

NELSON: Oh, I see.

DONNA: That's wonderful, dear.

DONALD: Yeah, yeah. Yo, dig. There're a couple of things I want to drop on y'all. This is for you, Pops. *(Hands him an envelope)*

NELSON: What's this?

DONALD: Go on. Open it.

NELSON: What in the world . . . ?

DONALD: You know my latest album, *Star Crossed Lovers*, it went platinum last week. That's practically unheard of in jazz, so I'm doing all right. So, Pops, considering how hard you've worked all your life to keep the All African People's deal afloat, I told my agent to sign the royalties from this album over to you. That's your first payment.

NELSON: I don't know what to say.

DONNA: "Thanks," is what people normally say in a situation like this.

NELSON: Thanks, son. *(They embrace)*

DONALD: I thought it would let a little pressure off you, Mom. *(Kisses Donna)* The other thing I wanted you guys to know is that I'm planning to get married.

(The band plays a soft conga and bass rhythm.)

DONNA: Oh, baby, that's wonderful!

NELSON: Who is the lucky girl?

DONNA: Do we know her?

DONALD: Nah, I don't think so. Here's her picture. I met her in New York. She hasn't come down here yet. She's dying to find out about New Orleans though.

DONNA *(Looking at the picture)*: Donald, you're not serious about this, are you?

NELSON: What's wrong?

DONNA: What's wrong?!

DONALD: There it is!

DONNA: This is a white girl! That's what's wrong!

DONALD: She's not white.

DONNA: Natural blond and baby blue. If she's not white you have a real serious problem 'cause "creole wannabes" are worse than "real white folk."

NELSON: Let's try to get a handle on the big picture here.

DONNA: Nelson, you take your handle and stick it where the sun won't shine. I didn't struggle through life to raise what I thought was a strong, intelligent black man to have him run off with some no-count white girl.

NELSON: Donna . . .

DONALD: She's not white, Mom. She's Puerto Rican.

(The conga-bass rhythm ends.)

DONNA: That makes a whole lot of difference, huh!

NELSON: The African cultural influence is very strong in Puerto Rican culture. They have a whole different take on race. I have some very strong comrades in the Movement . . .

DONNA: This is not about some abstract movement. This is about my son. And I don't want half-white grandchildren not knowing what they are or who they are.

NELSON: It's not a question of skin color, Donna, it's a question of consciousness. Does she understand the relationship between class, race and the struggle for justice? What does she think about—

DONALD: She thinks I love her! And I think she loves me. And that wraps it. This is my life. I'm not just the focus of your arguments about politics. I'm flesh and blood and feelings. And I'm a horn player, a jazz man. That's all. *(Donna turns her back on Nelson and Donald)* Look, I love you guys, but I got to go. I'll let you know when the wedding is. I guess we'll have to do it in New York. If you think you can handle it, you'll be welcome. I won't bring her down here till I feel like you'll be comfortable with her.

(Donald moves to leave, but Nelson makes a pleading gesture for him to come closer to his mother. Donald gives her a quick kiss. She does not respond. He exits.)

DONNA: Where did I go wrong? Lord knows I did the best I could do. I needed more help from you.

NELSON: You sound like it's all over. We're not done yet. *(Comes closer, tries to embrace her softly)*

DONNA: Aren't we?

(Lights fade.)

SCENE 4

Lights rise on the rural Appalachian house. Mother and Billy are arguing.

BILLY *(Chasing Mother around, agitated)*: You think them's not this'n don't you. This'n couldn't be that or know 'bout this or understand that . . . why not? Why can't I be anybody? I got no job, no children, no wife, house, no past, no future. *(Mother leaves the house, crossing upstage to face the band)* If this'n is whatever you think I am, then why can't I be whatever I think I am. Why can't this'n? *(Lights fade on Billy. Mother remains with the band)*

(Lights rise on the New York tenement house. Father is singing "La Ultima Copa," a cappella:)

FATHER:

Eche, amigo, no más; écheme y llene,
Hasta al borde la copa de champán
Que esta noche de farra y alegría
El dolor que hay de mi alma quiero ahogar.
Es la última farra de mi vida,
De mi vida, muchachos, que se va,
Mejor dicho que se ha ido tras de aquella,
Que no supo mi amor nunca apreciar.

(He continues to sing as a spotlight rises on Mother. She sings "Green-
wood Sidee'o," a cappella, overlapping with Father.)

MOTHER:

Then she returned to her father's hall
All alee and lonely.
Saw two babes a-playing at ball
Down by the Greenwood sidee'o.
O babes, O babes if you were mine
All alee and lonely.
I'd dress you up in scarlet fine
Down by the Greenwood sidee'o.

Besides the Lord, it is this land that has been the most comfort to me.
And it is Billy who has helped me to stay here. The only time my husband ever spoke directly to me in forty-four years, to tell me to do
somethin', was to buy this land when we got the chance. Land is about
raising family, generation after generation; not just its coal, timber,
ground for one generation to use up. You don't say I'll be a mother till
this child goes off on its own, then I won't be its mother. It ain't no
short-term thing . . . I'll live here on this land till I don't need it no
more, then I'll jist stop caring for it?

FATHER: Dear Brother, It was a great party after all. Lots of food, *pasteles,*
gandules, and the rice with the real *sofrito* you sent up from the island.
We can never find *sofrito* here. Maybe someday we'll sell the stuff ourselves. Oh, there was lots of rum, lots of Palo Viejo, lots of domino . . .
the more we played and drank, the more we cried. I didn't cry, nor drink.
But you know, at midnight some people were reminded of the island by
the smells in the kitchen, you know . . . Oh, and the music. We played
Daniel Santos, Felipe Rodríguez . . . *(Sings:)*

Eche, amigo, no más; écheme y llene,
Hasta al borde la copa de champán

Loved him till he filled her heart
Down by the Greenwood sidee'o.

(*Mother rests her head on Billy's shoulder. Lights fade on the rural Appalachian house.*

Silhouettes and patterns come up on all three scrims: Billy and Mother face each other, joining hands; Father and Angela face each other, with her standing at a distance; Donna and Nelson stand side by side.)

DONNA AND NELSON (*Sing*):
The price of peace is charged in blood
And this a time for struggle,
When love songs made of fluffy stuff turn dry and brittle
Blow away.
What good's a parasol in heavy rain?
A dainty cake to starving masses?
Did crazed Nero stain his place in time
With Love's lyric?
All light unweighted things
Like feathers, flutter in the wind.

(*Lights fade.*)

SCENE 7

Father is dressed in white behind the New York tenement scrim. Angela sits on the trunk, her back to the audience, looking at her father.

FATHER: It is a dangerous thing to forget the climate of your birthplace, to choke out the voices of dead relatives when in dreams they call you by your secret name. It is dangerous to use weapons and sharp instruments you are not familiar with. (*Slowly takes off his white hat and suit*) It is dangerous to disdain the plaster saints before which your mother kneels, praying with embarrassing fervor, that you survive in the place you have chosen to live. (*Lights fade on Father*)
ANGELA: Jesús, María y José. To forget is a dangerous thing.

(*Nelson comes from behind the New Orleans scrim and crosses to Angela. She gets up and joins him. They address the audience:*)

NELSON: Read these living words.
ANGELA: Love the lives these words are made of.

NELSON: Know these lives to be your own,
ANGELA: And then, you'll know a love song.

ANGELA AND NELSON *(Sing)*:
    Made of sweat and bread and blood.
    You sing the tune you know I would
    If I could promise you a love song.

(Lights rise on a Musician, who enters playing guitar.)

ALL *(Sing)*:
    If you were me
    And I was you,
    Would I still do
    The things I do?
    Would you still say
    The words you say?

    Would we feel joy?
    Would we feel pain?
    Would every day
    Still start the same,
    A hope and a prayer
    For a love that's true?
    If you were me
    And I was you.

    There is no cure,
    No magic pill
    That can change
    Every ill.
    But . . . maybe
    If we could see
    What it's like
    To be you and me.

    If you were me
    And I was you
    Would I be black,
    Would you be blue,
    To see what life
    Put me through?
    What would you do?

HARD COAL: LIFE IN THE REGION

Bloomsburg Theatre Ensemble

"When I Go to America" (from left to right): Tom Byrn, Daniel Roth, Peter Brown and Seth Reichgott.

GERARD STROPNICKY AND MARLIN WAGNER

Introduction

In 1976, a group of young actors came to tiny Bloomsburg, Pennsylvania, to study with the legendary acting teacher Alvina Krause, who had retired there. Although Krause had trained a number of actors who went on to great success in Hollywood and New York, she in fact believed that "theater must be built on a bedrock of concern for the community." Krause's last protégés took her up on that: as the Bloomsburg Theatre Ensemble (BTE), they have made professional theater in their rural, largely blue-collar hometown (population 8,000) in the foothills of the Poconos for the past twenty-five years. Krause's community philosophy remains at the core of BTE's mission.

Over time, an ensemble assumes an investment in its community, as the community assumes investment in its ensemble. Although this can be true in urban as well as rural ensembles, it may be more obvious among the country cousins. (I'm also thinking of the Appalachian audience members who, when watching Roadside Theater's shows based on local history, felt free to stand up and correct the actors if they felt the play got a fact wrong.) Researching an article for *American Theatre* some years back, I asked BTE's co-founder Laurie McCants what sort of feedback the ensemble gets from the local community. "It's very direct," she said, laughing. "Our post-show discussion groups take place on Main Street."

Local audience members, seeing theater made by the familiar faces of their long-standing ensemble, may find it easier to invite the play's ideas and themes into the context of their own lives. This is important because theater offers its audience the experience of examining the underlying significance of the ordinary events of life. A community that supports a long-standing professional ensemble can thereby make a real contribution to its own sense of identity, purpose and meaning. Of course the ensemble has an awesome responsibility in that relationship as well. BTE sees itself as the community's court fool, which is to say the speaker of truth and revealer of wounds that others may fear to name. "The audience feels challenged by us, and so they're loyal," McCants says.

BTE received national media attention in 1996 when it premiered *Letters to the Editor*, an original piece based on letters to the local newspapers dating back to Bloomsburg's first settlers. Although *Letters* had an irresistible charm, it also expressed the darker dimensions of small-town attitudes, which was provocative to local audiences.

Similarly, *Hard Coal* is an original, ensemble-created work that documents the rise and fall of the culture born of Pennsylvania's anthracite coal boom. While celebrating the region's deep roots, the play does not spare its audience the realities of the brutally overworked class from which many Bloomsburg citizens are descended.

—F.L.

ACKNOWLEDGMENTS

We would like to thank all those who contributed their time, tales, expertise and enthusiasm to *Hard Coal*: the ensemble, staff and trustees of BTE; our collaborators Karen Bamonte, Guy Klucevsek and Rand Whipple, who brought provocation and vision to the piece; and our designers April Bevans, A. C. Hickox and F. Elaine Williams for their evocation of time and place.

For music and lyrics: "Nightfall," music by Guy Klucevsek, lyrics by Guy Klucevsek, from the writings of Nicho Allen; "Mauch Chunk Mountain," music by Guy Klucevsek, lyrics by Guy Klucevsek, from the writings of Philip Ginter; "Abraham Williams," music by Guy Klucevsek, lyrics from an advertisement by Abraham Williams in the *Luzerne Federalist*, March 1805; "Air Apparent," music by Guy Klucevsek; "When I Go to America," arranged by Guy Klucevsek, from a Serbian folk song, lyrics traditional; "The Hudson Coal Company Trio," music by Guy Klucevsek and cast, lyrics from "Handling Explosives," from *Handbook for Miners* (International Correspondence Schools, 1928); "Over the Coals," music by Guy Klucevsek, lyrics from a poem by James Sweeney Boyle, ca. 1910; "Avondale Mine Disaster," music by Guy Klucevsek, from an American folk song, lyrics traditional, 1869; "Women's Work Fugue: Spin Cycle," music by Guy Klucevsek; "Miner's Lament/Down in a Coal Mine," music by Guy Klucevsek, lyrics by J. B. Geoghan, for an 1872 stage show; "Soup Song," music by Guy Klucevsek, lyrics by Laurie McCants and Guy Klucevsek, from Eckley Miner's Village "Ethnic Mosaic" cookbook; "Old Miner's Dance," music by Guy Klucevsek; "Hey, Love," music by Guy Klucevsek, lyrics adapted by Guy Klucevsek, from a poem by Ondrej Kostovcik, ca. 1885 (from family memoirs supplied by Matthew Stretanski); "Old Miner's Refrain," arranged by Guy Klucevsek, lyrics traditional; "Tunnel Running," arranged by Guy Klucevsek, from the Slovak-American folk song "The Lonely Miner of Wilkes-Barre"; "Me Johnny Mitchell Man," music by Guy Klucevsek, lyrics by Con Carbon, 1902; "Mitchellisms," music by Guy Klucevsek, lyrics by Guy Klucevsek, from the writings of Johnny Mitchell; "Baer (Naked) Truisms," music by Guy Klucevsek, lyrics by Guy Klucevsek, from a letter by George Baer to

William Clark, July 1902; "I Want to Be Born," music by Guy Klucevsek, lyrics adapted by Laurie McCants, from "The Hymn of Jesus" (*The Acts of John*), translated by Robert Bly.

————

Bloomsburg Theatre Ensemble would like to thank the following for their support: the Pennsylvania Anthracite Museum Complex (Chester Kulesa of the Anthracite Heritage Museum, Scranton; William Gustafson of the Museum of Anthracite Mining, Ashland; Keith Parrish of Eckley Miner's Village, Weatherly); the Blaschak Coal Company, Mahanoy City; the Bloomsburg School of Dance; the Bureau of Deep Mine Safety (Pennsylvania Department of Environmental Protection), Pottsville; the Children's Museum, Bloomsburg; the Institute for Cultural Partnerships, Harrisburg; the F. M. Kirby Center for the Performing Arts, Wilkes-Barre; Knoebels Amusement Park and Resort, Elysburg; the National Mine Health and Safety Academy, Beckley, West Virginia; the No. 9 Mine Wash Shanty, Lansford; Sedesse's Coal Museum, Lykens; WVIA-FM (Erika Funke); and the Luzerne County Historical Society.

We would also like to thank the following individuals: Leonard Ciszek of Shenandoah Valley Middle School; Marge Killian, for collecting email; Carmen Latona of Wyoming Area High School; Sally Teller Lottick; Harry Martenas; Chris Ring, creator of *Carbon Knight*; Joseph G. Rudawski of MMI Preparatory School; Dr. Lew Santini; Matthew Stretanski, for permission to use Ondrej Kostovcik's poem for "Hey, Love;" and Ken Wolensky, coauthor of *The Knox Mine Disaster*.

The Pennsylvania Council on the Humanities provided funding for consultation with these experts: Harold Aurand of Penn State, Hazleton; Perry Blatz of Duquesne University; Stephen Couch of Penn State, Schuylkill Haven; Trude Check-Tuhy and Philip Tuhy of the Slovak Heritage Society of NEPA; Richard J. Donald, retired miner and educator; Thomas Dublin of SUNY Binghamton; William Gustafson of the Museum of Anthracite Mining, Ashland; George Harvan, photographer; Ben Marsh of Bucknell University; and George Turner, professor emeritus of Bloomsburg University.

PRODUCTION INFORMATION

Hard Coal: Life in the Region was created and directed by James Goode and Laurie McCants. The music and lyrics were by Guy Klucevsek, the choreography was by Karen Bamonte, the projection design was by Rand Whipple, the set design was by F. Elaine Williams, the costume design was by April Bevans, the lighting design was by A. C. Hickox and the production stage manager was Jennifer Smith.

The cast included Peter Brown, Tom Byrn, Elizabeth Dowd, Samantha Phillips, Seth Reichgott and Daniel Roth, with McCambridge Dowd-Whipple, Grier Wilt, Brian Burrows, Zach Ferro, Laura Mazol and Andrea Solomon. The musicians were Guy Klucevsek (accordion) and Dillon Wright-Fitzgerald (violin).

The creation and production of *Hard Coal: Life in the Region* was supported by funding from AT&T, the Rockefeller Foundation, the Mid Atlantic Arts Foundation "Artist as Catalyst" program, Meet The Composer, the Pennsylvania Humanities Council and Theatre Communications Group/Metropolitan Life Foundation.

CHARACTERS

The play is performed by an ensemble of four adult men, two adult women, a female teenager and a young girl and boy. The following historical figures appear in the play:

NICHO ALLEN, PHILIP GINTER AND JAMES TILGHMAN, eighteenth-century settlers, each credited with the discovery of anthracite in Pennsylvania.

ABRAHAM WILLIAMS, Welsh immigrant who advertised his mining skills in a Wilkes-Barre newspaper in 1805.

MRS. JOHN FLANIGAN, nineteenth-century British immigrant.

DAVID DAVIES, nineteenth-century Welsh immigrant.

REVEREND PHILLIPS, early twentieth-century minister who served men and boys in the coal fields.

MRS. O. W. SEABERG, high-society coal baron's wife, 1930s.

JOHNNY MITCHELL, influential and revered union organizer who at age twenty-two, in 1898, became president of the United Mine Workers.

GEORGE BAER, railroad magnate; leader of the anthracite operators during the 1902 strike.

PVT. STEWART CULIN, officer in the Coal and Iron Police (private forces hired by company owners).

WILLIAM F. CLARK, clergyman and miners' advocate who corresponded publicly with George Baer.

THEODORE ROOSEVELT, twenty-sixth president of the United States (1901–1909).

SOPHIA COXE, prominent coal operator's wife, called "The Angel of the Anthracite Fields" because of her philanthropic work.

All other characters are fictionalized versions of miners, their families and descendents, reporters, mining operation owners and coal region residents.

SETTING/SET

The set evokes a Pennsylvania coal town; structures of rough-hewn wood with doors and windows suggest the simple "company houses" of the miners and their families. Sheets of corrugated metal are sometimes lowered from above; on these, and on the sides of the "houses," projections of photographs or illustrations, indicated in the script as "image," and captions for scenes, indicated as "title," are displayed.

At the opening of the play, there is a laundry line stretched across the space, filled with clothes that suggest the lives of the people who lived in these towns: work clothes, nightgowns, "Sunday best" shirts. These clothes will serve as a projection screen later in the piece. There is also a large, rolling, two-level set of steep wooden steps, with a platform above and a platform below. At times, characters enter and exit from a trapdoor center stage. This is rolled on and offstage at various points during the play.

Buckwheat, pea, chestnut, stove, egg and steamboat. These are a few of the names given to the various sizes of anthracite coal as it is sorted and shipped to consumers. Each size has its own value in the marketplace.

As we explored the heritage of the anthracite region, we discovered stories of various sizes: from small "buckwheat" voices to large "steamboat" epics. Each story, too, has its value, and there were so many stories that selection was very difficult. Our criteria came from our sense of responsibility: as residents of this region, to be objective, and as contemporary artists, to be fantastic.

The impetus for *Hard Coal* was born as we traveled around Northeastern Pennsylvania taking our educational touring shows to schools all over the region. The fading legacy of anthracite was all around us, yet we were surprised that most young people had no knowledge of the industry that brought their grandparents to this country. Indeed, textbooks on Pennsylvania history often had no mention of anthracite. Our first stage exploration of the culture was *Patchworks: Life and Legends of the Coal Towns*, which toured regional schools in 1997 and showcased at the Network of Ensemble Theatre Festival in 1999. That project inspired us to create for our mainstage *Hard Coal*, a multimedia music-theater piece developed from documentary source material.

One of the more recent historical events depicted in *Hard Coal*, the story of Centralia, is well known to residents of Northeastern Pennsylvania. Centralia was once a booming coal town not far from Bloomsburg. In the 1960s, a fire at the town dump ignited an outcropping of coal. The fire spread underground, eventually under the entire town. A federal buyout program relocated all but a few die-hard residents. Today, Centralia is only a crossroads with a few scattered houses, and smoke rising from the ground as the fire continues to burn. For this sequence we used images from *Carbon Knight*, a regional comic book set in Centralia, written by Chris Ring.

There are two events whose exclusion from *Hard Coal* deserves comment. We did not cover the "Molly Maguires," the secret society of Irish immigrant miners, because their story has been told often and well. And one day we hope to bring to the stage the fascinating drama of the Lattimer Massacre of 1897, when nineteen Eastern European miners, who were striking, were gunned down by civil authorities.

ACT ONE

A Schoolgirl emerges from behind the clothesline. She is in a contemporary Catholic school uniform, giving a class report.

SCHOOLGIRL: Anthracite. A-N-T-H-R-A-C-I-T-E.

      Anthracite is a type of coal which is ninety to ninety-eight percent carbon. It was formed during the Carboniferous Age three hundred and sixty million years ago, when this part of the world was covered by a great swamp.

      (Holding up a sample) Here is a piece of anthracite. As you can see, it has a shiny surface. It is difficult to light, but once it is lit it burns with a beautiful pale blue flame, which doesn't need a lot of attention to keep burning. Of all the different types of coal, anthracite is the one that gives off the greatest heat value, making it the most valuable of all the coals. However, it is also the least plentiful. Almost all of the world's anthracite supply is found in nine counties of Pennsylvania.

      Anthracite is also known as *hard coal.*

(She holds the anthracite before her. Three colonial men, dressed in eighteenth century attire—James Tilghman, Nicho Allen and Philip Ginter—emerge from the darkness, regarding the anthracite with curiosity and wonder.)

JAMES TILGHMAN: On the banks of the Susquehanna has been found a great fund of stone coal . . .

("Nightfall," a plaintive aria, sung to the accordion and fiddle's drone, plays. James Tilghman begins a slow-motion dance, which introduces some of the movement motifs used throughout the piece: reaching, digging, searching, listening, praying . . .)

NICHO ALLEN:

Nightfall, found myself too far from home
Built a fire under a ledge at the foot of Broad Mountain
Fell asleep
In the night, I was awakened by a strong light and a great heat
Mountain on fire!
Mountain on fire!
Daybreak
And I saw that the rock in the ledge was coal
Ignited by my campfire.

JAMES TILGHMAN: . . . A *very* great fund of stone coal. A few Indians living in this valley say that it can burn . . .

(He continues his dance as Philip Ginter steps forward and sings "Mauch Chunk Mountain," another plaintive aria, sung to a pulsing accordion and fiddle.)

PHILIP GINTER:

I first came to Mauch Chunk Mountain
Some years ago.
When I saw the black rock I knew
It must be stone coal.
It must be stone coal.
In exchange for my discovery
I got a small tract of land and a sawmill.
Hundreds of fortunes were made
But it ruined me
My land and sawmill were taken
And now, once again, I am a poor man.

JAMES TILGHMAN: This bed of coal, situated as it is on the banks of the river, may some time or other be a thing of great value.

(The three men reach for the Schoolgirl's anthracite, but she eludes them and runs off. They run after her.
"Air Apparent," a slow waltz inspired by Appalachian folk music, plays. The melody is simply stated at first, then it builds to a full and rich resolution by the end of the scene.)

IMAGE: *An opening montage of faces of miners, women and children, spanning a period from the 1880s to the 1970s, is projected on the laundry and set.*

(Abraham Williams's head and shoulders emerge from the floor, through the trapdoor.)

TITLE: "An advertisement from the *Luzerne Federalist*, Wilkes-Barre, 1805."

ABRAHAM WILLIAMS: I take this method of informing the public that I understand miners' work. I have worked the greater part of twenty-three years in the mines of Wales, and four and a half years in the copper mines in New Jersey. If anybody thinks there is any coal on your lands, or wants to sink wells, blow rock or stones, I understand it, wet or dry, on the ground or under the ground. I will work by the day or by the solid foot or yard, or by the job, at reasonable wages.

(He sings his "ad" for himself, a cappella, in a Welsh folk song style:)

> I work cheap for country produce,
> But cash I think I won't refuse,
> Despise me not nor take me scorn,
> Because I am a Welshman born,
> Now am a true American,
> With every good to every man.

Thank you.

(Abraham Williams goes back down the trapdoor.)

TITLE: "Mrs. John Flanigan, 1818."

(Mrs. Flanigan enters and takes down laundry from the clothesline.)

MRS. FLANIGAN: On the sixth day of September, my husband, myself, five children, and some laborers set out from Connecticut for the Susquehanna. We were bound for Plymouth . . .

TITLE: "To my mother in Wales, 1834."

(David Davies enters and begins to idly throw chunks of coal into a bucket.)

DAVID DAVIES: I did not think a year ago that I would be writing to you from this wilderness near Carbondale. I cannot blame anyone but myself because nothing would do but that I should come to America . . .

MRS. FLANIGAN: We were bound for Plymouth, where my husband planned to mine the anthracite with blast powder *(Explosion)* instead of the old way of digging it out the side of the hill. Our conveyance was a two-horse covered lumber wagon.

DAVID DAVIES: America . . . Work here is very stagnant at present and the outlook is poor. This makes everyone here want to return home to Wales. I wish I could persuade Welsh people to believe the truth about this country.

MRS. FLANIGAN: I bore up under the dreary journey, and preserved my courage pretty well, till we struck the logway on the Easton and Wilkes-Barre turnpike, when I was forced to give vent to my feelings, and wept like a child.

DAVID DAVIES: If you spent a year here seeing nothing but poor cottages with chimneys smoking so that Welsh people could not breathe in them, and the jolly Welsh women losing their rosy cheeks and smiling eyes—what would your feelings be?

MRS. FLANIGAN: At the end of eleven of the longest days of my life, we landed in Plymouth.

DAVID DAVIES: What would your feelings be?

MRS. FLANIGAN: Had I but foreseen the trials and misery of the long journey ahead, I should never have consented to have left my old home and friends. *(Explosion; she exits)*

DAVID DAVIES: What would your feelings be? You would sigh for the lovely land you had left. *(Exits)*

TITLE: "From *A Conversation on Mines* instruction manual, 1864."

(This dialogue is performed with stylized movement before a home-made backdrop of a mine tunnel. Punctuation is highlighted by primitive offstage sound effects, made by the other actors. The Father and Son enter as if in a nineteenth-century play. The Father wears a very fake "old man" beard, and the Son—played by an adult—wears a "little boy" sailor suit and straw hat.)

SON: As you have been in mines, Father, from early life, and your ancestors have had, during generations past, a practical knowledge of them,

I shall be glad when convenient to have a little conversation with you on mines.

FATHER: If I can give information by which you, Son, and the public may profit, I shall have great pleasure in so doing; and as we have just now a little leisure, I shall be glad to answer, to the best of my abilities, any questions respecting mines and mining.

SON: Very good. I presume, Father, that mines require much care and attention to produce a good profit for the employers, and ensure the safety of the men. I wish to know, Father, have you adopted many ways of working out coal since you were first engaged in mining?

FATHER: Yes, I have adopted many ways, because I know the same way of working will not answer with safety and economy in all mines. The nature of the roof, floor, coal and gasses is not alike. One plan of working coal may answer well at one mine, but not at every one.

SON: Does the roof, floor, coal and gasses vary much then, from mine to mine?

FATHER: Yes. At one mine the floor is soft, but hard in another; in other mines the roof and floor are both soft, in others both hard; in some mines the seam of coal is very thick, but in others very thin; also the seam of coal is flat in some mines, but dips or rises very much in others.

SON: I see now, Father, in my "mind's eye," why so many plans are adopted. As you say, one is because the floor is hard, another because it is soft; one is adopted for this thing, another for that. Therefore, a miner's object should always be to adopt the best plan for whichever seam of coal he happens to be working out.

(At this point, the Schoolgirl comes out and stands to the side of the melodrama scene. At points, she holds up placards printed in nineteenth-century style script: ADOPT THE BEST PLAN: ROOM AND PILLAR, LONG WALL, QUARRYING OR PIT.)

FATHER: Yes.

SON: I shall be glad to know, Father, how or by what methods coal is worked out?

FATHER: One method is called "room and pillar," another is called "long wall," another is called "quarrying" or "pit."

SON: I am glad, Father, for this knowledge I have received from you. At your next convenience I shall ask to understand the different methods you have called "room and pillar," "long wall" and "quarrying" or "pit." Thank you.

(Father, Son and Schoolgirl bow, then exit.)

TITLE: "From *Mrs. Beeton's Book of Household Management,* 1891."

(Housekeeper enters, followed by a young Irish Parlor Maid. "Women's Work Fugue: Spin Cycle" underscores the scene. It is a weaving, cyclical "work song" version of "Air Apparent," both gentle and driving, indicating the comfort and drudgery of life's daily routine.)

HOUSEKEEPER: "Cleanliness is next to godliness, and order is the next degree." As the housemaid, you are the handmaiden of these virtues. Whatever the habits of the master and mistress, you will find it advantageous to rise early. In the winter, after opening the shutters, your first duty is to prepare the fire. Sweep up the ashes, deposit them in your cinder pail. This has a wire screen inside to sift the cinders out of the ashes. Now, put a double handful of cinders in the bottom of the grate. Put on them a layer of dry paper. On the paper lay some small sticks of wood crosswise. Place another double handful of cinders and bits of coal on top of the wood. Open the draughts. Light the paper. Gradually add more coal and cinders until there is a beautiful pale blue flame. Then partly close the draught, there should be just enough air to promote combustion. Throw the ashes away into the ash can. Any extra cinders can be reserved for use in the kitchen stove.

(She turns to leave the parlor, but pauses in the doorway as the "master" and "mistress" enter the room; then she exits. During the following dialogue, the Irish Parlor Maid prepares the fire as instructed, then exits.)

TITLE: "From *Harper's New Monthly Magazine*, 1857."

(This scene is performed as a nineteenth-century drawing room drama "courtship" scene, full of beating hearts and romantic innuendo.)

MAN: There are probably but few persons in this "land of the free" who have not, at some time or another, enjoyed the novelty and genial warmth of an anthracite fire.
WOMAN: Often has a pleasant, jocund story been related and many tender vows have been made and sealed before the flaming minister upon the hearth. Night is turned into day . . .
MAN: . . . and the gaudy chandeliers of the fashionable salon give luster to the eyes of beauty by its brilliant jets.
WOMAN: But it is on a cold winter's night, when we hear the wind fret and howl around us, that we realize in a more grateful sense the glowing qualities of our anthracite friend.

MAN (*Caressing her*): The process of mining coal is simple: a miner and a laborer cut away all the coal, it slides behind them. Now we find the cars loaded with coal and hauled safely to ground level by mules. At the surface, it's emptied at the breaker. As the coal slides down the chutes, boys pick out the slate and impure coal, and it is truly astonishing to observe with what wonderful celerity and exactness they discover and seize the unwanted rock.

WOMAN (*Rebuffing his advances*): They often perform their work carelessly, however.

MAN: Then the consumer commits the blunder of denouncing the quality of the coal instead of the careless breaker boys.

WOMAN: Although the social and moral condition of our mining population is not as good as many of us would like to see, it is infinitely superior to that of the same class in Europe.

MAN: It is composed almost exclusively of foreigners from England, Ireland—

WOMAN: Scotland—

MAN: Wales—

MAN AND WOMAN: Germany.

WOMAN: But what *is* coal?

MAN: Although coal is plain and unpretending in its physical aspect, it can, nevertheless, claim relation with a celebrated member of the higher order of mineral aristocracy.

WOMAN: You refer to . . .

MAN (*Presenting her with a ring*): The diamond, whose beauty cannot easily be exaggerated.

WOMAN: Both are almost identical in composition, yet are wholly dissimilar in the role they play in the domestic economy of man. (*They embrace and exit*)

PARLOR MAID (*Reentering*): I was a young girl in Ireland, just married, when the potato rot came, you know. It was an awful sight to see, it was. I thought to myself, Poor Ireland's done now. People were passing around letters from America, and well sure it sounded fine there. There's land, and work for all, and the sun shines always there. I thought, That sounds like the place for us. (*Exits, clearing parlor furniture as she goes*)

TITLE: "When I go to America."

(*Four Immigrant Men enter with luggage and boisterously sing and dance to a rowdy, upbeat, Eastern European folk tune, "When I Go to America":*)

IMMIGRANT MEN:

> From America, when I go, I will send to you my photo.
> Leafy mountain, rushing water, good-bye, darling, I'll be gone.
> Leafy mountain, rushing water, good-bye, darling, I'll be gone.
>
> When I'd traveled halfway o'er then, I recalled the dress you wore then.
> Leafy mountain, rushing water, good-bye, darling, I'll be gone.
> Leafy mountain, rushing water, good-bye, darling, I'll be gone.
>
> If you are beset by sorrow, from your purse then take my photo.
> Leafy mountain, rushing water, good-bye, darling, I'll be gone.
> Leafy mountain, rushing water, good-bye, darling, I'll be gone.
>
> But the picture speaks to no one; with your sorrows you must go on.
> Leafy mountain, rushing water, good-bye, darling, I'll be gone.
> Leafy mountain, rushing water, good-bye, darling, I'll be gone.
>
> Soon there'll be an end to sadness, when together we'll know gladness.
> Leafy mountain, rushing water, good-bye, darling, I'll be gone.
> Leafy mountain, rushing water, good-bye, darling, I'll be gone.

IMAGE: *Montage of photos of immigrants arriving at Ellis Island, projected onto the set and the sides of the men's luggage.*

(The jocund tone turns somber as the men move in slow-motion through the projected images of scared and lonely immigrants. They exit one by one, leaving an Italian Immigrant alone onstage.)

ITALIAN IMMIGRANT: Well, I came to America because I heard the streets were paved with gold. When I got here I found out three things: first, the streets weren't paved with gold; second, they weren't paved at all; and third, I was expected to pave them.

(He exits as the Proctors enter, followed by three assistant miners, called "Buddies" in mining slang.)

TITLE: "Miner's examination, 1890s."

PROCTOR 1: The examination for Miner's Certificate in Competency was conducted in the Pine Street School in the city of Hazleton . . .

PROCTOR 2: . . . the use of which was granted by the city controllers.

PROCTOR 1: The examining board was composed of the honorable Eckley B. Coxe, John W. Scott, Michael Mulligan and J. M. Lewis.

(The Proctors exit. Three Buddies read in thoughtful tones from the examination and mark their answers. They sit on their suitcases, or use them as desks. Their movements are slow and abstract, suggesting deep thought and careful consideration.)

BUDDY 1: What is your name?

BUDDY 3: What is your age?

BUDDY 2: Where were you born?

BUDDY 1: State what experience you have had in the anthracite coal mines, and what you were employed at, and at what mines.

BUDDY 2: What is your first duty on entering the mines?

BUDDY 3: Upon entering your chamber in the morning you discover three props broken . . .

BUDDY 1: Suppose you were required to remove a prop . . .

BUDDY 2: Suppose there were a dangerous piece of rock hanging . . .

BUDDY 3: Suppose you drilled a hole (four feet, six inches), and in charging the hole . . .

BUDDY 1: Suppose you struck a blower of gas, how would you proceed . . .

BUDDY 2: How would you fire a hole in a place . . .

BUDDY 3: How would you prepare dynamite in a frozen condition . . .

BUDDY 1 *(Overlapping)*: What should a miner do in each of the following cases: before allowing his laborer to commence work in the morning . . .

BUDDY 2 *(Overlapping)*: after firing each shot . . .

BUDDY 3 *(Overlapping)*: before commencing to prepare a charge of powder for a blast . . .

BUDDY 1: when he discovers any dangerous condition of the roof.

(Having completed the exam, the men stand and present them to unseen examiners.)

BUDDY 3: Witness!

BUDDY 2: Witness!

BUDDY 1: Witness!

(They exit.)

TITLE: **"Breaker Boys." And "From the *Tamaqua Evening Courier*, 1902."**

(Reverend Phillips and a Boy enter. Their dialogue occurs in the fore-ground, while in the background the patch town dwellers are about their business of going to work, which involves moving out the stair unit and setting it out as a breaker for the "Over the Coals" sequence.)

REVEREND PHILLIPS *(To audience)*: On a railroad track near the mining town of Edwardsville, I met a child on his way to work. The child certainly did not look a day over eleven years old. *(To Boy)* How old are you?

BOY: Thirteen goin' on fourteen.

REVEREND PHILLIPS: And you work in the breaker?

BOY: Sure, and so does all the other lads in the town when they're not strik-ing. You haven't got it in for me? I suppose you are some kind of a company detective, ain't you?

REVEREND PHILLIPS: No, no. I'm a traveling minister visiting the town. Tell me a little about your work in the breaker.

BOY: Well, that's it over there. Four hundred lads works in that building. We go to work at seven in the morning and stay until six at night. We have half an hour at noon for eatin'. We sort over the coal as it comes out. We pick out the slate and the slag. That's all we do, see?

REVEREND PHILLIPS: Rather hard work.

BOY: Yes, until you get used to it. The coal dust's pretty bad. Sometimes it gets into your eyes and makes you kind of blind. The breaker isn't heated in winter, so you get used to bein' cold all day. But I don't mind it no longer. The only thing I kick about is the way the coal cuts my fin-gers. Say, isn't it too bad they can't invent a way of keepin' coal from wearing a feller's fingers off'n his hands?

(The Reverend looks at the Boy's hands.)

Red tips.

REVEREND PHILLIPS: How long have you worked in the breaker?

BOY: Six years.

REVEREND PHILLIPS: Then you must have been seven years old when you began picking coal?

BOY *(Quickly)*: My papers was OK. They says I was thirteen when I started to work. And that's what I was.

REVEREND PHILLIPS: Did you ever go to school?

(We hear the sound of a breaker whistle. Other boys enter, take their places on the breaker, and start miming the action of sorting coal.)

BOY *(Laughs)*: School! Hey, mister, you must be a green hand. Why, lads in Anthracite doesn't go to school. They works in the breaker.

(He joins the other boys on the breaker and sorts coal; the Reverend exits.)

IMAGE: *Breaker Boy photo montage.*

(A woman who has been sorting coal with the other boys steps forward as a Breaker Boy and sings:)

BREAKER BOY:
> Over the ice, they pull the coals,
> Their fingers rent by a hundred holes;
> You may trace the path torn digits tread
> By the crimson stream on the iced chute shed.
> Their heads are bowed; their bodies cramped,
> A painful look on their features stamped.
> Their knees are pressed against aching breasts,
> While bones are bent in their tender chests
> And lungs are crushed like slaves oppressed.
>
> From morn till night with a groaning sound,
> The merciless coals destroy their bloom;
> From morn till night in the breaker's gloom,
> The massive screens whirl round and round.
> And still they list to its doleful grind;
> And still they toil till their eyes go blind;
> And frowning phantoms haunt the walls,
> While deep and deeper the dark gloom falls
> And the picker's soul for respite calls out.
>
> Pitiless coals dash madly by
> With doleful chatter and mocking cry,
> But still they bend in the dreary gloom,
> The floating dust and the sable pall.
> They hear the knell of their bitter doom
> As they watch the coals from the segments fall.
> For over the coals, ay, over the coals,
> They dwarf their bodies and blight their souls,
> From morn till night as the breaker rolls on.

(We hear the sound of a breaker whistle. The boys exit, as Mrs. O. W. Seaberg, a 1930s high-society matron, enters.)

MRS. O. W. SEABERG: It's almost here! Hundreds have already made reservations for this year's annual banquet of the Anthracite Club of New York. Don't delay in making your reservation. As before, the banquet is in the Grand Ballroom of the Hotel Astor. It's informal. Tables seat ten to twelve, six dollars a plate. (The tasteful menu invites overeating!) There'll be surprises; a few short, informative addresses; celebrities from all branches of the industry (including the railroads, who are becoming more intimate in the anthracite family circle). Music by the Hudson Coal Company Trio . . .

(The Barbershop Trio and Con McCole enter.)

BARBERSHOP TRIO *(In three-part harmony)*: Hudson! Coal! Company!
MRS. O. W. SEABERG: . . . and Con McCole will repeat his famous sketch—
CON MCCOLE: "The Handprint of the Molly Maguires."
MRS. O. W. SEABERG: It's a memory worth keeping. Yours for Anthracite, Mrs. O. W. Seaberg, Banquet Chairwoman. *(Exits)*

TITLE: "'Handling Explosives,' from *Handbook for Coal Miners*, International Correspondence Schools, 1928."

BARBERSHOP TRIO:
Never open a metal keg of powder with a pick or metal object.
Never allow powder to remain exposed; keep it in a well-locked box.
Never guess at the quantity of powder to be used; always measure it.

Never withdraw a shot that has missed fire; drill a fresh hole.
Never light two or more shots at the same time.
Never return to a shot that has failed to explode till ten minutes after lighting it.

Never fire a shot without making sure that the coal dust nearby is well wet down.
Never take more than one day's supply of explosives into the mine at one time.
Never use weak detonators.

Never use a short fuse.

TITLE: "Irene Wieczorek, born in Nanticoke, 1923."

(Irene and her boyfriend enter dancing a polka.)

IRENE WIECZOREK: Well as far as I know, my father was born in Pennsylvania, in Nanticoke to be exact. And Mom was born here. Now Mom's parents were married here but Pop's came from the old country. Where in Poland I don't exactly know. Mom and Pop settled in Nanticoke. As far as that, we weren't strictly Polish but we were to the sense that we were Polish and we all attended parochial school . . . and of course they always wanted everybody to get married good. Not that you had to marry rich, but Mom, she wanted you to have a good husband and a good life. The oldest married a Swedish boy, and Betty married a Polish, and now I am going with a Russian. Teresa married a Dutch and Timmy married a Russian girl and Sylvie married a Polish. So we always say we are a League of Nations!

(They polka off as the stair unit is rolled center stage. We hear the sounds of a football game. Tommy and Dan enter and sit on the unit as if it were stadium bleachers. They have Yuengling beers in hand.)

TITLE: "You might be from the region if . . . 1997."

TOMMY: You might be from the region if you say "ain't ya" more than once in a sentence.
DAN: You call your friends "yous guys."
TOMMY: A tree comes between a two and a four.
DAN: You go out pickin' "mushies."
TOMMY: You were ever on camera during *The Land of Hatchy Milatchy.*
DAN: (Extra points if you ever met Miss Judy.)
TOMMY: Your home is within walkin' distance of at least tree Cat'lick churches.
DAN: (Or buildings that used to be Cat'lick churches.)
TOMMY: You consider kielbasa one of the major food groups.
DAN: (Along with pierogies, halushki and Yuengling.)
TOMMY: You tell your wife you have to "swing by the hosie a while."
DAN: You can never get that black haze out of your clothes, no matter how hard you try.

(Big cheer as they watch a play on the field.)

TOMMY: Wanna go to Knoebels? *(The "K" is pronounced in "Knoebels")*
DAN: Let's try out the new roller coaster!
TOMMY: The Twister!

(They exit as a phone rings. Receptionist, wearing a telephone headset, rushes to her desk to answer phone.)

TITLE: **"From the National Mine Health and Safety Academy course catalog, 1998."**

RECEPTIONIST: Good morning, National Mine Health and Safety Academy, how can I help you? . . . Uh-huh . . . The new courses we're offering this year are: Advanced Inspection Seminar, Mine Emergency Procedures, Roof Control Seminar, Advanced Metal Inspection and a computer course on Portable Applications for Laptops . . . OK, the course on Mine Emergency Procedures deals with emergency events including explosions, fires, flooding, etc., and covers detection of gasses, oxygen breathing apparatus, tactical procedures for rescue teams, and strategy and management of mine emergencies. Why don't I send you a new catalog? . . . No problem . . . First, may I ask you, ma'am, how long have you worked in the anthracite coal mines?

(As the lights fade on the Receptionist, other actors have set up the telegraph. On one side of the stage is the sender, tapping out the news as recited by the Reporter. Across the stage, the receiver is transcribing the telegraph. At the center of the stage is an Avondale Miner, beginning a slow-motion version of the Avondale dance; he is joined later by other men and women. The movement evokes reaching, digging, reaching, listening, praying, panic, death.)

IMAGE: *Newspaper headline:* SEPTEMBER 6, 1869. AVONDALE.

REPORTER: September 6, 1869. Special dispatch to the Scranton *Weekly Republican.* At the coal breaker, built at Avondale, about a mile south of Plymouth, over one hundred men and boys had gone back to work after a strike. The ventilating furnace at the bottom of the shaft was relit, and the last man to go down that morning was the stable boss with a bundle of hay for the mules. Maybe it was the dry hay that started the fire. Fire spread up the shaft and ignited the wooden breaker. The surface engineer saw the blaze of fire shooting up from the shaft, which was the only outlet from the mine below. He ran and blew the breaker whistle. *(Breaker whistle)* The breaker was built on top of the shaft leading to the mine—to save the expense of hauling coal from the mine to the breaker.

IMAGE: *Newspaper headline:* AWFUL DISASTER! AVONDALE COAL BURNED.

Telegraph wires along the Lackawanna and Bloomsburg tracks crackled with pleas for help, and horse-drawn fire equipment from Wilkes-Barre, Scranton, Kingston and nearby towns were soon on their way to the scene of the conflagration. *(Fire bell)*

(Avondale Mother enters reading a newspaper to her son; telegraph stops.)

AVONDALE MOTHER: While this was the scene aboveground,
REPORTER AND AVONDALE MOTHER: one hundred and eight men and boys were in the bowels of the earth buried alive beneath this mass of fire.

(Telegraph resumes.)

REPORTER: September 8. After two days of frenzied effort, crews were able to clear out the poisonous gas. By now, volunteers from all over Northeastern Pennsylvania have poured in and rescue squads have been formed. 6:45 A.M.: The hope that anyone would be found alive is dashed.

(Telegraph stops.)

IMAGE: *Engraving—dead miners in the chamber.*

Sixty-seven men and boys were found huddled together in one chamber.
AVONDALE MOTHER *(Reading from newspaper)*: Some of the dead were kneeling;
REPORTER AND AVONDALE MOTHER: some were sitting hand in hand, as if they had vowed to live and die together; some lay on the ground, as if they had fallen while fleeing; and others lay as if pressing their face into the earth in the hope of extracting from it a breath of pure air . . . in another chamber every man had stripped off his clothing to use it in stopping the crevices of the embankments . . .

(Telegraph resumes.)

IMAGE: *Engraving—bringing the bodies out.*

REPORTER: A hoisting apparatus was built and each time the cage was lifted, the horse pulling the cable traveled in a circle of more than a mile. Then began the long, tedious ordeal of bringing each body to the surface. Each trip took eight minutes.

IMAGE: *Flames; names of the dead projected on the miner's bare back, then on the walls of the set. By the end of the scene, the set is literally covered with names.*   .

Names of the dead, condition of each when found:

AVONDALE MOTHER *(Reading from newspaper)*: Palmer Steele, Denison Slocum, John Bowen, William Powell, David Jones, Thomas Williams . . . *(Continues reading from list; overlapping with Reporter)*

REPORTER *(Overlapping with Mother)*: 9:45 A.M., the fifth body rescued is that of William Williams, a boy about fourteen years of age, who had only worked one day . . . 11:00 A.M., the ninth body, that of an unknown man, was found a long distance from the rest. He is lying on his face, and was much disfigured. He has a black mustache and also a new pair of shoes . . . 3:00 P.M., the twenty-sixth body is that of Evan Hughes, Plymouth. Face bloody; wife in crowd screaming. 5:08 P.M., The fifty-second and fifty-third bodies, man with son in his arms. John Burtch and John Burtch, Jr., age twelve . . . 7:14 P.M., the sixtieth body, name unknown, face pale; head turned back. He is an Irishman . . . 5:52 A.M., the ninety-ninth body is Daniel Givens, age seventeen; mouth open . . . 6:03 A.M., the one hundredth body is Dave Johnson of Plymouth; leaves a wife and one child . . . Some adequate conception of the disaster may be gathered from the fact that in Avondale there are left only nine heads of families. *(Telegraph stops)*

AVONDALE MOTHER *(Reading from newspaper)*: It took seventy men to dig the graves.

(The Welsh melody of "The Avondale Mine Disaster" is heard. The accompaniment is a minor, sometimes dissonant drone.)

TITLE: **"The Avondale Mine Disaster."**

TELEGRAPH RECEIVER *(Solo at first, later joined by other singers one by one)*: Good people all, both great and small, I pray you lend an ear

And listen with attention while the truth I will declare;
When you hear this lamentation, it will make you weep and wail,
About the suffocation in the mines of Avondale.

On the sixth day of September, in eighteen sixty-nine,
Those miners all then got a call to go work in the mine.
But little did they think that day that death would soon prevail
Before they would return again from the mines of Avondale.

The women and their children, their hearts were filled with joy
To see the men go work again, and likewise every boy.
But a dismal sight in broad daylight soon make them all turn pale,
When they saw the breaker burning o'er the mines of Avondale.

From here and there and everywhere they gathered in a crowd,
Some tearing off their clothes and hair, and crying out aloud,
"Get out our husbands and our sons, for Death he's going to steal
Their lives away without delay in the mines of Avondale."

But all in vain, there was no hope, one single soul to save,
For there is no second outlet from the subterranean cave.
No pen can write the awful fright and horror that did prevail
Among those dying victims in the mines of Avondale.

Sixty-seven was the number that in a heap were found.
It seemed they were bewailing their fate in underground.
They found the father with his son clasped in his arms so pale.
It was a heartrending scene in the mines of Avondale.

Now to conclude and make an end their number I'll pen down.
One hundred ten of brave stout men were smothered underground.
They're in their graves till the last day, their widows may bewail,
And the orphans' cries still rend the skies 'round the mines of
   Avondale.

(All exit as lights fade.)

TITLE: "Centralia."

(The title dissolves into flames.
    The back side of the stair unit is used as the porch of one of the
remaining houses in Centralia. A boy, Jason, dressed in 1980s school

clothes sits on his porch. He is working on a school report about the history of the Anthracite region; he has a book bag, school notebook, etc.)

MOTHER *(Offstage)*: Jason! You get that report done or you won't get to go to Knoebels, you hear me?

JASON: Mom, I'm working on it, I'm working on it. *(To himself)* Chill out, Mom. *(Returning to report; reading aloud from notebook)* "The job of picking out all the slate, pieces of timber and rocks was done by eight- to sixteen-year-old boys called breaker boys. They were supervised by a breaker boss who was not afraid to use his whip or stick on any boy who was slow, talkative or inattentive." *(Under his breath)* Hey, Mom, you big mean old breaker boss. *(He gets up to look to see if Mom is looking, and sneaks a copy of the comic book* Carbon Knight *out of his book bag)* All right!

IMAGE: *Cover of* Carbon Knight #1: *Carbon Knight, all aglow, is bursting forth from the smoking Centralia ground.*

(Two adult actors stand at a microphone; they are using empty Pringles cans for a reverb effect.)

VOICES: CARBON KNIGHT!
JASON: Carbon Knight!

(Reading from the comic:)

JASON AND VOICE 1: A new hero from the heart of the coal region!

(Jason's voice fades out as Voice 1 takes over.)

VOICE 1: Centralia, P.A. Thirty years ago. An underground mine fire has been discovered in a small town located in the heart of the Pennsylvania coal region. Centralia's champion is . . .

(Chief McKnight, played by an adult actor, springs onstage as if brought to life by Jason's imagination. Brilliant light illuminates the stage. Chief McKnight and Jason pantomime the story in comic book "panels.")

IMAGE: *Page 1,* Carbon Knight #1: *Chief McKnight saving girl.*

JASON AND VOICE 2: Chief McKnight!

VOICE 1: . . . the courageous chief of the fire department, who saved many a Centralia child from the burning inferno. His efforts to stop the fire are thwarted by a meddling government agent.

IMAGE: *Page 2,* Carbon Knight #1: *close-up of bad guy.*

VOICE 2 *(As bad guy)*: Chief McKnight! No one was supposed to go down there until my team and I arrived. I'm taking over command of the situation!

IMAGE: *Page 2,* Carbon Knight #1: *close-up of McKnight.*

JASON AND VOICE 2 *(As Chief McKnight)*: This situation is an underground coal inferno. If I had waited for you that little girl would be dead! This whole area is going to be swallowed up if we don't stop it.
VOICE 1: Chief McKnight's wife, Tina, is frightened.
VOICE 2 *(As Tina)*: Please don't go back down there. It's too dangerous. Let the government men handle this. *(As Chief McKnight)* I have to go with this other government guy to show him through the tunnels. I have to go if it means saving this town. It's my job and there's always a danger. *(As Tina)* I know all that, but you're also a husband and a father, and . . .
JASON AND VOICE 2 *(As Tina)*: I love you. *(As Chief McKnight)* I love you, too.

IMAGE: *Page 7,* Carbon Knight #1: *Chief McKnight, in his protective Freon suit, accepts a locket from his lovely wife, Tina.*

VOICE 2 *(As bad guy)*: Come on McKnight! Just get going!
VOICE 1: Down underground, in their protective Freon suits, the two men make their way through the burning tunnels.
VOICE 2 *(As bad guy)*: Out of my way, McKnight, I don't take orders from you.
JASON *(As Chief McKnight)*: You don't care if Centralia is destroyed, do you?
VOICE 2 *(As bad guy)*: I don't get paid to care.

IMAGE: *Page 10,* Carbon Knight #1: *fight scenes.*

JASON AND VOICES: KRAK! THWAK! SMACK! K-THWAK!

VOICE 2 *(As bad guy)*: You shouldn't have tried to play hero, McKnight. You're out of your league! Small-town hicks like you will never understand the power I and those I work for possess!

JASON AND VOICE 2 *(As Chief McKnight)*: These are people's lives you're playing with.

VOICE 2 *(As bad guy)*: Still playing the hero, McKnight? Too bad you won't be remembered that way!

IMAGE: *Page 12,* Carbon Knight #1: *fight continues.*

JASON AND VOICES: SLAM! KRAK! ZAKOW!

VOICE 2 *(As bad guy)*: AAAAAAAAAaaaaaaahhhhh! *(He's fried in the fire)*

VOICE 1: Chief McKnight watches in horror as his opponent is fried in the fire. He tries to save him, knowing that he, too, will probably die. *(As if on a wristwatch two-way radio)* Chief McKnight, what's happening down there?!

VOICE 2 *(As Chief McKnight)*: I'll tell you if I make it out of here. I've got to get this guy up to the surface, but my Freon suit took quite a jolt, it's going berserk on me!!

VOICE 1 *(On radio)*: Chief, you have to get out of there now! Regardless of the heat down there, you could freeze alive!

VOICE 2 *(Freon suit on overload; electronic sound)*: BEEP! BEEP! BEEP!

VOICE 1 *(On radio)*: Chief, you're out of time! Get out of there now!

IMAGE: *Page 15,* Carbon Knight #1: *Chief McKnight running through the mine tunnel.*

(Counting down): 5 seconds . . . 4 seconds . . . 3 seconds . . .

JASON *(Simultaneously, as McKnight)*: Move! Getting cold! Move! Cold! Freezing!

JASON AND VOICES: BARROOOOM! *(Chief McKnight freezes)*

IMAGE: *Page 16,* Carbon Knight #1: *Chief McKnight freezes.*

MOTHER *(Through window)*: Jason! You've got five seconds to show me that report and then we're outta here!

JASON: Gotcha, Mom. *(He returns to comic book)*

JASON AND VOICE 1 *(Whispered)*: Centralia, P.A. . . . Today.

VOICE 1 *(Whispered)*: Once again, the children of the town are swallowed up by the earth.

IMAGE: *Page 23*, Carbon Knight #1: *boys falling into subsidence.*

FFFRRRRRUUUMMMBBLLEEE!

IMAGE: *Page 23*, Carbon Knight #1: *"HHHEEELLLLLPPP!"*

JASON AND VOICE 1: Hellllppp!!

IMAGE: *Page 25–26*, Carbon Knight #1: *Carbon Knight, all aglow, emerges from the rock.*

VOICE 1 *(Over Jason's faint continuing cry)*: What? Who? How? Where? He barely remembers his own name. He has no idea where he is or how long he's been there, but he catches something that long dormant ears struggle to hear. It is a faint cry . . .
JASON: Helllpppp!
VOICE 1: It triggers something in his awakened soul, something he was. Something he is. *(Chief McKnight slowly unfreezes)*
JASON: It is a cry for help.
VOICE 1: And when he hears it . . .
JASON AND VOICE 1: HE MOVES!

   (Chief McKnight is transformed to Carbon Knight.)

IMAGE: *Cover,* Carbon Knight #1: *Carbon Knight bursting forth from the smoking Centralia ground.*

MOTHER *(Offstage)*: Five . . . four . . . three . . .
JASON AND VOICES: CARBON KNIGHT!!!

IMAGE: *Cover,* Carbon Knight #1: *Carbon Knight, now transformed—he's all aglow and enormous.*

MOTHER: two . . . one.

   (She comes out onto the porch. Lights restore to the real world. The figure of Carbon Knight is stuck in the real world and tries to sneak off.)

IRISH:

>Beef cut up to stew,

LITHUANIAN:

>drippings from the ham,

ITALIAN:

>brodo di carne,

POLISH:

>noodles made by hand.

IRISH:

>Onions, carrots, celery;

LITHUANIAN:

>warm fresh duck's blood;

POLISH:

>vinegar;

ITALIAN:

>mmm, poco vino;

ALL WOMEN:

>let it simmer.

ITALIAN:

>Chi mangia bene, bene dorme
>Chi bene dorme, non pecca.
>Chi non pecca, va in Paradiso,
>Allora
>Chi bene mangia va in Paradiso.

ALL WOMEN:

>He who eats well sleeps well.
>He who sleeps well goes to Heaven,
>Therefore,
>He who eats well will go to Heaven.

>He who eats well sleeps well.
>He who sleeps well goes to Heaven,
>Therefore,
>He who eats well will go to Heaven.

ITALIAN:

> Mangia;

LITHUANIAN:

> valgik;

POLISH:

> prosche, yeshch;

IRISH:

> ith;

ALL WOMEN:
> Eat!

(The breaker whistle. The Women move the stair unit upstage. The lights go out on the Women as they come up on the "mine" area. It is lunch break.)

MINER 3: Whatcha got?
MINER 1: Babka.
BOY: Bologna.
MINER 3: Bean soup.
MINER 2: Pork sandwich.
BOY: Pierogie. *(Gets up and tries a couple of dance steps)*
MINER 1: Bumbleberry pie.
MINER 2 *(To Boy)*: Hey, what are you doing?
BOY: I'm trying to do the jig you were doing the other day at lunch.
MINER 2: Come on, we'll show you how it's done.

(The Miners dance a jig as the "Old Miner's Dance," a sad yet spirited drinking song, plays.)

Okay, now you try it.

(The breaker whistle. It's quitting time. The Women move the stair unit downstage so that the Miners can load themselves into the cage. The hoisting signal rings, four long bells.)

Men up!

IMAGE: *Film of miners coming up out of the cage.*

For forty years and over, I have toiled about the mines,
But now I'm getting feeble, old and gray.
I started in the breaker and went back to it again
But now my work is finished for all time.
The only place that's left me is the almshouse for a home
Where I'm going to lay this weary head of mine.

MINER 4 *(Spoken)*: I went to work in the breaker the day I was fourteen years
old. I worked for fourteen days straight and my pay was fourteen dollars and fourteen cents. So, I got the fourteen cents and my ma got the
fourteen dollars. I saved a dime, and spent the four cents.
ALL MINERS: On candy.
MINER 4: Yes, sir, on candy!

ALL MINERS *(Sing)*:
Where are the boys who worked with me in the breaker long ago?
There are many now who've gone on to their rest
Their cares of life are over, and they've left this world of woe,
And their spirits now are roaming with the blest.

*(Miners 1, 2 and 4 stumble home. Miner 3 lingers at the bar. The Girl
comes to bring him home.)*

GIRL: Grandpop, Ma wants to know where you are.
MINER 3: Well, I'm not here. I just left.
GIRL: Come on, Grandpop. Let's go home.

*(The Girl leads Miner 3 home through the patch town at night: dark
houses, a few lights. From the open windows can be heard the sound
of coughing. A screen is flown in. The set is closed in to make a dark,
claustrophobic space. Hank, a retired miner in a wheelchair, is wheeled
onstage by his adult Daughter. He has oxygen tubes in his nose; he has
difficulty breathing and talking.)*

IMAGE: *X-rays of lungs suffering from black lung disease.*

(Doctor and hospital Residents enter and gather around Hank.)

DOCTOR: This patient is seventy-one years old, exhibits shortness of breath
and his sputum is black . . .
RESIDENT 1: Anthracosis, a form of pneumoconiosis, caused by the accumulation of coal dust in the lungs. Often takes ten to twenty years for

symptoms to appear. Can contribute to other respiratory diseases such as pneumonia, tuberculosis . . .

DOCTOR: Common name?

HANK: Black lung.

DAUGHTER: Dad, let them answer.

RESIDENT 2: It was first described in the sixteenth century in Germany. Probably the most widely known occupational disease in America.

RESIDENT 3: My grandpop had it. He used to take me to his favorite saloon— I was only about ten years old or so—and I was fascinated by this sort of trough they had underneath the bar stools. The old guys would be drinking—they said it helped wash down the coal dust—and they would spit this black spit into it and every once in a while the bartender had this flushing device that he used, and all the black spit would go down the drain. Then it'd fill up again. I watched that for hours. I loved it . . . *(Hank has a coughing fit)* The disease is distinctive for the blue-black marbling of the lungs caused by the dust accumulation.

(The Residents whisper/chant "blue black blue black . . ." The lights pull down to a tight spot on Hank, and the X-rays of black lung disease fade into a dark blue-black light, like the surface of anthracite. Residents 1 and 2 are positioned on either side of Hank's face, in profile.)

RESIDENT 1: Black lung . . . Blue damp . . .

RESIDENT 2: Black damp . . . Blue curling flames . . .

RESIDENT 1: Black spit . . . Blue coal under the skin . . .

ALL RESIDENTS *(Chanting, in Gregorian style)*: Dampness, dust, darkness.

RESIDENT 2: Dust.

RESIDENT 1: Darkness . . . Lack of light, insufficient ventilation, full coal . . .

RESIDENT 2: Open pits, acid runoff, subsidence . . .

RESIDENT 1: Culm banks, mine fires and . . .

ALL RESIDENTS: Illness . . . *(Chanting, in Gregorian style)* Dampness, dust, darkness.

RESIDENT 2: Dust.

RESIDENT 1: Darkness.

RESIDENT 2: Black damp, black lung, black spit, blue damp . . .

RESIDENT 1: Blue damp, blue curling flame, blue coal under my skin . . .

ALL RESIDENTS: Black, blue, black, blue . . .

(The Residents fade away; a faint spot stays on Hank as he watches the next scene.)

IMAGE: **Blue-black light fades into a movie loop of a miner traveling through a mine tunnel.**

(Through the movie images of the mine tunnel, a Miner is seen running, falling, stretching, collapsing. The haunting "Tunnel Running" plays. Lights fade on this; Hank's Daughter joins him.)

DAUGHTER: Dad was one of two men who survived a cave-in. It was just him and Davy. They were trapped in a monkey (that's the little carved-out space on the side of the tunnel where you can get out of the way of the cars). It was real cold, of course, and dark. They were trapped for five days. To stay warm, they took turns breathing down each other's shirts, in the back.

HANK: That's a trick I learned in the service.

DAUGHTER: Well, at one point (Dad's told this story a million times) in front of them appeared a full vision of this man, and Dad said, "Davy, what is that," and Davy's lookin', and Dad's lookin', and Davy says it looks like some kind of thing . . .

HANK: A holy vision thing.

DAUGHTER: They'd never seen anything like it before. The man was wearing a red gown. Big velvet things in the front . . .

HANK: . . . and a cross . . .

DAUGHTER: . . . and a cross, and his hat cocked in the back there. It was there till they come out. And that cross lit up, that they could kind of see. It was there from the time everything come down on them, when everything settled, that cross was there. All at once they saw the vision. Lots of people have pooh-poohed this story. But Dad knows what he seen.

HANK: Davy seen it.

DAUGHTER: Dad's the only one that can back it up, now.

HANK: If Davy was here, he'd back it with the same words.

DAUGHTER: When they got to the hospital, Dad told 'em about the vision. Someone said, "How was he dressed?" Dad described him, and then someone showed him a picture—

HANK: It was the Pope.

DAUGHTER: Dad had never seen the Pope before. It was like Dad was buried alive, and the Pope was watching over him, helping him to call on some kind of strength—a superhuman inner strength—and bringing him back from the dead, from the grave.

(Daughter wheels Hank offstage. The stage is very dark. A Nipper Boy is dimly illuminated, sitting, waiting.)

OFFSTAGE VOICE *(Speaking thoughts of Nipper Boy)*: Dampness, dust, darkness. By a big door under the ground, I wait. Keep it closed . . . it guides the fresh air to the miners. Stay awake . . . Open the door when the coal cars pass. In goes the good air, out goes the bad. Stay awake . . . Draw birds in the dirt to pass the time. Don't scare the birds!

IMAGE: *Illuminated cross, which morphs into a Red Cross symbol.*

(Dimly seen through the Red Cross symbol are Residents 1 and 2. The Nipper Boy is still there, waiting.)

ALL RESIDENTS: Chapter Seven: Artificial Respiration.

RESIDENT 2: If a man has been completely knocked out

RESIDENT 1: and has the appearance of being dead

RESIDENT 2: as is frequently the case in

ALL RESIDENTS: shock,

RESIDENT 2: or what's known as

ALL RESIDENTS: after-damp,

RESIDENT 1: his heart may continue to beat for several minutes after he stops breathing.

RESIDENT 2: Artificial respiration is then the only way of restoring life.

ALL RESIDENTS: In goes the good air, out goes the bad.

RESIDENT 1: When properly done,

RESIDENT 2: and persisted in,

RESIDENT 1: it will force the man to breathe,

ALL RESIDENTS: whether he wants to or not.

RESIDENT 2: Why, we had a case of this kind in one of our mines when artificial respiration was kept up

ALL RESIDENTS: for over forty-five minutes,

RESIDENT 2: and the patient is still working for us to this very day.

ALL RESIDENTS: To this very day.

(Lights fade on Nipper Boy. Lights up on First Aid Announcer.)

FIRST AID ANNOUNCER: On the baseball field outside Shamokin, this year's First Aid Competition was held.

ALL RESIDENTS: Chapter Eight: First Aid.

FIRST AID ANNOUNCER: The winning team, from the Brisbin colliery, will represent our region in the nationals at Pittsburgh.

RESIDENT 1: The following is a list of injuries most commonly found in our coal mines:

RESIDENT 2: Crushes, fractures, dislocations, burns, wounds to the skin, hemorrhages and

ALL RESIDENTS: shock.

RESIDENT 2: Still other injuries that affect the major veins and arteries require a knowledge of

RESIDENT 1: the location of these veins and arteries and a practical application known as

ALL RESIDENTS: pressure points.

FIRST AID ANNOUNCER: The events were (1) man lying on live wire, remove and treat; (2) fracture of nose caused by kick of mule, stop bleeding and dress; (3) explosion of keg of powder causing—

(Explosion. The First Aid Announcer is blown up.)

IMAGE: **Red Cross symbol morphs into a diagram of the circulatory system.**

ALL RESIDENTS *(Sing)*:
> The temporal connected to the facial
> The facial connected to the carotid
> The carotid connected to the subclavian
> Now press as hard as you can.

(Lights up elsewhere on Nurse and Doctor. The Nurse is reading a list of injuries from a clipboard; the Doctor is deciding who is at fault.)

NURSE: Killed in breaker while playing with a rope and throwing it around a revolving shaft.

DOCTOR: Carelessness of victim.

NURSE: Fingers crushed while spragging mine buggy.

DOCTOR: Avoidable.

NURSE: Skull fractured falling down manway.

DOCTOR: Unavoidable.

NURSE: Face and hands burned in explosion of gas; he was smoking.

DOCTOR: Carelessness of victim.

(A pool of light comes up, showing a bleeding, unconscious man being treated by a First Aid Worker.)

ALL RESIDENTS *(Sing)*:
> The subclavian connected to the axillary
> The axillary connected to the brachial
> The brachial connected to the radial
> Now press as hard as you can.

NURSE: Legs cut off while cleaning rollers in the breaker. Breaker engineer started machinery not knowing he was there.

DOCTOR: Carelessness of engineer.

NURSE: Bruised testicles by stick of timber striking him.

DOCTOR: Unavoidable.

NURSE: Chest and shoulder injured by falling down manway.

DOCTOR: Carelessness of victim.

ALL RESIDENTS *(Sing)*:
> Now press as hard as you can
> Keep that pressure a-comin'
> Gonna have to press a little bit more
> 'Fraid that just ain't enough
> Better call on your superhuman strength
> Dampness dust darkness dampness dust darkness . . .

(The bleeding, unconscious man dies.)

IMAGE: *Circulatory system morphs into a horizontal red line.*

FIRST AID WORKER: Ashes to ashes, dust to dust.

DOCTOR *(Looks at an X-ray he is holding)*: When I look at black lung X-rays like these, chances are the names on the charts end in S-K-Y or S-K-I. *(Checks name on X-ray)* Yep, Lipensky. *(Lights fade on him and Nurse)*

TITLE: *"The Great 1902 Strike."*

(The men enter and sing a rousing union song, "Me Johnny Mitchell Man," as they shift the set and furniture:)

MEN:
> Oh me belong fer union
> I'm good citizen,
> Seven, mebbe 'leven year, vorkin' in beeg 'Merica
> I'm vorkin' for de black heat, down in Lytle Shaft,
> In de Nottingham, Conyngham, and ev'ry place like dat.
> I've got lotsa money saved
> Nine hoondret, mebbe ten
> So strike can come, like son-of-a-gun,
> I'm Johnny Mitchell man.
>
> Oh, I'm a' no afraid for nottink, Joe,
> Me dey never shcare,

So call em shtrike tomorra night.
Dat's de biz'ness, I no care.
Right here I'm a' tell ya, Joe,
Me not schabby fella;
Good union man, citizen,
I'm Johnny Mitchell Man.

(A suggested gym. A boxer is sparring in the background. Men are conversing as they watch him. The sound of a boxing ring bell.)

ANGRY MAN: It's the twentieth century, for God's sake! How much longer are we going to put up with this?

MAN WITH NEWSPAPER: Hey, listen to this, some kid wrote a letter to the president . . .

THIRD MAN: Teddy Roosevelt?

MAN WITH NEWSPAPER: No, the president of the union, Johnny Mitchell.

ANGRY MAN: How much longer do the coal company presidents and the railroad presidents think we're going to take this?

THIRD MAN: So what's the letter say?

ANGRY MAN: I'd like to see George Baer step out of his fancy office at the Philadelphia & Reading Railroad and spend ten minutes in a mine.

MAN WITH NEWSPAPER *(Reading)*: Dear Mr. Mitchell, I want to send a letter to Santa Claus but I don't know how to direct my letter . . .

ANGRY MAN: A decent American wage, is that so much to ask for? An eight-hour day?

MAN WITH NEWSPAPER: . . . and I saw your picture in a magazine and I think you look like you would be able to help me send it. Your little friend, Garry.

THIRD MAN: Think Johnny Mitchell can help the kid?

MAN WITH NEWSPAPER: Of course. He's our man, Johnny!

BOY: He's Father John!

ANGRY MAN: He's Johnny d'Mitch! And he can help *us*!

("Mitchellisms," a driving, rabble-rousing chorus, plays as the boxer becomes Johnny Mitchell.)

MITCHELL *(Speaking to a large crowd)*: Gentlemen. The supreme crisis in the history of the Anthracite region is approaching. You and I know that no miner should work under the conditions which you are now working under. *(Crowd cheers)* But don't underestimate the strength of our opponents. They can afford to fight. As a matter of dollars and cents, they could afford to close the mines for months. They could afford to spend several million dollars on this fight and make it all back, while we, with quaking hearts, ask for each paycheck. When money is placed on one side of the balance, and human life on the other, money outweighs life in innumerable proportion. *(He sings:)*

> There is nothing on earth so cheap as human life
> Every ton of coal has a splash of blood on it.
> There is nothing on earth so cheap as human life
> Every ton of coal has a splash of blood on it.

CROWD:

> There is nothing on earth so cheap as human life
> Every ton of coal has a splash of blood on it.
> There is nothing on earth so cheap as human life
> Every ton of coal has a splash of blood on it.

MITCHELL *(Spoken)*: When I first came to the Anthracite region, I found the miners disorganized and separated by ethnic prejudices and religious animosities. Let us look to the future, when strikes shall be no more, when peace and justice shall be secured for all. *(Sings:)*

> I look forward to the time when strikes shall be no more
> When peace and justice shall be secured for those who toil
> When labor and capital work together in harmony
> For the welfare of our country and its commonwealth.

CROWD:

> We look forward to the time when strikes shall be no more
> When peace and justice shall be secured for we who toil
> When labor and capital work together in harmony
> For the welfare of our country and its commonwealth.
> For the welfare of our country . . .

(The song is halted by the entrance of George Baer. All back away to make room for him.)

IMAGE: *Photo of George Baer.*

BAER: As president of the P&R Railroad, and a broad-gauge businessman, I see the drift of change. I'm always willing to hear the grievances of my employees. You can talk to me. You've no reason to let a soft-coal man from Indiana talk you into a strike. For a strike in this day and age will be a fight to the end. It will be a long strike. What will you do when the grocers cut off your credit, when the saloons shut their doors, and you get cold? A strike's not a vacation; what will you do, read books? How long will it be till you're hungry?

HECKLER 1: How long will it be till you're broke?

HECKLER 2: You think we'll go back to work before winter?

MITCHELL: Gentlemen, I could appeal to you in the names of your wives and your children, but I won't do that. You know better than I how long they can starve. Experience has shown me that miners can live longer with nothing to eat than anyone else in this world. If you strike, if *we* strike, we strike until we all win, or we all go down in defeat.

CROWD *(Sings)*:
    There is nothing on earth so cheap as human life
    Every ton of coal has a splash of blood on it.
    There is nothing on earth so cheap as human life
    Every ton of coal has a splash of blood on it.

    We look forward to the time when strikes shall be no more
    When peace and justice shall be secured for we who toil
    When labor and capital work together in harmony
    For the welfare of our country and its commonwealth.
    For the welfare of our country and its commonwealth.

(The men raise strike signs in various languages.
    Baer and Mitchell square off, facing each other. The boxing bell rings twice. A Referee comes between them. They go to opposites sides of the playing area, sit on benches.)

REFEREE: Never in history has such a spectacle been presented! One hundred and forty-seven thousand men and boys in a solid, unbroken labor force on one side; the capitalists on the other.

(The boxing bell rings twice again.)

(Like a train conductor) Scranton!

(A gunshot rings out. Screams. The crowd parts, revealing a Mother cradling her wounded son.)

MOTHER: The first blood of the strike has been shed, and as usual the victim is perfectly innocent. He is Charles McCann, a thirteen-year-old boy. He was shot in the leg by those men *(Points to a Guard; crowd seizes him)* brought up from Philadelphia to guard the mines.

GUARD: We didn't know the little fellow was shot until we were arrested.

BOY: We were going to the swimming hole. I just peeked through the fence to see the guards.

GUARD: They were ripping down parts of the fence! Someone outside was shooting. I think the boys or someone was shooting off a cannon. Stones were thrown at us. I'll be glad to get out of this hot region. So will my chums. I never thought we'd get in such a mix as this and if we get out safely we'll be mighty glad, I can tell you.

(The boxing bell rings twice.)

REFEREE: Branchdale!

(A scab, Henry, approaches the strikers, who have an American flag.)

STRIKER 1: Well if it isn't Henry Gottshal. Where you think you're going, you scab?

HENRY: I'm just going in to check the pumps, Pat. You know they got to keep working or the mines will flood.

STRIKER 1: Let 'em.

HENRY: Let me by. *(They struggle, and the flag falls on the ground)*

STRIKER 1: Now look what you done.

STRIKER 2: The only way you're going to get to work, Henry, is to walk on the American flag.

STRIKER 1: If you do that, we'll have to shoot you.

(Henry attempts to lift the flag out of his way.)

ALL STRIKERS *(Assaulting Henry)*: Get your hands off that . . .

(The struggle continues until the sound of a police whistle. Everyone freezes.
The boxing bell rings twice.)

REFEREE: Shenandoah!

PVT. STEWART CULIN *(Entering)*: On the first day we were stationed in Shenandoah, we escorted some workers through a mob calling out: "Scab." *(Previous scene continues, with strikers chasing Henry off, yelling, "Scab!")* This insult is also expressed in gesture, by scratching the cheeks with the fingers of each hand. On still another occasion, we arrested some men who were illegally mining coal during the night. Another time, a gray-haired Irish woman cried after us:

IRISH WOMAN *(From the crowd)*: God bless ye, and may ye die of the hunger.

HARD COAL 97

PVT. STEWART CULIN: We bought a brown puppy from one of the Lithu-anian children for a dime; we have named him Striker. These children have never heard of George Washington, and could not tell me the name of our president.

(The boxing bell rings twice.)

REFEREE: Wilkes-Barre!

WILLIAM F. CLARK: To Mr. Baer, President of P&R Railroad. Dear Sir, while it is true that the coal strike is not a religious matter, I pray God to send the Holy Spirit to reason your heart. Take Christ in your business and consider the labor unions as a brother.

GEORGE BAER: My dear Mr. Clark, I do not know who you are. I see that you are a religious man, but . . .

(He sings "Baer (Naked) Truisms," a majestic tenor aria:)

> I beg of you not to be discouraged.
> I beg of you not to be discouraged.
> The rights and interests of the laboring man will be protected,
> Protected,
> But not by the labor negotiators,
> Certainly not by the labor negotiators,
> But by good Christian men to whom God, in His infinite wisdom,
> Christian men
> To whom God has given control of the property interests of the
>   country.
> To whom God has given control of the country.
>
> I beg of you not to be discouraged.
> Pray earnestly that Right may triumph.
> Remembering Lord God omnipotent still reigns,
> Still reigns, still reigns,
> And when He reigns . . .

MITCHELL *(Spoken)*: It pours.

SCHOOLGIRL *(Skipping rope)*:
> Old King Coal was a jolly old soul,
> And a jolly old soul was he;
> When he felt in the humor
> He'd rob the consumer
> And chuckle with fiendish glee.

(The boxing bell rings twice.)

REFEREE: New York City!

A NEW YORKER: To the Editor of the *New York Times*: Coming across the river today I heard a man express the hope that the mine owners may spend eternity in a place where the question of heat is purely academic . . .

A BAKER: We, the New York Retail Baker's Association, finding the means of our livelihood menaced by the lack of coal, appeal to you, President Roosevelt, to end the reign of terror in the coal fields. Very soon, all factories, including our own, will close down. Suffering, disease and death stalk close behind the present hardship and privation. The strike must end.

(The boxing bell rings twice.)

REFEREE: Washington, D.C.! End of the line!

(The Referee becomes President Theodore Roosevelt.)

ROOSEVELT: The catastrophe of a winter fuel shortage requires me, as your president, to use whatever influence I can to end a situation which has become intolerable . . . We are upon the threshold of winter, the future terrors of which, with a coal shortage, we can hardly yet appreciate. I fear there may be fuel riots as bad as any bread riots we have seen . . . I appeal to your patriotism, that you meet the crying needs of the people and bring to an end this bitter strike through arbitration.

(Mitchell jumps up and shakes Roosevelt's hand. Baer takes his time, he bypasses Mitchell, shakes Roosevelt's hand. Baer and Roosevelt exit together, as chums.

The boxing bell rings twice. Again, we are at the gym. Mitchell is again the sparring boxer in the background. Men are conversing as they watch.)

ANGRY MAN: A decent American wage, was that so much to ask for? An eight-hour day?

MAN WITH NEWSPAPER: You talk like we lost the strike! We won!

ANGRY MAN: Won? Money isn't everything. Did the union get recognized? No. We're back where we started.

MAN WITH NEWSPAPER: Yeah? Watch this. *(To a Boy)* Who's President of the United States?

BOY: Everybody knows that. His picture's on the wall, next to Jesus. It's Johnny d'Mitch!

(They exit; fade out on gym.)

TITLE: "Sophia Coxe (1841–1926): 'The Angel of the Anthracite Fields.'"

IMAGE: *Photo of Sophia Coxe; film clips of birds flying.*

(The Schoolgirl, barefoot, dressed in a white turn-of-the-century girl's dress, emerges from the shadows. In each of her hands she has a sheet of paper, folded so that they gently flap in her hands like a bird. She gently "flies" the papers across the stage and delivers them to two women awaiting her on the side of the stage. Woman 1 is standing; Woman 2 is sitting on the floor of the stage. When she has delivered the sheets of paper, the Schoolgirl returns to the main playing area, which is suggestive of a dusty patch town street. She looks a little lost, she spins idly.)

IMAGE: *Photo of Mining and Mechanical Institute, 1902.*

WOMAN 1 *(Reading from her paper)*: From a typewritten manuscript donated to the archives of the Mining and Mechanical Institute, a college preparatory school for miners' children founded in Freeland in 1879 by the prominent coal operator Eckley B. Coxe, and endowed by his widow, Mrs. Sophia *("Sophia" is pronounced with a long "I")* Georgiana Coxe, known to thousands of people of this and past generations as the "Angel of the Anthracite Fields."

WOMAN 2 *(Reading from her sheet of paper)*: As a child, I lived in the small mining village of Drifton . . .

SCHOOLGIRL *(Playing hopscotch)*:
God made bees and bees made honey.
God made man and man made money.
Pride made the devil and the devil made sin,
So God made a coal pit to put the devil in.

(A group of men, each holding a pure white book opened in his hands like wings, "flock" together in a cluster, gently flapping the "wings" of their books, circling like birds around the Schoolgirl. She reaches for the books, but the men hold them just out of her reach. Then they flock out of sight. The Schoolgirl is angry. She yells after them:)

God made a coal pit to put the devil in!

WOMAN 1: After her marriage, Sophia Coxe left the social life of Philadelphia and spent all her remaining years living among and helping the
working people of this region.

*(From the shadows emerges the figure of Sophia, dressed in white with
a white lace cap. She approaches the Schoolgirl. During the following
dialogue, Mrs. Coxe and the Schoolgirl mime a gentle give-and-receive
sequence, with some distance between them.)*

WOMAN 2: When I was tiny, she brought me milk every morning.
WOMAN 1: As she did for all the households with children.
WOMAN 2: She taught me the names of the flowers in her garden.
WOMAN 1: Solomon's seal, anemone, bloodroot . . .
WOMAN 2: Every Christmas, at Cross Creek Hall, beside the Christmas tree
bright with candles, Mrs. Coxe gave every child in the town two pres-
ents . . .
WOMAN 1: One useful . . .

*(Mrs. Coxe mimes the gesture of wrapping a warm muffler around the
Schoolgirl's neck. She enjoys the warmth.)*

One pleasurable . . .

*(Mrs. Coxe mimes giving a doll to the Schoolgirl, who cradles the doll
in her arms.)*

WOMAN 2: She cared for me when I was sick.
WOMAN 1: She cared for all who were sick or injured or crippled or blind.
WOMAN 2: It seems incredible to me that these many years after the death
of so rare and vital a woman as Sophia Coxe, there exists no biogra-
phy of her life, no monuments or placards listing her thousandfold
gifts to the poor people of our region.

*(Mrs. Coxe and the Schoolgirl laugh. Mrs. Coxe puts her finger to her
lips and then to the Schoolgirl's, as if they have a secret.)*

IMAGE: **White clouds floating by.**

WOMAN 1: She truly believed that such gifts would cancel her credit in
Heaven if she put her name on them.

(The men flock on; one has a largish white book. They give the book to Mrs. Coxe, who gives it to the Schoolgirl, who lifts it up in her hands like a bird.)

WOMAN 2: Sophia . . .
WOMAN 1: Sophia . . .
WOMAN 2: Best of all, she gave me books.
WOMAN 1: The bard, Blake, the Bible . . .

(A soaring spiritual, sung in soprano, "I Want to Be Born," plays. Mrs. Coxe and the Schoolgirl listen to the song, then dance as the lyrics repeat.)

WOMAN 2:
> I want to be born . . . and I want to give birth.
> I want to hear . . . and I want to be heard.
> I want to join with you . . . and I want to be joined.
> I want to make you beautiful . . . and I want to be beautiful.
> If you look at me . . . I will be a lamp.
> If you see me . . . I will be a mirror.
> If you knock on me . . . I will be a door.
> If you are a traveler . . . I will be a road.
> This is my dance . . . Answer me with dancing. *(Repeat)*

(The men and Mrs. Coxe are gone, leaving the Schoolgirl, who comes to the Women and takes their hands. They leave the stage together.)

TITLE: "The Knox Mine Disaster, January 22, 1959."

IMAGE: *Newspaper headline:* 12 MISSING AND 33 RESCUED AFTER RIVER BREAKS INTO MINE NEAR PITTSTON, **Wilkes-Barre Record,** *January 23, 1959; vintage news footage of the whirlpool created in the Susquehanna River when the Knox mine collapsed; later footage depicts the failed attempts to stop the whirlpool by filling up the hole with empty railroad cars.*

(Onstage, below the enormous image of the whirlpool, a Trapped Miner tries to escape. He moves in a stylized variation of the Avondale dance: reaching, digging, reaching, praying, reaching . . . A woman kneels over a washtub, whooshing a shirt about in circles in the water. These actions continue throughout the following scene. Another Knox Miner, dressed in suit and tie, stands stage right. Above him on a bench stands a newspaper Reporter.)

REPORTER: What was your position for the Knox Coal Company?

KNOX MINER: Assistant foreman.

REPORTER: And what was your job that day?

KNOX MINER: I went with a couple of laborers and rockmen to finish up the work of extending the slope into the second level vein.

REPORTER: Was this extension of the slope beyond the danger line, the stop line?

KNOX MINER: Well, the stop line had been re-drawn by the company.

REPORTER: Re-drawn?

KNOX MINER: Well, yeah. There was real good coal under the river there, and so a few years ago, the company re-drew the red line on the map so they could get in there and get that coal.

REPORTER: When did you realize that something was wrong that day?

(A Boy enters trailing a red toy train.)

KNOX MINER: Fred and Frank, my laborers, called me over to check out the props, the timber ceiling supports, you know. There was this sound coming from them, this shrill cracking sound. That's not good.

(A Wilkes-Barre Woman comes out to sit on the floor next to the rocker. She has a scrapbook. Nearby, the Boy plays with the train.)

WILKES-BARRE WOMAN: My pop told me he kept having the same dream over and over again. In the dream, he said, we were all asleep in the house, and there was this big crack in the ceiling and the whole ceiling came crashing down on us.

IMAGE: *Looped video of railroad cars going down into the whirlpool.*

KNOX MINER: I no more than put my foot in the place and looked up than the roof gave way. It sounded like thunder. Water poured in like Niagara Falls.

WILKES-BARRE WOMAN: Just a few days before, I heard Pop say to Mom, "If that river comes in, we'll be drowned like rats."

KNOX MINER: You know what I want to know? How come we were told to keep mining? Just a week or so before, the inspectors ordered all work stopped, 'cause, you know, where we were was illegal. The company just ignored that and told us to keep on mining. How come?

IMAGE: *Newspaper headline:* CORRUPTION IN MINES, **Sunday Dispatch.**

WILKES-BARRE WOMAN: We saw that story in the paper about that guy, that August Lippi, the union boss who kept pleading the Fifth.

IMAGE: *Newspaper photo, with caption:* LIPPI TAKES OATH BUT THEN CLAMS UP.

(Trapped Miner assumes a frozen position, back to audience, focusing on the projected image of Lippi on the screen above him.)

IMAGE: *Looped footage of televised hearings, featuring Lippi.*

REPORTER: At the hearings held to investigate the disaster, August J. Lippi, president of District 1 UMWA, repeatedly invoked the Fifth Amendment, but was ultimately exposed as a secret, part owner of the Knox Coal Company, in blatant violation of labor laws. Although he escaped conviction on this crime, and also on charges of manslaughter and conspiracy, he was finally convicted of income-tax evasion and bank fraud. However, the legal system never actually found any individuals or organizations guilty for causing the events of January 22, 1959. The Knox mine disaster is repeatedly referred to by the people of this region as the tragedy that signaled the end of anthracite mining in this part of Pennsylvania.

IMAGE: *Knox whirlpool.*

KNOX MINER: That was it. Greed. That's all, just greed. You can name a book "Greed" and write forever on it in the Anthracite, from the first mines that were ever opened. That's all it was, all the time.

WILKES-BARRE WOMAN: You know, years later, I had this dream that Pop came into my bedroom and he told me not to worry about him, not to miss him so much.

REPORTER: Names of the dead: *(He reads from a list, continuing under the scene as it proceeds)* Samuel Altieri, John Baloga, Benjamin Boyar, Francis Burns, Charles Featherman, Joseph Gizenski, Dominick Kaveliskie, Frank Orlowski, Eugene Ostrowski, William Sinclair, Daniel Stefanides, Herman Zelonis.

(The Trapped Miner removes his shirt.)

IMAGE: *Names of the dead are projected on the Trapped Miner's bare back, then on the screen above him.*

KNOX MINER: Did anybody ever leave anything for a coal miner? Is there a park ever donated by a coal company? Not one. They left nothing for you. All the streets are named after them. All the shafts are named after them. And they never left nothing.

WILKES-BARRE WOMAN: And when I woke up from that dream in the middle of the night, the rocking chair next to the bed was rocking to and fro, to and fro, and there was nothing there. Nothing. *(Exits)*

(The Schoolgirl enters and comes center.)

SCHOOLGIRL: Hard coal is still being mined today. It's used for paint, water filtration and heat.

GARAGE OWNER *(Enters from house, crosses to rocking chair)*: My wife and I run a garage; our electric heat bills used to be out of sight.

IMAGE: *The logo of Blaschak Coal Company:* IT'S NOT JUST COAL . . . IT'S ANTHRACITE!

GARAGE OWNER'S WIFE *(Joining him)*: I suggested we try an anthracite stove.

GARAGE OWNER: I was skeptical, but I decided to give it a try. It was the best thing we've ever done.

(The rest of the cast enters one by one, "warming themselves by a stove.")

GARAGE OWNER'S WIFE: Our customers love the steady, even warmth. They sit in rocking chairs near the stove, watch the beautiful pale blue flames, and enjoy the heat while waiting for their cars.

GARAGE OWNER: It's the kind of warmth that . . . makes you feel good.

IMAGE: *Photo montage of faces: miners, women, children, looming large over the actors grouped around the "stove."*

(Lights fade to black.)

END

Select Bibliography

Bartoletti, Susan Campbell. *Growing Up in Coal Country.* Boston: Houghton Mifflin, 1996.

Bodner, John. *Anthracite People: Families, Unions and Work, 1900–1940.* Harrisburg: Pennsylvania Historical and Museum Commmission, copyright © Commonwealth of Pennsylvania, 1983.

Dublin, Thomas. *When the Mines Closed: Stories of Struggles in Hard Times.* Ithaca, NY: Cornell University Press, 1998.

Korson, George. *Minstrels of the Mine Patch: Songs and Stories of the Anthracite Industry.* Hatboro, PA: Folklore Associates, 1964.

Miller, Donald L. and Richard E. Sharpless. *The Kingdom of Coal: Work, Enterprise, and Ethnic Communities in the Mine Fields.* Philadelphia: University of Pennsylvania Press, 1985.

Ring, Chris. *Carbon Knight*, a regional comic book set in Centralia. Lunar Studios, 50 1/2 N. Market St., Elysburg, PA 17824.

Wolensky, Robert P.; Kenneth C. Wolensky and Nicole H. Wolensky. *The Knox Mine Disaster, January 22, 1959: The Final Years of the Northern Anthracite Industry and the Effort to Rebuild a Regional Economy.* Harrisburg: Pennsylvania Historical and Museum Commission, copyright © Commonwealth of Pennsylvania, 1999.

BLOOMSBURG THEATRE ENSEMBLE

Bloomsburg Theatre Ensemble was founded in 1978 in a small town in rural Pennsylvania. With start-up support from the town council and area patrons, BTE presented two plays in the Central Columbia Middle School "cafetorium," which became their home for the next three summers. In 1980, BTE purchased the Columbia movie theater in downtown Bloomsburg and reopened it in 1983 as the Alvina Krause Theatre, named in honor of the legendary acting teacher who was BTE's founding inspiration. BTE celebrated its twenty-fifth anniversary during the 2002–2003 season. On the mainstage of the Alvina Krause Theatre, BTE has produced more than one hundred and fifty plays. This production history includes American and European classics by Euripides, Shakespeare, Molière, Chekhov, Beckett, Shaw, Miller, Wilder and Williams, as well as adventurous contemporary plays such as *Molly Sweeney*, *The Baltimore Waltz*, *Arcadia*, *The Laramie Project*, *Ambition Facing West* (the world premiere of the revised version), *Oleanna*, *The Firebugs*, *Lebensraum*, *Whispering to Horses*, *The Women of Lockerbie* and *Rain. Some Fish. No Elephants.* Ensemble-written adaptations of literature include Dickens's *A Christmas Carol*, Barrie's *Peter and Wendy*, Carroll's *Alice's Adventures in Wonderland* and *A Midnight Dreary* (based on poems and stories by Poe).

In line with its mission: "We are dedicated, over time, to our community, to theater as a patient but powerful instrument of understanding and social change, and to one another as artists," BTE has recently devoted its energy to creating original works based in regional history and folklore. *Hard Coal: Life in the Region* and *Letters to the Editor*, which dramatized letters to local newspapers from colonial times to the present, are examples of this work.

BTE tours schools annually with *Theatre in the Classroom* (TIC), original forty-five-minute pieces based on American history or international folk literature. In 1991, TIC's *Along the Susquehanna: Tales from Pennsylvania's Native Americans* performed in five African nations on a tour sponsored by the State Department's United States Information Service. Other educational projects include theater classes offered throughout the year for area children, teens and adults, as well as season-long internships for early-career theater artists. Bloomsburg University theater majors receive professional experience in a summer BTE-BU co-production. BTE also hosts the annual Noh Training Project, and is the only location in North America to provide intensive training in the classical theater-dance of Japan. BTE continues its training through collaboration with major national artists, such as Daniel Stein (*Bend Till It Breaks*), Karen Bamonte and Guy Klucevsek (*Hard Coal: Life in the Region*), Anthony Clarvoe (*Ambition Facing West*) and Joan Schirle of Dell'Arte International (*School for Wives* and *Human Hearts*). *The Alexandria Carry-On*, a multimedia music-theater piece created and directed by ensemble member Laurie McCants, in collaboration with composer/performer Theo Bleckmann, premiered at BTE in 2004 and was performed at the Bibliotheca Alexandrina in Alexandria, Egypt, the following fall. *The Alexandria Carry-On* continues to tour to theaters, universities and libraries in the United States and abroad.

Today, BTE combines the artistry of the resident ensemble with a dedicated professional staff of administrative and production personnel, backed by a regional board of trustees and numerous volunteers. With local support from businesses and Ensemble Circle Donors and through major funding from national and regional foundations, BTE continues to grow as an organization and artistic force. It is a theater dedicated to awakening the imagination, provoking questions and emboldening the spirit.

BERLIN, JERUSALEM AND THE MOON

Traveling Jewish Theatre

Left to right: Corey Fischer, Albert Greenberg and Naomi Newman.

F. SIMON

Introduction

Once, while addressing a group of students, Traveling Jewish Theatre cofounder Naomi Newman stopped and said with sudden fervor, "Look, you have a story, and once you know what it is, you must tell it, you have a *responsibility* to tell it."

Our stories connect us to personal history, as well as the histories of our community, culture and civilization. Over the years I've come to understand that Newman's statement has been more than this ensemble's ethos: it has been their crusade. "This work is not about making a living," TJT's cofounder Corey Fischer once told me. "It's a way of being in the world."

In 1978, Newman and cofounders Fischer and Albert Greenberg began making theatrical experiments, attempting to simultaneously explore contemporary issues and the most ineffable, mystic qualities of their mutual Jewish heritage. They applied the rabbinic *midrash* tradition of literary exegesis—an Iron Age hermeneutics, still used by Torah scholars—to playwriting and performance, and forged a unique non-narrative approach to creating text, music and extended movement. TJT's original pieces are structured like poems, play like dance, and stir emotions and ideas as only the theater can. Helen Stoltzfus joined the company as co-artistic director in 1986. As a non-Jew she brought a whole new dimension to the theater's work.

For TJT, storytelling has been not only the basis of tradition, but also liberation. Like the real-life philosopher Walter Benjamin, a character in *Berlin, Jerusalem and the Moon*, this ensemble assumes the mantle of the divine fool, showing us that courageous, conscious engagement with history—personal and collective—can free us from history's effects.

—F.L.

PRODUCTION INFORMATION

Berlin, Jerusalem and the Moon was originally performed by Corey Fischer (Jacob, Walter), Albert Greenberg (Angel, Izzy) and Naomi Newman (Woman, Else, Edie), with original music by Albert Greenberg and percussion and keyboards by Jim Quinn. The original set and lighting were designed by Jim Quinn.

The text for Walter (page 127) is adapted from "Theses on the Philosophy of History," Walter Benjamin, from *Illuminations*, Hannah Arendt, ed., Schocken Books, Inc., New York, 1969; English translation copyright © 1968 by Harcourt Brace Jovanovich, Inc.

SETTING/SET

The play is performed in an open space with white walls. There is an alcove upstage center that serves as a kind of stage-inside-a-stage, where characters can appear in silhouette. Suitcases "bandaged" with cheesecloth are used to define and alter the space.

Darkness. Lights slowly reveal the Angel of History, dressed in a ragged coat and top hat, a cross between a circus ringmaster and a shell-shocked survivor. He is seated on one of a group of suitcases that are wrapped in cheesecloth. The suitcases are placed in an alcove that is formed by an upstage archway. Just before the lights come up, we hear a piano chord and the Angel begins to sing, "lu lu lu . . ." He continues singing over the chords as the lights come up. As he sings, he discovers two pieces of paper in his coat pockets, which he takes out and uses as wings. His movements carry him out of the alcove and into the central playing area.

ANGEL OF HISTORY *(Singing)*:
>Some are clean-shaven, some are hairy, some give birth and take flight;
>Some believe, some don't believe in anything,
>Some are black and some are white.
>And they're all called the children of Israel,
>Whether they like it or not,
>In hotel rooms and in the desert,
>In L.A. and in Elat.
>Yes they're all called the children of Israel.
>And who was Israel?
>Israel was Jacob, many, many, many years ago
>Many, many, many years ago,
>Many, many, many years ago . . .

(Drums begin. Chords continue a few more beats.)

Many, many, many years ago . . .

(The Angel crosses upstage left. A Woman enters and begins chanting the biblical text of the Jacob story in Hebrew, while the Angel chants in English.)

WOMAN *(Chanting):*
> Va yi va ter Ya'akov l'vado . . .

(Jacob, naked to the waist, suddenly appears from behind the suitcases, staring straight ahead in terror.)

> Va yay avek ish i mo ad a lot ha scha char . . .

(Jacob climbs over the suitcases and quickly moves center stage as his left arm rises slowly to full extension, straight up.)

ANGEL OF HISTORY *(Chanting):* And Jacob was left alone and someone or something wrestled with him until the rising of the morning star.

(During the following, Jacob's right arm and hand take on the role of the "other" with whom he is wrestling. The index finger of Jacob's upraised arm points down at him. He looks up at it in terror. He tries to escape it. It grabs his throat, then his arm, as he keeps wrestling with it.)

WOMAN *(Chanting):*
> Va-yi-va-teyr Ya-a-kov l'-va-do
> Va-yey-a-veyk ish i-mo ad a-lote ha-sha-char
> Va-yar ki lo ya-chol lo va-yi-ga b'chaf Ye-re-cho
> Va-tey-ka-kaf ye-rech Ya-a-kov b'hey-av-ko i-mo
> Va-yo-mer shal-chey-ni ki-a-la ha-sha-char
> Va-yo-mer lo a-sha-ley-cha-cha ki im bey-rach-ta-ni . . .

(Jacob's left arm "flees" to the left, and then suddenly moves across his body, ending with a blow to his right hip. His leg bends in pain.)

ANGEL OF HISTORY *(Chanting):* And when it saw that it could not prevail against Jacob, it touched the hollow of his thigh and Jacob's hip was put out of joint as he wrestled with him.

(Jacob struggles to pull his left arm off his thigh.)

WOMAN (*Chanting*):

> Va-yo-mer ey-lav ma shme-cha va-yo-mer Ya-a-kov
> Va-yo-mer lo Ya-a-kov yey-a-mer od shim-cha
> Ki im Yis-ra-el ki sa-ri-ta im E-lo-him
> V'im a-na-shim va-tu-chal . . .

(The left arm flees again. Jacob grabs it with his right hand and pulls it toward his face.)

ANGEL OF HISTORY (*Chanting*): Then it said, "Let me go, for the dawn is breaking," and Jacob said, "I will not let you go till you bless me."

(It stops at Jacob's ear.)

And it said, "What is your name?"

(Jacob moves the hand to in front of his mouth and releases a breath.)

And he said, "Jacob."

(The hand pulls away from Jacob's mouth and makes a gesture of hurling something to the ground. It then rises up and slowly descends in a gesture of blessing, ending at Jacob's heart. Jacob remains transfixed. He opens his eyes. He tries to take a step. He discovers his wound, his infirmity, and slowly limps away.)

And it said, "Your name is no longer Jacob, your name is Israel . . ."
WOMAN (*Simultaneously*): V'Yisrael . . .
ANGEL OF HISTORY: For you have wrestled with the divine and the human and have overcome . . . *(Exits)*

WOMAN (*Chanting*):

> Ki sarita im Elohim v'im anashim va thuchal . . .

(Drumming stops. Jacob exits, limping.
   The lights fade to a glow on the white suitcases upstage. An accordion plays "The Café Theme," a melody in the style of Kurt Weill, in a slightly melancholy cabaret style. Izzy the K enters in a black leather jacket. He is a hyper, streetwise comic in the Lenny Bruce mold, except that his obsessions are not drugs and sex, but Germans, Zionism and the Middle East conflict. He is also obsessed with Kafka. With a great flourish, he places three suitcases center stage: a large one in the center, with the other two on either side, at an angle. The music fades.)

IZZY: Welcome, ladies and gentlemen! Welcome to Kafka's Kafé in Tel Aviv. A land of mystery. A land of the red sun. Yeah, it's true, Kafka wanted to open a café in Tel Aviv, but he died. Which is just as well, because Kafka was a hunger artist and there wouldn't be any food in Kafka's Kafé, only more ideas.

Now, obviously Kafka couldn't be with us this evening, but in a way he is . . . in a way he is . . . I want to tell you a little story about just what a funny guy he was. You see, at the end of his life, the tuberculosis that he had carried for so long had moved into his throat. *(Transforms into Kafka with a deep, raspy voice)* "'Josephine the Mouse Singer' is the last story I write. She does not so much sing, as squeak!" *(Transforms back)* Squeak! *(Tries to milk the audience for a laugh. Not getting much of a response, he continues)*

So you see, if Kafka were alive today, he'd be a komic—a komic with a capital 'K.' *(Puts on dark sunglasses)* You know the kind. The kind most people think of as sicK! SicK of all the b—hypocrisy that passes for real life. Take the Middle East . . . Please! Beirut. Jerusalem. Why, we hear the names of those quaint little places and we get filled with all kinds of moral outrage. Opinions. Then we order another cappuccino, or buy a new jacket. Oh, you like my jacket? German leather . . . bought it in Israel. *(Pause)* German leather, bought it in Israel. Connections past and present. Connections . . . *(Cabaret music fades up again)* So come with me now, ladies and gentlemen, to Kafka's Kafé in Tel Aviv! On the menu this evening . . .

(Walter and Else enter from right and left sides of alcove and freeze.)

Germans in the desert!

(Walter and Else bow to each other and cross. They sit on small suitcases, using a large suitcase as a café table.)

Not just any Germans, but Weimar Germans. Between-the-World-Wars Germans. Between being Jews and . . . Germans. Ladies and gentlemen, for your intellectual and emotional discomfort—Walter Benjamin, the most famous obscure critic of German culture; and Else Lasker-Schüler, the most famous forgotten poet of German history. Here they are, ladies and gentlemen, in an imaginary meeting, in an imaginary café. Caught in a never-ending wrestling match—which is their struggle, their salvation, their obsession. *(Turns away, observing the following scene)*

WALTER: Tell me, Else, what do you dream of in Zion?

ELSE: I dream of in Zion, what I dreamt of in Germany—a new Zion. A just society, where people can live together with love.

WALTER: That is a beautiful dream. But it is only a dream.

ELSE: You know, Walter, you haven't changed one bit, since we met back in Berlin in the twenties.

WALTER: Else, we never met.

ELSE: Yes dear, we did.

WALTER: No, no, no, I'm certain we did not.

ELSE: Well Walter, you wrote about it yourself.

WALTER: How could I have written about it . . .

ELSE: In the *Berlin Chronicle*, "Else Lasker-Schüler drew me to her table."

WALTER: Well, maybe we did.

ELSE: Yes. *(Beat)* Did you think I was beautiful?

WALTER: Actually, I thought you were a cross between an archangel and a fishwife.

ELSE *(Laughing)*: I see, Walter, you were afraid of intelligent women?

WALTER: No, no . . . I was afraid of—

ELSE: Of artists.

WALTER: Will you let me finish my sentence?

ELSE: Why?

WALTER: Why?

ELSE: Yes, why?

WALTER: Because it is mine.

ELSE: So, what is so marvelous about your sentence?

WALTER: It is not that it is marvelous, but it is an attempt to capture—

ELSE: Everything with the mind.

WALTER *(Standing)*: And what is wrong with the mind? Besides, for me the mind was never just the mind—

ELSE *(Standing)*: No, Walter, for you the mind was God.

WALTER: I wouldn't quite say that—and you've done it again.

ELSE: What? What have I done?

WALTER: Not allowed me to finish my sentence.

ELSE *(Crossing in front of him)*: Oh. Go ahead. Something about attempts.

WALTER: For me the sentence was an attempt to capture history.

ELSE: Walter, you cannot capture history—you can only live it.

WALTER: And understand it.

ELSE: Oh, I see, you have found a way to understand what happened to our moment of history in Berlin?!

WALTER: That was your moment, Else. You were in the center of all of that. I was only on the side.

ELSE: Side. Center. Top. Bottom. It was all incredible: such art, such passion, such brilliance.

WALTER: Such inflation, such excess, such bad taste. I had not planned to speak about this.

ELSE: Well, you see how history works, Walter. Plans make very little difference.

WALTER: No one knows that better than I.

ELSE: I know, I know. You didn't plan to end up the way you did on the Spanish border.

WALTER: I planned nothing. My life was a series of accidents. It was all because of the little hunchback, Buchlichmanlein. It was a nursery rhyme that my mother use to sing to me about the little hunchback man who follows you around, makes you trip, distracts you . . . Ever since then he has followed me around, and he makes me stumble . . . *(Sits on hat)* He distracts me. Ach, you see . . . I tell you this . . .

ELSE *(Comforting him)*: "Storytelling is reaching its end, because wisdom is dying out."

WALTER: Else, you committed that to memory. I am touched.

ELSE: Walter, I read every word you wrote.

WALTER: "Wisdom is dying out, as is the idea of eternity . . ."

ELSE: "Warmth is ebbing from things . . ."

WALTER: ". . . and the German spring that never comes is but . . ."

ELSE AND WALTER: ". . . one of many, many signs that German nature is decomposing."

ELSE: Oh, Walter, I wrote something so like that. I'm sure you know it.

WALTER: As a matter of fact, Else, I'm not so familiar with your work. But, please, don't take it personally.

ELSE: I won't. Well, maybe I will a little. I wrote: "My mother land is soulless. / Roses no longer grow there. / Winter has played with death in every nest."

WALTER: When did you write that?

ELSE: Oh, I don't usually remember. But that one . . . 1933.

WALTER: Did you get out?

ELSE: Did *we* get out?

(Drum roll. Izzy comes between Walter and Else, knocking over the large suitcase and then standing on it.)

IZZY: 1933, the Nazis come to power, through the will of the people. Democracy! 13.8 million votes. Now Else and Walter know it's time to start moving. *(Walter and Else pick up their suitcases and freeze)* Walter, he tries to take everything, his books, his chair, his armoire. *(Walter exits)* But, Else, she really flees. *(Else arcs upstage)* She takes nothing at all. You see, she went practically overnight from winning one of Germany's great literary awards—the Kleist prize—to being beaten on the streets of Berlin.

(Else moves downstage as drum roll and bell sounds continue under the following scene.)

ELSE: I was on my way home from the café when they stopped me, three of them in brown shirts. And with an iron bar they beat me on the arm and the leg and over the head. I looked into their eyes and their eyes were completely dead. So when they left me, bloodied and bruised on the street, I got up. And without going to my room, without getting anything, I went directly to the railroad station.

(She turns and quickly walks upstage into another space, which is the railroad station. We hear chimes and sounds of the station. She looks around, lost.)

And now I don't know where to go.

(A Faceless Stranger in a white mask enters. She goes to him.)

Excuse me, I would like to ask you a question—
FACELESS STRANGER *(Interrupting)*: Do you have the time?
ELSE: The time? It's twenty-five to five.
FACELESS STRANGER: Thank you. *(Exits)*
ELSE: Oh my God, it's so late.

(Another Faceless Stranger enters, sits on a suitcase.)

Excuse me, I know you are a stranger, and I am a stranger, and this is all very strange; but where would you go if you had to go?
ANOTHER FACELESS STRANGER: Pardon Madame, je ne comprends pas.
ELSE: Ah, mais je parles un peu de Francais.
ANOTHER FACELESS STRANGER: Excuse me, I don't speak French. Auf weidersehen, Fraulein. *(Exits to upstage alcove)*

(First Faceless Stranger crosses downstage. Else moves to him.)

ELSE: Please, tell me, do you have a ticket?
FACELESS STRANGER: Yes.
ELSE: That is so good. Now if you would just tell me your destination, that would be so kind.
FACELESS STRANGER: But I could lie to you. I could tell you anything.
ELSE: Well then lie, LIE. I must know where someone else is going.
FACELESS STRANGER: I am going to the Moon. *(Exits to alcove)*

ELSE:

Never has my life been so naked
So exposed to time

As if I stood
Behind the end of days
Between gaping nights
Alone.

(The other stranger, Another Faceless Stranger, crosses downstage and stands frozen.)

Please tell me where you are going. I must know where someone else is going.

ANOTHER FACELESS STRANGER: They are going everywhere.

ELSE: Not they. You, here now, in a body next to mine. One last person, in this place where I am not sure there are any human beings left. One little gesture where you will say, *ja*, I am going somewhere, too.

ANOTHER FACELESS STRANGER: I am going to Zurich. *(Crosses upstage to alcove)*

ELSE: ZURICH! I hate Zurich: where they lock everything up and hide the keys. *(Pulling herself together)* I will go to Zurich.

(The Faceless Strangers walk back and forth slowly inside the upstage alcove. They drone in unison the German word for farewell, "Ade.")

(Sings:)
    Ich bin ausgegangen in stiller Nacht,
    in stiller Nacht wohl über die dunkle Heide;
    Hat mir niemand Ade gesagt.
    Ade! Ade! Ade!
    Mein Gesell war Lieb und Leide!

(She exits. The second Faceless Stranger takes the mask of the first Stranger and exits. This Faceless Stranger transforms into Izzy, puts on sunglasses and continues the Mahler song in English, in a jazz rendition.)

IZZY *(Singing)*:
    I go out alone
    Into the silent night
    Into the silent night
    I must wander in darkness alone
    No one comes to me to say good-bye
    Good-bye Good-bye
    Bye bye bye. Bye bye bye. Bye bye bye.

(Explodes toward the audience) Love that Gustav Mahler. That baptized German-Jewish music. Talk about a dialectic. Talk about a dialectic. You see Else, here? She is going to Zurich. But she won't stop there. She's on the road to Zion! Talk about a dialectic. Talk about a dialectic.

Why I was just talking to a German friend of mine the other day—hey, some of my best friends are German. And I said, "Severing . . ." And he said *(Rolling the "R" in the back of his throat)*, "SeveRING . . . RING."

"Uh, excuse me, SeveRING. Do you mind if I call you 'Ring' for short? Tell me, Ring, what do Germans, today, think of Zionism?" *(Takes off sunglasses. His eyes are exaggeratedly open)*

"Vell, ve don't like ze Zionists zo much. And ze French don't neizer."

Now I know that, I know that. I mean, who likes the Zionists? The British? The Bulgarians? Berkeley? No, I figure the Zionists have two friends—Jerry Falwell and Vanessa Redgrave. And that's it! So I said, "I'll tell you what, Ring, I'll tell you what. We're coming back! Every one of us! Back to Berlin!"

So, that's how it starts, you see, as a little joke. But, then I get to thinking, I get to thinking, Why don't they want us in the goddamned desert? What's the big deal? And then, it hits me. They miss us. The Germans really miss us!

No, I'm serious, I'm serious. We've got a lot in common. We're blood relatives. And I understand the Germans, I understand them. I mean, they're a defeated people, and I understand that. But, you've got to understand, the Germans have given the Jewish people the greatest gift we have ever been given . . . Freedom From Guilt!

Think about it! Think about it! We don't have to *love* the Germans. They don't even want us to *love* them. *Love* is not even in the script. I mean, you know how American Jews are, don't you? *(Edie enters, sits on suitcase upstage. She's heard this act before)* You know how American Jews are, *don't you*? They're just like Californians, they *love* everybody!

Now don't get me wrong, I love this country. I do. America is one of . . . America is "The Greatest Country in the History of Motion Pictures." But the thing about America is, and thing about being a Jew in America is . . . is that in America you can just *disappear. (Makes large arm gesture)* I mean, come on, how many of you have just disappeared? *(Gesture)* But in Germany! Why, the Germans would never let a Jew just . . . *(Gesture)* Never! Again.

(Edie and Izzy are now in the railroad station.)

EDIE: Next on the menu, Americans, with *no* identity. Now, ladies and gentlemen, for your continued discomfort, I give you Izzy, the most famous obscure critic of everyone and everything; and Edie, yours truly, the most famous neglected wife in American history. Caught in a never-ending wrestling match, which is their obsession . . .

EDIE AND IZZY: Their compulsion, their addiction.

(Loud train sounds. Edie and Izzy go upstage to pick up suitcases, quibbling. Their lines are inaudible. They slam suitcases down at the same time. Edie is behind Izzy as they wait in line.)

EDIE *(Continuing the argument)*: But Izzy, it's crazy. What are we going to *do* in Berlin?

IZZY: Return.

EDIE: Return?

IZZY: Yes. Berlin used to be a Jewish city before the war.

EDIE: You want a Jewish city, let's "return" to New York.

IZZY: We're from New York.

EDIE: Exactly, that's why it's a dumb idea to go to Berlin.

IZZY: What do you mean, dumb idea?

EDIE: Come on, you know what happened. Everybody knows what happened.

IZZY: Of course I know what happened. I'm interested in what is happening.

EDIE: What are you going to do? Go over there and picnic on the graves?

IZZY: Partly, yeah. I wanna eat the past.

EDIE: Good. I think you should go. *(Starts to leave)*

IZZY *(Grabs her arm)*: No, no, no. I think *we* should go.

EDIE: Hey wait a minute, wait a minute. I am not a bicycle or a computer that you can take with you wherever you want to go.

IZZY: Look, we left some of the best parts of ourselves over there.

EDIE: Not me. What I've lost, I can't find in Berlin.

IZZY: I know it's upsetting.

EDIE: You're right. It's very upsetting. But I don't even know how upsetting it is because I don't know how serious you are.

IZZY: I am very serious. I am deadly serious. We can't go to Poland . . .

EDIE: I said you're upsetting me . . .

IZZY: We can't go to Saudi Arabia . . .

EDIE: Why can't you get the idea out of your head?

IZZY: . . . but Germany.

EDIE: You're Jewish. I am Jewish.

IZZY: And you sing German music. *(Singing)* Ich bin ausgegangen . . .

EDIE: Very funny, honey.

IZZY *(Singing)*: . . . In stiller Nacht. In stiller Nacht wohl über die . . .

EDIE: Yeah. Well, it used to upset my father, a lot.

IZZY: But you did it.

EDIE: I did it.

IZZY: You upset your father a lot.

EDIE: Yes.

IZZY: How did you feel about it?

EDIE: I thought it was beautiful music.

IZZY: You thought it was beautiful music. Why German music?

EDIE: I am not going to Berlin. My father could not stop me from singing German songs . . . and you think I'm going to live in Berlin? . . . I am getting so upset, I don't know what I'm saying anymore.

IZZY: Say that again. I really like that last bit of logic.

EDIE: I said, "I am getting upset."

IZZY: No. Before that.

EDIE: I said, "I don't know what I am saying."

IZZY: You know what you said . . .

EDIE: I know what I said . . .

IZZY: What did you say?

EDIE: I said, My father could not stop me from doing what I wanted to do.

IZZY: Which was?

EDIE: Which was . . .

IZZY: What?!

EDIE: To marry you.

IZZY: No, no, no. He couldn't stop you from singing German songs . . .

EDIE: That's right. And he couldn't stop me from marrying you. And he was right both times.

IZZY: Why couldn't he stop you from singing German songs?

EDIE: I AM NOT GOING TO BERLIN!

IZZY: Right, right. Nobody's going anywhere. (Gets on his hands and knees) Baa . . . Baa . . .

EDIE: What are you doing? Get up! OK, OK. Maybe if I could understand where you got the idea. If I could just get into the contours of that mind. Where did you get the idea?

IZZY (Jumps to his feet, erupting with energy): I look around at the world today and I see the same catastrophe right around the corner . . . only I can't tell if it's real or my paranoia . . . or . . .

(Drum roll. Walter and the Angel of History enter running with suitcases. They circle the stage. Edie begins running also. It is as if all three are running from some unseen threat. At some point during the running, Edie exits. The drums stop abruptly. The Angel drops his suitcase downstage right as Walter cowers in the upstage left corner. The Angel stands on his suitcase and sings, while Walter wanders, as if looking for a path that is not blocked.)

ANGEL OF HISTORY *(Singing)*:

Praise to Walter Benjamin and his generation.
Praise to those who are leaving home fresh with
the scars of separation.
Praise to the seekers and the wanderers who look
for other possibilities
in strange rooms, in boarding houses,
storytellers of untellable stories.
Praise to the survivors who bear the guilt of
those who will not survive.
Praise to those who learn the holy tongue
in places other than they desire.
Praise to the maker.
Praise to the taker.
Praise to the maker and the taker of possibilities.

(The Angel retreats upstage center, turns back. During the song, Walter has arranged his two suitcases as a lecture podium. As the Angel finishes his song, Walter wipes his forehead with his handkerchief and begins to speak.)

WALTER: My name is Walter Benjamin. I am here to speak to you on the nature of possibility. Our possibilities in these times, yours and mine. Let us begin with the possibility of the known. The possibility of what has gone before. *(Crosses to stage left wall, takes out red chalk)* And let *(Writing)* "Berlin" stand for that possibility. Berlin, the flowering of culture. Tolerance. The glory of the intellect. The power of language. The German language in which we placed our faith, our ambition, our love . . . and now that language is turned against us like a weapon, so for us, this first possibility does not exist. *(Crosses out "Berlin")*

For the second possibility, we shall take the example of my friend Bertolt Brecht, who is in exile in Denmark. He wants me to come visit him, but I do not know if I will go. His possibility is Marxism. And for Brecht, and perhaps even for myself, this unique brand of Marxism is still a viable possibility. However, Marxism, as currently manifest in the Soviet Union, leads to such phenomena as socialist realist art! . . . to dictatorship in the name of the proletariat, and it does not address our specific problems as Jews, so for us as Jews, the second possibility does not exist.

The third possibility *(Crossing stage right)* is one that is very poignant and close to us as Jews. Let Jerusalem stand for the possibility of a homeland. My dear friend Gerhard Scholem—who now calls himself Gershom—has emigrated to Palestine and he wants me to do the same. He wants me to learn Hebrew and to help build the culture of the new land and I have begun to do so. *(Writes on stage right wall in red chalk the Hebrew characters for "Yerushalayim")* Yeru: the city of, Shalayim—from Shalom—peace. *(Looking at what he has written)* Yeru-shalayim. The city of peace. *(Pause)* And each year I announce my imminent departure to Palestine. And each year I cancel my plans because I am still attached to this first possibility— *(Crossing toward stage left wall)* which does not exist! *(Crossing back to stage right wall and crossing out "Yerushalayim." Crosses back to "podium." Pause)*

The only remaining possibility is to describe impossibility. Which I shall now continue to do with the assistance of my personal icon, which I carry with me at all times. *(Announcing)* The Angel of History! *(The Angel runs back to his downstage position on the suitcase)* His face is turned toward the past. Where we see a chain of events, he sees one single catastrophe, which keeps piling wreckage upon wreckage, and hurls it in front of his feet. The Angel would like to stay. He would like to awaken the dead, and make whole what has been smashed, but *(Begins "sculpting" Angel's body as he speaks)* a storm is blowing from paradise and it has got caught in his wings with such violence that the Angel can no longer close them. This storm irresistibly propels him into the future, to which his back is turned, while the pile of debris before him grows skyward. *(Pause)* This storm is what we call progress.

(Walter quickly gathers his suitcases and exits. The Angel makes harsh breathing sounds as he remains frozen, arms upraised, head twisted. The lights fade slightly.

A drum roll begins. The Angel runs off in a panic.

Else enters. She places her suitcases downstage right and collapses to the ground, exhausted.

Walter enters carrying two suitcases, passes Else, then recognizes her. He places his suitcases downstage left and hurries to Else's side.)

Else?

ELSE: Walter?

WALTER: I thought you were in Zurich. *(Helps her up onto the suitcase)*

ELSE: I was. But they closed my play about peace after only two nights. And another beating, this time by the Swiss. In the post office. And anyway, I keep losing my keys. And you? *(Motions for him to sit down next to her)* I thought you were dead.

WALTER *(Sits on suitcase)*: No, no. It's only 1937. I still have three more years. I manage quite well. I slip into Denmark to visit Brecht, and then I come back to Paris. I even manage to sell an article or two . . . under an assumed name. *(Else drops her gloves. Walter picks them up)* And once in a while I give a lecture at the antifascist society.

ELSE: Oh Walter. You are so stubborn! You know what is going to happen *(Taking gloves from him)* and you still refuse to leave! It's over!

(Walter and Else freeze. Izzy enters and crosses downstage center. He speaks very rapidly.)

IZZY: What do you do with a chimpanzee in Germany? What do you do with a half-crazed chimpanzee when you're a Nazi? Well, you get yourself a beaten-till-he's-half-blind-German-Jewish poet, Erich Muhsam, Else Lasker-Schüler's friend, and you stick him in a cage with that chimpanzee and you wait for that ape to tear him to bits. But the chimpanzee puts his arms around the poet who speaks kind words to him. What do you do with a loving chimpanzee who hugs a prisoner when you're a Nazi? Well, you torture that ape before the half-blind eyes of the poet and then you murder the poet.

(Izzy exits abruptly making monkey sounds softly: "Hoo, hoo, hoo.")

ELSE: Hope lies elsewhere.
WALTER *(Crossing away from Else)*: America?
ELSE: No. Zion.
WALTER: Now you sound like Gerhard.
ELSE: Oh Walter, why do you refuse to see it?

(Walter takes a newspaper out of his pocket. He sits on the suitcase where he left it, downstage left, and pretends to read.)

WALTER: I see perfectly well, Else. I see your dream of Zion being devoured by history.
ELSE: There will always be a dream of Zion, and not just for the Jews. And if we can no longer dream it, then some child will.
WALTER *(Shouting)*: GOD WILL NOT BE SO CRUEL AS TO GIVE US MORE CHILDREN! *(Catches himself, looks to see if anyone has noticed his outburst)*
ELSE: *(Crossing behind him)*: Walter, that is obscene. You are dead, like this beloved Europe of yours. But I will build a new Zion in Palestine. *(Exits)*
WALTER: Then I will haunt you, Else, in your promised land.

(Izzy enters playing the Mahler tune on a saxophone.
Walter puts his newspaper away. He secretively takes a piece of bread from his pocket . . . eats . . . realizes he's dropped several small

pieces of bread on the ground, picks one up and eats it. As Izzy, still playing the saxophone, crosses behind Walter, Walter senses his presence and quickly exits.

Izzy stops playing. He crosses to the spot where Walter dropped his bread, reaches down and picks up several crumbs. He puts bread crumbs in the "Berlin" wall. Edie walks to him. She clears her throat, but he walks right by her and goes to the "Jerusalem" wall. She follows, reaches out and touches his shoulder. He turns with dark glasses on, they stare at each other in silence. She turns away from him and walks to center stage, rejected.

Edie sees Else's scarf on the ground. She picks it up and absentmindedly plays with it. The actor uses the scarf to switch between the characters of Edie and Else.)

EDIE: That settles it. I am not going to Berlin. We can't even talk . . . He's crazy.

ELSE: What are you doing, flailing around and gasping like a dying fish?

(Edie is bewildered. She looks around for the source of the voice.)

EDIE: Huh? What?

ELSE: I said you look like a dying fish.

EDIE: Look, whoever you are, I got plenty of people pushing me around. I don't need you.

ELSE: You need me. I am one of your mothers, and you had many. Sarah, Hagar, Rachel, Leah, Miriam. I heard all their voices. And now you will hear them, and also mine.

EDIE: Not interested. I'm resigning from your club. Your voices drive me crazy—fading in and out. I can't decipher the messages.

ELSE: Can't, can't, can't. Are you going to spend your entire life saying no?

EDIE: You got it. I can't be a woman and I can't be a Jew. And I can't be either, because I can't be both. So, you know what I'm gonna be? I am gonna be nothing.

ELSE: Oh, I see, you call all of that anger and fear "nothing."

EDIE: You are really upsetting me.

ELSE: Of course I am upsetting you. Now, you listen to me. I too began my life silenced, immobilized, surrounded by chains. But I stuck my fingers through the chains, and then my tongue, and then my hair. Do you know what patience it takes to liberate yourself hair by hair?

EDIE: Liberate?! Yeah, the Bible says a Jew means: Get out of Egypt. Don't be a slave. And then it says: A woman is a man's property. And, when you give birth to a girl child you are unclean for twice as long. With a woman everything is twice as— You go through the same shit as the man and then you get an extra dose when they turn on you. *(She doesn't want to know or say it)* I know a woman who was raped by a Jewish man on the train to Auschwitz.

ELSE: Only fools feel no grief. And only fools let their grief stop them. I have lived it all: poet, woman, Jew. And yes, the world fears us. We are too . . . inconvenient, too messy, too full of blood. But even though our blood is in danger we cannot freeze it. It is life pounding through you. So whether you like it or not, you are a woman. And whether you are in Berlin, Jerusalem or the Moon, you are a Jew. Take from me the courage to live who we are.

EDIE: Every night my mother put me to bed singing Yiddish lullabies. But when she died they wouldn't let me sing the Kaddish, the prayer for the dead, because I'm a woman.

ELSE: Enough! Take the fist out of your mouth. Let what has been forbidden to women come through your lips. Now, sing it now. Sing the Kaddish.

EDIE *(Hesitantly)*: Yit . . . yit gadal v'yitkad . . . *(Her voice cracks)* I can't. *(Sits down dejectedly on the suitcase)*

(Izzy enters stage right, carrying one of Walter's suitcases. Walter enters hesitantly behind him. Edie watches.)

IZZY *(Puts down suitcase)*: It's time, Walter. Time to tell your story. 1940. The lights are going out. *(Opening the suitcase)* Paris.

WALTER: Paris?

(He looks at Izzy, then down into the suitcase, then back to Izzy, who says nothing. He reaches down to the suitcase; Izzy crosses upstage. He slowly takes a Walter Benjamin puppet out of the suitcase.)

Paris. 1940. *(Indicating puppet)* A refugee from Germany. A Jew. He loves to haunt the rare book section of the French National Library. They call that place *enfer*, hell. *(In puppet voice)* But to me, it was paradise. I was working on a definitive study of Baudelaire and Paris of the nineteenth century. My writing obsessed me. It howled like a little beast all night if I did not water it at the most esoteric springs during the day. *(Back to normal voice)* The war begins. *(Drum roll starts)* And because he is a "stateless person"—a Jew without papers—he is rounded up by the French. *(Izzy crosses down to Walter and grabs the puppet by the collar)* Not by the Germans. *(Izzy stands with his back to the audience, arms outstretched)* And they hold him for ten days inside an open stadium *(Puppet moves behind Izzy's outstretched arms as if peering over a barrier)* along with six thousand other "stateless persons." And then, *(Izzy commandingly points downstage left)* they force him to march to a labor camp in Nevers. *(Walter and puppet cross downstage left)* He collapses once on the way. *(Puppet's head falls forward, Izzy grabs puppet's hair and pulls him upright)* After three weeks he is released. *(Izzy lets go, crosses behind Walter stage left. Puppet wipes brow)* He goes back to Paris. *(Walter takes one step back with puppet)* But now he is ready to leave France. *(Puppet searches for something in pockets)* Only, there are no visas available. Not to England, *(Puppet reaches toward Izzy, who shrugs his shoulders)* not to America. There is no place to escape to. The Germans invade. *(Izzy goose-steps stage right in front of Walter)* He flees to the south of France, to the unoccupied zone. *(Walter pivots upstage)* And now, friends of his in America are finally able to obtain a visa and a steamship ticket from Lisbon to America! *(Puppet holds out his hand to Izzy, who holds out his hand in return)* But in order to reach Lisbon, he must first cross through Spain. And in order to enter Spain, he must have an exit visa from the French and they will not give him one. *(Puppet's hand sinks)* So. *(Puppet lifts head)* He decides to cross into Spain in secret, at night, with three other refugees. *(Izzy crosses up left to Walter, kneels)* They must cross the Pyrenees, feeling their way in the dark, crawling on their hands and knees. *(Puppet "crosses the Pyrenees" using Izzy as the landscape. At the summit, he stops)* Finally, they reach Port Bou, the first town on the Spanish side of the border, *(Izzy turns, extends arm in a gesture of "halt!")* where they are stopped by Spanish border guards who tell them they must return to France, where they know that the Germans are waiting to deport them and murder them. *(Walter puts hands over puppet's mouth. Izzy takes puppet's arm and roughly leads him and Walter back to suitcase stage left. Walter sits with puppet. Izzy crosses up center)* They spend the night in a hotel room, under guard. *(Walter holds hand out as pillow for puppet, who places his head on it. Tries to sleep. Looks up. Puts head down again. Looks up again)* In that room, the refugee takes a small vial of pills from his pocket. *(Walter holds invisible pills. Puppet looks at them)* Morphine. *(Puppet voice)* It was enough to kill a horse! *(Walter and puppet exchange looks. Pause)* He takes the pills. *(Puppet grows faint. Lowers head. Breath sounds from Walter and Izzy)* The next day at seven in the morning, he says to his companions, *(Puppet voice, labored)* I have taken morphine . . . but please . . . tell them only that I am sick. *(Breath sounds. Puppet lowers head)* And then he falls into a coma. And twenty-four hours later, he is dead. *(Puppet dies with head up and slightly back, resting on Walter's chest. Izzy strides to Walter, grabs puppet violently, holding it upside down, places it in suitcase, snaps lid closed)*

(Having witnessed Walter's death, Edie now stands, and with a quiet calm she sings the Kaddish.)

EDIE:

> Yit-ga-dal v'yit-ka-dash sh'may ra-ba
> B'al-mah di-v'rah khir-u-tay
> V'yam-likh mal-khu-tay
> B'khay-yay-khon u-v'yo-may-khon
> U-v'kha-yay de-kol bayt Yis-ra-el
> Ba-a-gala u'viz'man ka-riv
> V'im-ru a-men.

IZZY: And you never knew that the next day the Spanish border guards let the rest of the party continue their journey to Lisbon and America.

(Pause. Izzy begins humming "The Café Theme" as Walter, with a slight hesitation, exits.)

We don't have to worry about that! That was 1940. This is 1996. Things are different now. The Jews have a homeland. Let me tell you a joke. It's a Middle East joke. It goes like this: You see, there's this Duck. And a Scorpion. And the Scorpion says to the Duck, he says, "Give me a ride across the river. I've *really* got to get across the river." And the Duck says, "Oh no no, are you kidding? You'll sting me. You'll kill me." Scorpion: "Why would I do that? Then we'd both . . . drown." So the Duck says, "OK . . . Get on." And the Scorpion gets on the Duck's back and they head out across the river. *(Distant Arabic chanting)* And they get halfway across the river and . . . *(Acts out being stung in the upper thigh, mimicking the wounding of Jacob in the opening scene. Winces in pain)* the Scorpion stings the Duck! And as they're *both* going under, the Duck says, "Why did you do that, man? Now we're both going to die." And the Scorpion says . . . the Scorpion says, "Don't you know? This . . . is the Middle East!" *(Loud drumming is heard)*

Oooooooh MAMA!

(Drumming ends. Regains his composure) OK. The last time I told this joke a guy comes up to me and he says, *(Takes off sunglasses; speaks in a deep, professorial voice)* "Excuse me, but I don't understand where you stand on the Middle East." Well, I stand everywhere, I don't need a position. Politicians have positions. Tantric yogis have POSITIONS. The Old Right, the New Left, the Old Left, the New Right. They've *all* got positions. I don't have to play that game. I'm not that schizophrenic. *(Professorial voice)* "But are you pro . . . or anti . . .

Zionist?" I'm pro-volone and I'm anti-pasti. I'm pro the dream . . . I'm pro the dream. Jews living together, not having to make an *excuse* for their survival. And I'm anti the corruption of the dream. But I don't want to get into that. *(Professorial voice)* "Why? What happens to you when you get 'into' that?" I get pimples, I get dandruff, my hair falls out, my foot begins to bleed, I have to limp, it's no good. *(Professorial voice)* "But, I still don't understand where you stand." Look, the Jews . . . escaped! *(Mimics an escape. Sits on a suitcase and pretends to float)* To the Moon! To create small islands of perfection. Of truth, justice and the American way. And they did it! Only they weren't on the Moon. They were in the goddamned Middle East. *(Izzy drops the "komic" mask)*

They forgot that there were people there. Arabs. Palestinians. Palestinians? Let the rest of the world worry about the Palestinians. Let the people of Berkeley worry about the Palestinians.

(Voice of a salesman) Yes, you too can have the ultimate Jewish experience: low-cost living among the beautiful hills of Judea and Sumeria. Treat you and your family to a luxurious home, complete with a two-car garage, two kitchens, complete internet access, surrounded by lush greenery, fruit trees, barbed wire and guard towers. Transform your paranoia into real fear for your life and for your loved ones.

(Voice of a Palestinian, playing it straight) What do the Israelis have to be afraid of? No one is confiscating their ancestral lands, no one is blowing up their homes, no one is stealing their water, no one is denying their right to self-determination. But, does the world care? So what if we are subject to arbitrary arrest and torture. So what if we have no right of return. So what if Jewish doctors inject AIDS into our children. So what if their women are whores who spread syphilis to our innocent young men. They say, never forget the six million. I say, never forget the four million Palestinians scattered all over the world like Jews.

(Voice of Israeli, or settler, playing it for keeps) Like Jews? The six million Jews are dead. They are never coming home. And why? Because the world hates us. Even the Americans only pretend to be our friends. So what if they give us billions of dollars? So what if the American Jews give us billions of dollars? They are not really Jews. They have rabbis who are homosexuals and they all marry goyim. At least the Arabs stick with their own kind. If the daughter of a Palestinian disgraces her family, they kill her. Like we killed Rabin and we will kill Shahak or Barak or anyone who is a traitor to Israel. Our allegiance is not to man, but to God and Torah.

(As himself again) So you see, we'll be so busy killing each other we won't have time to kill Palestinians . . . *(Begins to break down. Throws his arms around himself, as if he were in a straitjacket)* No,

there will always be time to kill Palestinians and blow up more houses and confiscate more land. And there will always be time for Palestinians to kill Israeli soldiers and teachers and children . . . *(Explodes out of the "straitjacket")* SO DON'T ASK ME ABOUT THE MIDDLE EAST!

(Regains his composure) Look, I was in Israel when Rabin was assassinated. And I was in the North. I took a walk on a hill. I was alone. *(Else enters, stands upstage right)* Only I wasn't alone. There was a woman there. An Israeli woman. And she looked at me. I mean, she looked at me. Like nobody ever looked at me before. Like I was family. And I looked out at the pink light, coming off the stones. And something was missing. So . . . I looked around my little cage. And I realized . . . that I have been hungry . . . for so long . . . that I can't find my soul.

(Else's head and face are covered by a black veil. She is singing a melody from Mahler's Das Lied von der Erde. *Walter enters upstage and watches her.)*

WALTER: Else, did you get out?

(She is used to being taunted. She answers, not knowing it is Walter asking.)

ELSE: Yes. I got out.
WALTER: And look what happened to you. The loneliest woman in Jerusalem. Eating, sleeping, writing in a rocking chair, in a room without a bed.
ELSE: So. There is day and there is night. I didn't expect to be the queen of Jerusalem.
WALTER: So what happened, Else?
ELSE: I was too old. To be a new child in a new land, one must not be tired. And I came dry and tired in my body. And so I dressed in extravagant clothes and I never knew whether I was hiding—or revealing myself.
WALTER: What did you want to hide, Else?
ELSE: I wanted to hide the gnarls in my fingers and the wrinkles around my lips. I wanted to hide that I cannot speak Hebrew, when I think everything I write is in Hebrew. But most of all, I want to hide that I am German. I am more German than I am Jewish. I am more German than I am a woman.
WALTER: Oh, Else. We are the same. It is stamped on our souls: Made In Europe.
ELSE: Walter! . . . I thought you'd never come.

WALTER: I didn't. I'm a ghost. And I'm haunting you as I promised I would. And you . . . I see you are becoming a legend here in Jerusalem.

ELSE: A ghost and a legend . . . how romantic. *(Crosses to him)* At least now I have someone to talk to. You know it's been very difficult for me here. Even the children . . . they follow me down the streets and they point their fingers and they laugh.

WALTER: But this is the land you dreamed of.

ELSE: Well . . . the land I dreamed of, I sometimes call "Misery-ael."

WALTER: I warned you of this. "The dream is devoured by history."

ELSE: Not devoured, chewed on a little.

WALTER: With very sharp teeth.

ELSE: For me, Walter, there is always a dream of Zion. And if I cannot find it on a map, well, then, I will find it in my heart.

WALTER: Else, you expect too much from your heart.

ELSE: You know, Walter, becoming a ghost has not made you any lighter. *(Takes Walter's hat off his head)*

WALTER: Yes, and becoming a legend has not made you any more discerning!

ELSE: Walter! Try to understand! For me, no matter what happened in the world, and no matter what happened to me, and no matter what they said I can be, must be, should be, won't be—I said, I will be. Life will be. And so I wrote my poems and I made soup kitchens for the Arab and Jewish children. Why, I even had a peace plan. I wanted to present it to the twenty-first Zionist Congress.

(Puts on Walter's hat, addresses audience) I said: "To solve the Arab and Jewish problem, it is simple. We will build an amusement park to which Arab and Jew will come. And together they will ride the same carousel and they will play the same wheel of fortune and they will eat the same reibepfannkuchen. But above the entrance there will be a sign, and it will say: FOR GOD!" *(Walter applauds)*

Ah, but Walter, they would not accept my plan.

WALTER: Hmmm. Now what did you say they were going to eat?

ELSE: Reibepfannkuchen.

WALTER *(Mocking)*: Reibepfannkuchen! And they turned you down?

ELSE: Yes, they turned me down. And they laughed. But while they were laughing, I was in a conversation with God. And God said: "Else . . ."

WALTER *(Imitating God)*: ELSE!

ELSE: Well, something like that. God said, "Else, if you would only . . ." *(Walter makes lightning and thunder noises)* Walter, stop it. This is very hard for me to talk about. God said, "Else, if only you would open up your eyes, and your heart, then you would see me in every face walking down the streets of Jerusalem . . . and Berlin. And you would know that you are the mother and the sister and the friend of each other. You are not hate . . ."

WALTER: Well yes, yes, but . . .

ELSE: "Else," he said, "You are my clown . . ." *(She playfully hides behind Walter, reaches around him into his breast pocket, magically pulls out an orange and presents it to him)* ". . . You do God's work."

(Lights change. Walter and Else exit. The Angel of History enters and takes down the drum that has been hanging on the wall of the archway. He takes a few steps back so that the drum is lit with the shadow of a crescent moon on its face. He sings the "lu lu lu" melody with which he opened the play as he crosses stage right. Drums come up under his singing. He reaches the corner of the stage as he ends the "lu lu lu" melody. The drums continue. The Woman enters and joins him. They begin chanting the Jacob text in unison.)

ANGEL OF HISTORY AND WOMAN:
    Va yi va ter Ya'akov l'vado . . .

(Jacob bursts onstage, runs to center. He has a wooden mask on his left arm. He recapitulates many of the gestures of the opening section: Jacob wrestling, this time with the mask. Near the end of the section, the mask goes on his face. He struggles to remove it, unsuccessfully.)

    Va yay a vek ish imo ad a lot ha shachar
    Va yar ki lo ya cho lo va yi b'chaf Yerecho
    Va tey ka kaf yerech Ya'akov
    B'hey avko imo va yomer shalcheni ki ala ha shachar
    Va yomper lo a-sha-lay cha cha ki im berachtani
    Va yomer Ya'akov va yomer lo va'akov
    Ye amer od shimcha ki im Yisrael, ki sarita im Elohim vi'm
    Anahim va tuchal
    Va yomer Ya'akov va yomer lo Ya'akov
    Ye amer od shimcha ki im Visrael.

(Jacob stops struggling against the mask. He holds his hands under his eyes to reflect the light up into them, and then extends his arms.)

    Ki im Yis-ra-el . . .

(Drums continue as lights fade to black.)

END

Traveling Jewish Theatre

TJT was founded in 1978 by Corey Fischer, Albert Greenberg and Naomi Newman, who shared a desire to create works of theater that, while grounded in the specifics of the Jewish experience, would be accessible to audiences of diverse backgrounds. In 1986, Helen Stoltzfus joined the company as co-artistic director. Forging a theatrical style influenced by the American avant-garde theater of the 1960s, vaudeville, liturgy and storytelling, and drawing on themes from Jewish history, legend, literature and folk tradition, the company has created scores of original works for the theater, with sources that range from the legends of the Hasidim to the assassination of Trotsky; from Yiddish poetry to the reclamation of women's wisdom; from the healing nature of storytelling to the challenge of interfaith marriage; and from the politics of the Middle East to African American–Jewish relations. TJT does not deal with social or political issues in isolation. It recognizes that the roots of theater lie in the realm of the mythic, the sacred and the communal; that theater can be an instrument of healing for people and cultures.

TJT has performed in more than sixty cities worldwide, including Chicago, New York, Berlin, Oslo, Jerusalem and Whitesburg, Kentucky. Members of the ensemble also teach solo performance, improvisation and ensemble creation privately and through TJT's professional-training programs. The company has also produced a four-part series for Public Radio International, entitled "Heart of Wisdom: Audio Explorations in Jewish Culture." TJT and its artists have received numerous awards, including a lifetime achievement award from the National Foundation for Jewish Culture, two TCG "New Generations" grants, and an award from the Kennedy Center Fund for New American Plays for *See Under: Love* by Corey Fischer.

In July 2002, Aaron Davidman, who had been working with the company for four years, became its artistic director. He works closely with founding members Corey Fischer, who remains active as a director, writer, actor and associate artistic director, and Naomi Newman, who also advises, directs, performs, writes and initiates projects. Founding member Albert Greenberg and co-artistic director Helen Stoltzfus have gone on to work on projects of their own and retain the titles of artists emeriti.

. . . NEVER DONE

Touchstone Theatre

Left to right: Peggy Pettitt, Haydee Cornfeld and Cora Hook.

INTRODUCTION

In the Fall 2000 issue of *The Drama Review*, Sara Brady leveled a charge of "non-radicality" at a collaborative production between Touchstone Theatre and Cornerstone Theater Company (Brady, 2000). The production, *Steelbound*, was a mythological rendering of the death of the steel industry in Touchstone's hometown of Bethlehem, PA. Brady asserted that *Steelbound* was indicative of a field-wide tendency among community-based theaters to appeal to politically ineffectual nostalgia rather than to the liberatory social strategies that she considered more appropriate to this work. In response to the charge, the collaborators, community cast members and others responded with a fusillade of letters that were subsequently published in *The Drama Review*, accusing Brady in turn of having too narrow a perspective on the politics of community-based art (McKenna *et al.*, 2001).

Reviewing the exchange at four years' distance, we might consider that while the Brady article was naive in its conclusions regarding the outcomes for which community-based theater is responsible, it was also probably inevitable that the politically charged production would end up in the sights of at least one harsh critic. If theater about the community has a responsibility to anticipate its political implications, then criticism of such work is responsible for anticipating the subtleties and complexities implied by such ambitious projects. The question of how community-based ensembles should frame their politics remains an open one, as does the question of how community-based art ought to be critiqued.

In the same year as the *Steelbound* debate, University of Chicago political philosopher Martha Nussbaum wrote about the humanizing, democratizing and community-building effects of the Greek dramas (Nussbaum, 2000):

> They ask their audience to ponder . . . what do we really care about and how can we best protect what we care about? In the process of thinking thoughts like these, we are brought close to one another, in common vulnerability and a shared set of commitments to human aid and to democracy itself.

Nussbaum—no political idealist, to be sure—considers simple, art-inspired acts like "thinking thoughts" and "being close" to represent nothing less than possibilities for a renewal of democracy. Action and change, like the vulnerabilities and commitments of which Nussbaum speaks, may take many forms. It is unreasonable to argue that something as expansive as a work of art or as complex as a community should be responsible for only one type of outcome. While community-based theater's social goals may at times call for immediate and visible political community action, they may just as easily call for more long-term (and therefore more indistinct) outcomes than the short-term goals of radical action. As discussed in the Introduction to this volume, an ensemble's contribution to community identity is never a small thing.

In an interview about . . . *Never Done*, Touchstone's contribution to this volume, ensemble member Cora Hook told me, "I have made my artistic choices with the idea that one of the actor's roles in society is to be a catalyst for other people's creativity, and not just the artists involved, but also the men and women that are interviewed, as well as everyone who comes to witness the stories being told." The egalitarian vision that inspired . . . *Never Done* was inspired by the birth of Hook's first child. "Walking with my new daughter, I saw all these people on the street, and suddenly thought that every one of them started out the same way that my daughter did." Hook took that idea to her friend Peggy Pettitt, and the pair began an artistic exploration of their disparate cultures. In time, they uncovered the fact that while their mothers were of different backgrounds, they had sung the same songs while working. Those songs became source material, and Hook and Pettitt began collaborating with another Touchstone actress on the theme of women and their traditional work. The research was based on interviews with women and men in the community, as well as historical readings and personal songs and stories.

. . . *Never Done* represents one important aspect of the identity woven by women's collective relationship to work. Like *Steelbound*, this play draws from a local context to offer its audience a new perspective on common identity. Yet also like *Steelbound*, it is impossible to suggest what commitments, action or change it may or may not influence, except perhaps to suggest that in providing perspective on an audience's history, the artists have demonstrated that it is worthy of examination, evaluation and care. What thought, what closeness, and what change may emerge from that care will likely be as multifaceted and challenging as the notion of community, as ensemble theater, as democracy itself.

—F.L.

Brady, Sara. "Steelbound and Non-Radicality in Community-Based Theater," *The Drama Review*: 44(3), 2000.

McKenna, Mark, *et al.* "Touchstone: How Radical Is Radical?" *The Drama Review*: 45(3), 2001.

Nussbaum, Martha. "Hope, Fear, Suspense: A Chance to Focus on What Democracy Means," *Newsday*, Currents & Books: Sunday, November 12, 2000.

Production Information

. . . *Never Done* was written by Touchstone Theatre ensemble members Jennie Gilrain and Cora Hook, and by guest artists Peggy Pettitt and Haydee Cornfeld in collaboration with Remy Tissier. The play was conceived by Cora Hook and directed by Jennie Gilrain. Costume and stage design was by Remy Tissier, lighting was by Judith M. Daitsman and musical direction was by Beverly Morgan. It was originally performed by Haydee Cornfeld, Cora Hook and Peggy Pettitt. . . . *Never Done* was supported, in part, by the National Endowment for the Arts and the Pennsylvania Humanities Council and through general operating support by The Shubert Foundation and the Pennsylvania Council on the Arts.

The letter to Annabee Williams is from the collected letters of Ida D. Williams, and was graciously donated by Jaye Austin-Williams. Lyrics: "Rosie the Riveter," by Redd Evans and John Jacob Loeb, 1942, Fred Ahlert Music Corporation, 2000, Van Ness Avenue, San Francisco, CA, 94109 (page 151); "What a Difference a Day Made," words and music by Stanley Adams and Maria Grever, Stanley Adams Music, c/o The Songwriters Guild, 1500 Harbor Boulevard, Weehawken, NJ 07087 (page 160).

Setting/Set

The stage is bare. Minimal props are used by the actors: a stool, a rope, a few sheets and three "welfare baskets" hanging from pulleys by ropes. (At Bethlehem Steel Mill, the locker rooms were called "welfare rooms." Instead of lockers, workers placed their belongings in round metal baskets with hooks attached, which hung from the ceiling by a rope-and-pulley system.)

The play is an investigation of women's work, in spirit and in gesture. (For example, the actors spent hours with a group of seniors, researching the sequence of tasks involved in doing the laundry before the invention of the automatic washer and dryer.) Time and place are fluid. The play begins out of time, with *Macbeth*'s three crones, and moves through many decades: from the 1930s (the time of our grandmothers) to the 1940s, '50s and '60s (our mothers' time), ending with our own time. All scene changes are created by the actors: a chicken farm, kitchens, a freight train, a steel mill, an elevator and a hospital birthing room. These changes are created simply, through movement and light. At times, one scene blends into another almost seamlessly, with a simple turn of the actor's body.

ACT ONE

Witches #1

Three Witches stand around a pot set at center stage.

WITCH 1: Sister, where have you been?
WITCH 2: Killing chickens.
WITCH 3: And you?
WITCH 1: Picking cotton.
WITCH 2: You?
WITCH 3: Threading bobbins.
WITCH 2: Sisters, look what I have.
WITCH 3: Show!
WITCH 2: Here I have a chicken's thumb. Wracked as homeward he did come.
WITCH 1: A drum! A drum!
WITCH 2: Our grandmothers come!

Washing laundry

The three Witches, now as three ladies, lift one sheet from a washtub with a giant stick. They approach the piles of sheets. A mimetic sequence of gestures is performed that reflects the work of laundry in the 1930s and 1940s.

Witches #2

They cross to a laundry basket set down center.

WITCH 2: Thrice the plucked chicken clucks.
WITCH 1: Thrice and once the wash is done.
WITCH 3: The baby cries, "'Tis time, 'tis time."

> *(They circle the laundry basket, adding their laundry to the pile as they speak.)*

WITCH 2: Round about the cauldron go. In the chicken's entrails throw.
WITCH 3: Cramps that often make us moan. Days and nights have thirty-one.
WITCH 1: Sweating and hot flashes got, boil 'em first in the charmed pot.
WITCH 2: Double, double,
WITCH 1: Toil and trouble,
WITCH 3: Fire burn
ALL WITCHES: And cauldron bubble.
WITCH 2: Hi-lich, hi-lich, hinkel drehk. Bis mah-dee-otts free gates ah-less wehk.

> *(Two Witches transform into chickens. They start to cluck. The Third Witch, Cora, picks up the washtub and starts to feed the chickens from it. Then she takes the washtub off and returns as the storyteller.)*

Chicken Plucking — Cora's Grandmother

Cora speaks, first as herself, then as her grandmother.

CORA: My grandmother grew up with chickens. Cora Eleanor Hook. Born 1874, or thereabouts, in Peculiar, Missouri. I barely knew her, except for one photograph. A chicken's-eye view through a wire fence. *(She poses, frozen, in profile)* Her body long and lean, like the limber jacks her brother used to make.

(She produces a limber jack toy and plays. Then she becomes the toy, dancing wildly. She then returns, exhausted, to profile, one arm flopping.)

My grandmother . . . Mother of Frankie Scott . . . My dad. With quick, twinkling eyes that seemed to say . . . "Gotcha."

(Chicken sounds as she grabs a chicken.)

CORA'S GRANDMOTHER: You see, Frankie Scott, that chicken's more afraid of you than you are of him. All you need to catch a chicken is to be quick. 'Cause they're not too bright. *(Chops head off. Lets blood drain)* Not like you, Frankie Scott. Not like you.

(Frankie Scott, played by Peggy, walks downstage. He stops and turns to Cora's Grandmother, who is dipping the chicken in hot water, then starts to pluck its feathers.)

Frankie Scott, you be careful about that horse now. And you tell that teacher to teach you good. I want you comin' home knowin' how to *read* your Bible.

(She finishes plucking. Frankie Scott assumes a new attitude: he is older; he leans against the wall, grinning.)

Now what you got that grin on your face for, young man?

(Singes hairs off chicken and guts it.)

You proud of yourself 'cause you graduated from high school? *(Wiping hand on apron)* Well I'm proud of you, too, Frankie Scott.

(She walks toward him, pulls some money out of her apron pocket and gives it to him.)

Now, I want you to go down to Kansas City and learn yourself some typing. Get yourself a good clerk's job with a good regular salary. Use that brain of yours.

(He turns away. She watches him go. She sings:)

> The old ways are changing you cannot deny.
> The day of the traveler's over.
> There's nowhere to go and there's nowhere to 'bide
> So farewell to the life of the rover.

(She returns to plucking another chicken. She ages more noticeably before the next interaction.

Frankie Scott turns back toward her. She looks at him hard before speaking this time:)

Frankie Scott, how many more books you gonna buy down there at that university? And not one of them a Bible. Hangin' 'round with those Methodists and Catholics. Drinking and smokin'. Just who do you think you are anyway? I don't understand you anymore. I don't know who you are anymore.

(She returns to work, then sings:)

> Good-bye to the tent and the old caravan,
> To the tinker, the gypsy and the travelin' man,
> And good-bye to the life of the rover.

(Haydee peeks out from offstage and makes a sound to get Peggy's attention. Peggy sneaks off as Cora's Grandmother looks the other way. Cora's Grandmother walks downstage and moves the laundry basket. Peggy sneaks by with a jump rope. Cora's Grandmother looks off. Peggy and Haydee start to swing the rope, singing: "Bluebells, cockleshells . . .")

Jump Rope—Bluebells

One end of the rope is attached to the wall. Haydee turns the other end while Peggy jumps. They sing a jump rope song. Then they run, giggling and squealing, to hang the other end of the rope, pulling it tight as a clothesline.

Hanging Laundry—Children Playing

Once the line is hung, Haydee becomes the mother, speaking in Spanish to her children, who are causing chaos with the laundry. Haydee disappears for a moment as the children continue to play. Peggy and Cora pull back two sheets, like curtains, and there is Haydee.

Treadle Pushing—Haydee's Grandmother

HAYDEE: Mi abuela Luisa Maria, mi abuelita. Era tan pequeñita, era tan bonita. Tenía unas manos tan chiquitas. Le encantaba coser.

PEGGY: Haydee's grandmother was born in 1881 and had nine daughters. Poor Grandpa, he was always trying to get a word in . . .

HAYDEE: Se sentabe en su maquina de coser la cual compro en 1929, y pago poco a poco con su pequeño salario. Pero nunca se quejaba, siempre se sonreia.

PEGGY *(Translating)*: She never complained. She always had a smile.

(Haydee is sewing in pantomime, with Cora and Peggy forming the cutting table out of a sheet.)

HAYDEE: Ah, y si, ella misma hacia sus patrones de coser, en esos dias no habia *McCall's* o *Vogue*. Yo lo enseñe a mis hijas a coser, y despues ellas misma se cosian su ropa.

CORA *(Translating)*: She taught all her girls to sew, and eventually they made their own dresses . . .

HAYDEE: Y la de sus hijos, nosotros no comprabamos en las tiendas, no. ¡Y ella cocinaba! Y era una intelectual al mismo tiempo. Le encantaba hablar de Constantinopla, historia y politica.

Pero una de las cosas que mas me impresiono de ella, fue que ella misma se cosio el camison, para que la enterraran cuando se muriera . . .

PEGGY *(Translating)*: She even made her own dress to be buried in.

HAYDEE: Me parece que la veo en el su pequeño cuerpo envuelta en el . . .

CORA *(Translating)*: I can just see it, her little body wrapped in it.

HAYDEE: Y colocandola en su lugar descanso, yo no estaba alla pero, ella siempre dos dijo, nunca se den por vencida, se debe luchar, se debe seguir adelante.

(She begins to sing a lullaby, "Muñeca Athule," to Peggy. Cora bundles the sheets that have been sewn. Haydee begins to hum. Peggy picks up the laundry basket, Cora the bundle. They walk slowly on a diagonal upstage, as Haydee moves downstage. As they march, they sing a few lines of the folk song "Bread and Roses": "As we go marching, marching . . .")

ODUN DE/BREAD AND ROSES

Peggy and Cora continue upstage, then turn and cross downstage. Peggy puts down the basket with the sheet bundle. Cora brings a stool for her.

COTTON PICKING—PEGGY'S GRANDMOTHER

PEGGY: I don't know about you, but all these sheets make me think of cotton. And the people who picked it. My grandmother was one of them. Fourteen years old in 1919. About my height, stocky, short woolly hair, big feet and big hands, loose-fitting clothes with a burlap bag across her shoulders. As far as you could see there was rows and rows of it. And everybody picked . . . the men, the women and the children.

You know what a cotton ball looks like? It's about that big . . . and you had to pick your weight. One ball after the other . . . and it hurt. You had to be careful when you went in to get it. It was enclosed in a kind of pod, rough and prickly. You had to open it and remove the stuff that weighed nothing. You had to reach around the other pods. That's why the hands were big, they were like tools. That's why children's hands were useful, they were small.

You worked from sunup to sundown. Pickin' one after the next.

(She looks up to the sky.)

One day she got hit by a pain, lifted her skirts, squat down and had a miscarriage. Kept on working without missing a beat.

I think she told us that story because she wanted us to know it's not always convenient for a woman to have a baby. She told us she prayed for it to happen. Fourteen years old. Down on her knees praying, *(Sings)* "Father, remove this cup from me." And I know she was telling the truth. Because my grandmother could pray. She prayed . . . *(Sings)* "Father, I stretch my hands to thee, no other help I know, if thou withdraw thyself from me, Lord, whither shall I go?" And she . . . my grandmother prayed . . . .Lord . . . *(Moaning)* Grandma could pray.

Prayer

Peggy's moaning becomes a song. Cora crosses to her, takes a sheet off the line.

Folding Laundry

Peggy and Cora fold the sheet together as Haydee folds another sheet. Peggy pulls yellow fabric from the basket as Cora pulls the basket away.

Cloth Dance

Drum music begins. Peggy dances. The dance begins as a sequence of cleaning gestures, using the fabric as a washrag. She mimes vigorously scrubbing the windows and then the floor, on her hands and knees. The work gestures build into a passionate frenzy, which evolves into a beautiful African dance with the same cloth-swirling movements. Peggy exits with the basket on her head.
The music continues with the stage empty for a moment.

Mask Dance

Cora enters with steel worker clothes, welding mask and gloves and dances. She begins backing up with her hands raised wide above her head. Then she slowly lowers her arms. Peggy and Haydee enter from offstage in work clothes.

Witches #3

WITCH 2: Speak.
WITCH 3: Demand.
WITCH 1: We'll answer.
WITCH 2: Say if you'd rather hear from our mouths . . .
WITCH 1: . . . or from the women who went before.

(Haydee and Peggy put on their hard hats.)

Rosie the Riveter

A recording of the 1940s song plays.

> While other girls attend their fav'rite cocktail bar
> Sipping dry martinis, munching caviar
> There's a girl who's really putting them to shame.
> Rosie is her name.
>
> All day long whether rain or shine
> She's a part of the assembly line
> Making history working for victory
> Rosie the riveter.

The Welfare Room

All three women lower their welfare baskets. They become workers at Bethlehem Steel. Cora is last. She turns to tie up her rope. They all start to change clothes. Cora, as Eleanor, realizes she has no soap. Peggy, as Anna-bee, reaches for her soap.

ELEANOR: Do you have any soap?
ANNABEE: What?

ELEANOR: Soap?

(Annabee starts toward her as if to give her some, then passes her without a word. Tension in the air is thick. Annabee speaks over her shoulder to Haydee, as Buena Ventura, but for all to hear.)

ANNABEE: They never speak to us unless they need something.

(Eleanor steps out of the scene and speaks to the audience:)

ELEANOR: When we would come out of there—when we were forging—our faces would be black, covered in soot. And our shoes were smoking and our glasses were always out of shape. And the only thing that took that black off was Lifebuoy soap. It was foamy.

(The three women meet at the sink. They wash.)

ANNABEE: Did you see that recipe for Betty Lou's brown sugar cake.
ELEANOR: Oh, I like Betty Lou.
BUENA VENTURA: I didn't see it.
ANNABEE: There wasn't any eggs in it!

(They laugh, then stop for a moment as Buena Ventura speaks to the audience:)

BUENA VENTURA: That mill enchanted us. The sounds. The fire. The heat.

(Eleanor and Annabee laugh again.)

ELEANOR: I can't wait until this war is over and I can have some eggs and butter!
BUENA VENTURA *(To Annabee)*: I see you got a letter.
ANNABEE: Yeah. It's from my sister.
ELEANOR: The one who's a WAC?
BUENA VENTURA: Stationed in South Carolina?
ELEANOR: I always wanted to join the WACs.
BUENA VENTURA: Not me.

(Buena Ventura and Eleanor dress slowly as Annabee steps out, looking at the letter. The others stop dressing as Annabee reads the letter out loud:)

ANNABEE: July 23, 1944. Dear Annabee, I know you want to join the WACs, but I despair for you in this army whose total theme is Jim

Crow. As a Williams you are too pigheaded to be able to make yourself submissive to these intolerant conditions. It isn't that it cannot be done, in fact, it *will* be done, but it is so difficult on those with a rugged individualistic disposition. So keep that in mind, should you insist. It is so easy to get life in the guardhouse for a little or nothing. You will have to just grit your teeth and bear it. It will hurt awful bad, worse than a bullet from Hitler's guns, but you will have to take it. If you make a real attempt to adjust yourself to this strange discipline, then you will be grateful for the rest of your life, because you will have lost fear of any living condition. Smile . . .

(Eleanor steps out and again speaks to the audience:)

ELEANOR: I would've loved to have gone in the army. But I couldn't. My periods were just too heavy. I'd have such cramps. I remember when I was at school, I'd have to cross my legs when I stood up to answer a question or there'd be a flood.

    Eleanor Graver, metallurgical engineer at Bethlehem Steel, 1943 to 1945.

ANNABEE *(To audience)*: Annabee Williams, welder at Bethlehem Steel, 1942 to 1944.

BUENA VENTURA *(To audience)*: Buena Ventura Martinez, machinist at Bethlehem Steel, 1941 to 1943.

(They all cross to center and sing "Don't Sit Under the Apple Tree."
    Peggy and Cora move to opposite sides upstage with their backs to the audience, as Haydee finishes the song by herself:)

HAYDEE: " . . . no, no, no . . ."

BUENA VENTURA/MATIANA

Cora and Peggy play various roles throughout Haydee's storytelling.

HAYDEE: Buena Ventura was born in 1922. She came here with her parents from their farm in Mexico at the age of six months.

    Don Pedro Gonzalez, who was revered by the Mexican community for his kindness, was hired by Bethlehem Steel to go down to the Mexican border to recruit workers.

(She becomes Don Pedro. She puffs on a cigarette, then puts it out on the floor. Pad and pencil in hand, she starts to call names. As she calls

names, the others line up to enter an imaginary boxcar on a freight train.)

DON PEDRO: Juan Garcia, pal tren, Roberto Rivera, pal tren, veinte y nueve, treinta. *(Slams train door shut)* Jacinto Aguilera, pal tren, Pancho Gonzales, pal tren, José Maria Martinez, pal tren por favor.

(Haydee becomes José Maria and climbs into the train. He checks out the space and moves between Peggy and Cora, who play Mexican workers sitting in the boxcar.)

JOSÉ MARIA: Hace frio . . . El piso es muy duro . . . Esta oscuro . . .
WORKER: Cerilla, mano?

(José Maria strikes a match on her foot and lights Worker's cigarette.)

JOSÉ MARIA *(To Worker)*: Eh, mano, ¿adonde que vamos? ¿Cómo es esto de B-e-len? ¿Palla pal norte? ¿Bethle—?
WORKER: Bethlehem.
JOSÉ MARIA *(Repeats pronunciation)*: Bethlehem.

(The train stops.)

(Sitting on the floor) Three trainloads, nine hundred and forty-one men and one hundred families in boxcars. *(Pointing to self)* José Maria Martinez, Matiana, mi esposa, y Buena Ventura, mi niña, arrived in Bethlehem and moved into the tent city on Bethlehem Steel property . . .

(Image of boxcar dissolves; the three women become the Martinez family, working in the kitchen.)

HAYDEE: José worked at the steel while Matiana worked at the sewing factory and had twelve children. Then, in 1941, when the United States entered World War II, Bethlehem Steel opened its doors to women. They flocked in. Matiana's daughters: Buena Ventura, Sofia, Elaria, Paz, they got their jobs there. Doña Matiana, she was a riot. On payday, she'd be standing at the door: *(As Matiana)* "Ventura, cheque, Sofia, cheque, Elaria, cheque." *(She takes the three checks and places them in her brassiere)*

(Scene in the kitchen of chaos. Haydee, as Doña Matiana, ad-libs in Spanish while she cooks and cleans.)

Vamos a cocinar . . . Tenemos que preparar las tortillas para su papa . . . Ay chicas . . . Todos que viven aquí, trabajan aquí . . . *(Shouting)* Francisca, pa la casa, la cena!

(As Haydee) The one thing Matiana was very proud of was that all her children graduated from high school. She used to say, "My Ventura graduated from Liberty High School in 1941, and now Ventura's daughter Ruthie has a master's degree in education."

(Cora, who has been scrubbing a floor downstage, stands up.)

The Doors Are Down at HDM

Cora speaks as Anna McGlaughlin Cassium:

ANNA: Ohh. This place would hum!

(She crosses to her welfare basket and puts on her hard hat. She crosses center and motions to Peggy to raise the crane. Peggy begins to raise it. Anna motions for her to stop. Peggy continues to raise the basket.)

STOP!

(She crosses to the audience.)

I worked at HDM at Bethlehem Steel during World War II. I was what they called a chain girl. There was a lot of us girls that worked there. A few fellows too. Another thing there was lots of was cranes. You hadda be on the alert or ya coulda caused a very bad accident.

I remember one New Year's Eve. I was working the night shift. It was just about midnight, and Vernie Mertaw decides that she wants to drive the forklift. The guys said, "Naw, Vernie, you can't do that. The load's too heavy. You'll tip right over." You got to understand, Vernie was a tiny little thing, no bigger than a finger. But she was Irish and stubborn. So she jumped right up on that forklift and she said, "Come on Annie, give me a hand." So I did! And we balanced that load perfectly. All the way to the end of the shop. We were just about at the doors when . . .

(The forklift crashes into the doors. The doors fall forward onto the ground. Silence.

Sounds of shouting and sirens are heard, made by Peggy and Haydee.)

Well, *(Anna hides behind her hat)* a little while later . . .

(Peggy swings a welfare basket slowly and makes the sound of a clock.)

Didn't the big boss man himself come down to see what was going on. Hello, Mr. Man.

(She takes off her hard hat and bows to "the boss." She hands her hard hat to Haydee, who puts it back on the welfare basket. Haydee raises the basket as Anna and "the boss" enter an imaginary factory elevator and ride it up.)

But, you know. Those guys in the shop . . . they didn't say a word. That's one New Year's Eve I'll never forget.

(She pops the cork on an imaginary champagne bottle.)

NEW YEAR'S EVE — AULD LANG . . .

All sing "Auld Lang Syne," as if at a New Year's Eve party at work.

ACT TWO

WITCHES #4

WITCH 1: Sister, where have you been?
WITCH 2: I've been a riveter.
WITCH 3: I've been a . . .
WITCH 1: I've been a . . .
WITCH 2: I've been a blast furnace helper.
WITCH 3: I've been a . . .
WITCH 1: I've been a welder.
WITCH 2: I've been an electrician.
WITCH 3: I've been a . . .
WITCH 1: I've been a . . .
WITCH 2: I've been a HOOKER . . . hooking up shells.
WITCH 3: I've been a SCREWER . . . screwing bolts.
WITCH 1: I've been a GRINDER . . . grinding edges.

LIP SYNC: MY LONELY NIGHTS ARE GONE

Peggy sings soulfully, standing behind Cora, who lip-syncs. Peggy reaches her arms forward, gesturing as she sings, so that they appear to be Cora's arms.

John Henry

Cora steps aside, revealing Peggy singing.

PEGGY:
> John Henry said to the captain,
> A man ain't nothin' but a man,
> Before I let a steam engine drive me down
> I'll die with a hammer in my hand . . .
> I'll die with a hammer in my hand.
>
> But John Henry had a little woman
> Her name was sweet Polly Ann.
> When John Henry got sick and had to go to bed
> It was Polly drove steel like a man, Lord
> It was Polly drove steel like a man.

And she raised a family, and made sure he got off to work on time with lunch in hand.

(She walks downstage.)

Mamie Enix

In the spice factory, Haydee and Cora do gestures of work as Peggy describes it, speaking as Tina Enix.

TINA: And as he poured liquid heat from one huge oversized container into another with a massive ladle and lifts, she maneuvered her way through a haze of hot steam, boiling water, scorching heat, scrub tubs and wash. Lifting one bag of bay leaves after the next and placing the jar that contained them onto a conveyor belt that moved things along . . . a handful of leaves, five or six, put that into the jar, screw the lid on tight and just move it along. They were solid. They were real . . . and handsome . . . ooo-weee! And muscled? And smile . . . chile! Everybody loved him. Bubbles, my husband. He never missed a day of work.

Everything they did, they did for us. So we'd have a better chance at everything. School. Jobs. Home. Everything.

Tremendous Discrimination

Peggy continues speaking as Tina Enix:

TINA: He worked in terrible, hot conditions there. Often worked a lot of overtime hours to take care of his family of three children and a wife. My father, Bubbles. He was quite a character in spite of the fact that he experienced tremendous discrimination . . . trying to get a job at the Steel and while there fifty years and throughout his employment . . . lack of advavancement. "Everything they did, they did for us." Terrible, hot conditions for more than fifty years.

> Father
> Mother
> Brother
> Cousins
> Sisters
> Sons . . .
> Years at the same job without advancement . . .
> Tremendous discrimination
> Tremendous discrimination
> Right here in Bethlehem there was tremendous discrimination.
> Throughout this country, tremendous discrimination!
> And everything they did they did for us.

Children's Games

Cora and Peggy, as little girls, chase and play, while Haydee, as mother, watches. The girls sing a medley of hand-clapping songs.

CORA AND PEGGY: Eeny, meeny, miney, moe, catch a . . . Eeny Meeny Josephiney . . .

(Haydee takes down the clothesline during the remainder of the games.)

Who stole my chickens and my hens . . . Miss Mary Mack Mack Mack . . . X marks the spot . . . Twenty-four robbers . . .

(Haydee exits. Cora runs offstage and hides. Peggy exits, looking for her. Cora reenters as Anna McGlaughlin Cassium.)

LUCY *(Crying)*: Ricky . . .

(Ricky laughs. Lucy's crying escalates.)

Ricky . . .

RICKY: Lucy, you have some 'splainin' to do. *(Ad-libs)* ¡Ay, Dios mio, esta mujer, caramba!

(Lucy continues sobbing as they exit stage left.)

Edith and Archie Bunker

(Haydee enters, as Edith.)

EDITH: Oh, I forgot Archie's pie.

(She opens the refrigerator as Peggy enters, as Archie.)

ARCHIE: Hey Edith, get me a beer wouldya.

EDITH *(Fussily)*: Sure Archie. Here you go. Sit here, make yourself comfortable.

ARCHIE: Where's the Meathead?

EDITH: I think he took Gloria to the movies.

ARCHIE: I don't know what's going on around here, all these people moving in . . . There's the two Negro families, then there's the Jews and the Puerto Ricans . . . they're like friggin' termites!

EDITH: Oh, but Archie, they're human beings too, Archie . . .

EDITH AND ARCHIE *(Singing)*: "Guys like us, we had it made. Those were the days."

ANDAR

Music plays. Peggy brings on Haydee's curlers and Cora's stool, dancing to the music.

CAFÉ CON LECHE

HAYDEE: I was thinking, An apple has a core and there are different kinds of breakfast. There's cereal and oatmeal and café con leche . . . You heard me right, café con leche! The other day my kid came home from school and said to me, "Mami, my teacher says that café con leche is not a real breakfast." *(Mutters curses in Spanish)*

Then on another day my other kid comes home from school and says, "My teacher told me that Guillermo is not my name. She said my name was Bill, and I don't feel like a 'Bill!'" *(Mutters curses)* And I said to them, "¡Tu vas a tomar café con leche and tu te llamas Guillermo!"

¿Quien ha dicho? ¿Quien tiene el derecho? Café con leche, café con leche . . . *(Muttering, the words fading as she begins to dance)*

(Cora enters and sits on the floor, center stage. Music continues. Peggy comes up behind her and tries to braid her hair.)

NAVIGATE

CORA: Peggy, I don't think it's going to work. I appreciate your efforts, but . . . Peggy, this is the way my hair is! It just does whatever it wants. I mean, ever since I was a little girl. When I was a little girl, it didn't matter so much. I remember when I was ten years old, I thought being a girl was great. Clearly we had many more options than a boy. We could jump rope, play house, dolls, ride a bike in the country, play ball—the worst anyone could call us was a tomboy. But, I mean, a boy—if he wanted to play dolls, or dress up . . . you know what you would call him . . . Clearly, being a girl was the best. Then something happened—puberty. I started to sprout breasts. I started to like boys, and I wanted them to like me. I remember running around the table after David Bergenstock. My face was flushed, red, excited. He turned around, saw me in this state, and said, "Who does she think she is?" I thought, Well, maybe I'm not supposed to play this game. Maybe I wasn't meant to be attractive. 'Cause, it seemed like the harder I tried to do anything, the worse it got. There's nothing more painful than really trying to be attractive, and it doesn't look good. So I gave up. But, you know, eventually you have to grow up, be an adult, look the part. But somehow the top never met the bottom. So, like a lot of white women, I ended up in therapy. And, I remember my therapist— it was a woman—and one day she asked me, "Do you ever remember wanting a penis?" No, no, NEVER! And then, late in life for this sort of thing, I became pregnant for the first time ever. You know, I don't think I ever thought I could get pregnant. My whole body started to change. I got round, I grew breasts. But something—a confluence of forces—were acting inside me and I had nothing to say about it. When my daughter was born, she was beautiful. And I had asked myself— how do I help her enjoy being a woman? How do I help her navigate?

(Haydee enters.)

I Never Wanted Babies

PEGGY: I listen to the two of you talk about being mothers, and it's amazing. You're incredible, both of you. I love being an aunt, a stepmother, grandmother, godmother, but I never wanted to have no baby, no sir, uh-uh. Just ain't my thing.

Daughter of a Single Mother

HAYDEE: Oh, Peggy, you're so funny. On the other hand, my mother always wanted to have a daughter. 1943—she had me, a woman. For a long time, I didn't know what was going on. You know, I asked her, "Mama, ¿donde esta mi papa?" And the answer was always the same: a muttered response, an empty response. And then one day we were laying on my bed. And I said, "Mama, ¿¡donde esta mi papa!?" It hit me like a ton of bricks—I felt like a mountain came crashing in on me and I felt I got lost in the shadows of the Earth. I remember just before I entered the first grade, my mother got a call from the nuns at the school saying, "I'm sorry, your daughter cannot be registered in our school." Then came the Union Club, you know, with all the fancy names and all the rich folks. It's not that she didn't have the money. And then, later on, seeing my half sisters across the street, wanting to run over and say, "I am your sister!" But I had an illegitimate identity. I was miserable. I was a figment of my imagination. The isolation was brutal. The despair of having to conform to the rules of society was asphyxiating.

Haydee's Mom

HAYDEE: But my mother gave me so much more. She breast-fed me. Every dress in my closet was made by her. You see, she was, and still is, a very artistic and talented woman. Ever since I was a little girl she enrolled me in ballet, piano lessons and painting. She was the first member of her family to own a Victrola. She'd go around the house dancing. But her real passion was opera. She loved *Carmen*. She'd get into position and do the flamenco. And then there was my piano teacher, Mr. Fooster. Every time he came to the house I'd say, "Oh, Mr. Fooster, could you please play Franz Liszt for me?" And he was from Spain, and he had a lisp, and he would say: *(Ad-libs very fast and very funny, in Spanish)* "Here's your position." *(Sings and mimes playing "Chopsticks" on the piano)* Ba-ba-ba-ba-ba-ba ba-ba . . .

Chopsticks

Cora enters singing the "Chopsticks" melody. She mimes the playing of a very regimented and stiff version on the piano. Peggy enters, also singing the "Chopsticks" melody. She mimes the steady playing of two bass keys on the piano. All three then sing their parts together.

Baseball and Politics—Cora's Mother

Cora stops and covers her ears. Peggy and Haydee sit and listen to Cora's story.

CORA: My mother was not musical at all. No. What she was, was baseball and politics. In fact, I remember she told me when she was growing up in Missouri they used to listen to the baseball games on the radio. But this was a *crystal* radio, which meant that only one person could listen at a time, 'cause you have to listen with the headphones. And so her oldest brother, who was handicapped, would sit in his big special car they had made for him and he would wear the headphones. In front of him he would have two sets of buttons, red for the St. Louis Cardinals and blue for the other team. He would set up the buttons before the game and at every play he would look up. *(Pantomimes setting up the buttons as players on the diamond and manipulating them to show action on the field)* And so my mother grew up *watching* baseball on the radio. Then she said in later summers her brother ran for public office. This meant at that time that you had to have a lot of starched white shirts. Now in Missouri in the summer that can mean several changes of shirts a day. It was my mother's job to keep the shirts starched and ironed. One day President Roosevelt was coming to speak in our town and my mother wanted to hear what he had to say because by God she might have something to say back. And she had to stay home and starch and iron the shirts.

(Cora mimes ironing shirts and begins singing "Take Me Out to the Ball Game." As the song continues, the others join in. Cora stops ironing. Haydee exits to bring on a stool for Peggy as she begins her next lines. The song ends.)

Vagina Heart—Peggy's Mother

Peggy moves the stool downstage to speak intimately with the audience:

PEGGY: That reminds me of my mom, because she loved basketball, and her favorite player was Magic Johnson. She used to say, "Magic Johnson's on the team." My mother was a simple woman. She was a welfare mother and she was missing her two front teeth and kind of shy about that. But to her everybody was a black somebody. You had a black Shirley Temple and a black Dorothy Lamour, and a black Clark Gable. She was like that. She was funny and quick-witted. Anyway, she passed away in '93 and that wasn't a bad thing because it was May and the weather was beautiful. And the hospital let us put our mattresses on the floor. That way she could have all her chicks around her. She was very happy. And it was a magic time—all seven of us together for five days and nights. Anyway, she knew that she was leaving this world and she wanted to be clean. So she asked me and my sister Pat to bathe her. Now this was a big deal 'cause my sister Pat is a Jehovah's Witness and I'm a Baptist and we both come from this little woman whose total claim-to-fame, bottom line, is: "I breast-fed all of them." Anyway, there was no shame. None whatsoever. And it was obvious that the cancer had ravished her body. But down there between her legs it was beautiful. The moles on the inside of her thighs were celestial, and the colors . . . It was the first time I realized that the vagina is shaped like a heart, like love, feeling, mother. And I told her so. I said, "Mom, the rest of you is a mess, but here you're beautiful." And she looked up at us and smiled and said, "Open wide. Each one of you come from here." As if to say, "I'm a welfare mother. Nobody. Supposed to be a source of shame for this whole country. But this is the door of life and every one of you came through here." The atmosphere in the room was tangible. She was transformed. I heard of Moses and Jesus, and God knows I love Jesus—Mahatma Gandhi—but there was this little black woman, a welfare mother, who was illuminated. Her breathing got slower. Her heart was being monitored and you could see it: ba-boom, ba-boom.

(Her hand gestures the line of the monitor with the ba-boom of the heartbeat. Then her hand, and the heart, come to stillness.)

Nothing. The only thing that was left in that room was the warmth that was the center of Helen.

HOLY, HOLY, HOLY—ELLA'S BIRTH

PEGGY: Now, when Cora's little girl Ella was born, her heart was monitored too, and she came into this world . . .

(Peggy again gestures the heart monitor, Ella's heartbeat accelerating to the point that Peggy's entire body is moving as quickly as she can.)

(To Cora) You remember?

CORA: Yeah . . . I was there. *(To audience)* And Peggy was there, too. And for both of us it was the first birth we'd ever encountered. I remember after Ella was born, Peggy said, "This is amazing! Women are having babies! Why isn't anybody talking about this?"

PEGGY: I guess it was all the history that was in that room. Because you have to realize that Cora's doctor was a black man, right here in Bethlehem. A hundred years ago this scene would not have been possible. And he's there looking like a football player, going, "Come on Cora, hit me with your best shot. Come on, come on Cora, PUSH." And I looked at my friend and she was changed and the ground we were standing on was sacred and the sky opened up.

(She gestures to the sky. They all sing a three-part chord. Cora is on the ground as if giving birth, Haydee behind her, Peggy as the doctor:)

Holy.

HAYDEE: Holy.

CORA: Holy.

(Blackout.)

END

Touchstone Theatre

Based in Bethlehem, Pennsylvania, Touchstone Theatre is a producing and presenting organization that fosters intercultural, international and community collaborations. Touchstone is dedicated to being an active force in the renewal of theater as a vital art form, and to pursuing the discovery of a theatrical vocabulary in which the emotional dynamics of image, movement and space are as important as the text, be it original or classic. Its resident professional acting ensemble tours nationally and internationally with selected original and ensemble-created works, and offers educational programs that contribute to serious training in the field, demonstrate the power of theater as a community-building tool, and inspire students of all ages to discover their own creative expression. The focus of its presenting season is original work by other innovative theater ensembles and solo artists. Visiting as well as resident artists generate and perform work in an ongoing dialogue with the rich diversity of the Lehigh Valley community.

Touchstone was founded in 1981 and grew out of the Lehigh University Improvisational Street Theatre Troupe (founded in 1972) and the People's Theatre Company (founded in 1977). It has toured its acclaimed original works for adults and children throughout the Mid-Atlantic states and abroad. Touchstone has performed at venues including Lincoln Center, INTAR Hispanic American Arts Center, New York City; Painted Bride Art Center, Philadelphia; Baltimore Theatre Project; the White House and the National Theatre, Washington, D.C.; Yerba Buena Center for the Arts, San Francisco; and the Alternate Roots Festival, Atlanta; and internationally in Morelia, Mexico; at the Edinburgh Fringe Festival, Scotland (where Touchstone received a Fringe First Award); at the seventh biennial International Puppetry Festival in Caguas, Puerto Rico; and at the 1993 Theatre of Nations Festival in Santiago, Chile. Touchstone has also made important contributions to education in Pennsylvania through more than twenty years of participation in the Arts in Education program of the Pennsylvania Council on the Arts and more than fifty teaching residencies in schools throughout the state.

NOTHIN' NICE

The Carpetbag Theatre

*Audience members with the cast (from left to right): Carlton "Starr"
Releford, Lloyd Joseph Martin, Sylvia Rupert (front) and Whitney Blue
(far right).*

Introduction

Arriving for the premiere of The Carpetbag Theatre's *Nothin' Nice*, the Austin East High School football team is in no good mood. They had been gathered on the football field earlier that afternoon for what was supposed to be a special summertime scrimmage, when their coach instead announced that he had in fact called them together to "see a play."

In the theater, adult community members in their Sunday best stop chatting to watch the team be seated in a tight, grumpy knot, house right. When a minister steps onstage to lead a prayer, the young men bow their heads respectfully, but afterward begin distracting one another. An adult lets out a sharp, "Shh!" and the boys go quiet.

The director of the organization sponsoring the premiere takes the stage to explain that today is in fact Knoxville's annual observation of Emancipation Day, which has been celebrated in East Knoxville since 1865. He asks us to join in singing the civil rights anthem "Lift Every Voice," but the teenagers roll their eyes and shift in their seats. In an instant, two stern-looking women in hats are standing in the aisle looming over them, conducting. The teens straighten up and sing.

Most every eye is on the team now, but once the song is done, the conductors return to their seats and the lights dim. The young men are on their own in a darkened auditorium, about to sit through a show they were tricked into attending. They're giggling and jabbing one another, and I have the impression that if the play can't hold them, nothing will.

East Tennessee's long relationship to the U.S. Civil Rights Movement is embodied in the work of The Carpetbag Theatre, one of only a few professional resident African American theater ensembles in the South. Since 1970, Carpetbag's plays have examined domestic violence, black history, feminism, the racial dimensions of environmental policy, capital punishment, urban economic development and other social justice and cultural issues. The ensemble's year-round schedule of residencies and performances keeps it on close terms with Knoxville's neighborhoods. *Nothin' Nice* was developed in community-based workshops over a two-year period, and the play's author, Linda Parris-Bailey, enumerates the play's themes according to what former Surgeon General Dr. M. Joycelyn Elders (1993–1994) calls "The Three P's: Poverty, Population and Pollution."

The play's main character, Lonewolf, is the same age as the players of the Austin East team, who jeer at first when Lonewolf's principled uncle lectures him. Environmental racism is a complex topic to absorb when you'd rather be out playing ball on a summer afternoon. However, as Lonewolf's crisis escalates during the course of the play, the teens listen more carefully to what the uncle has to say. When the attractive female lead enters, they whistle, but fall silent when they learn that she is the mother of Lonewolf's child. As each scene unfolds and the crisis intensifies, the boys grow increasingly still. At the play's tragic climax, the team is silent as stone.

The final scene plays like a call to action, and the house lights come up to rousing music. Lo and behold, the teens are already on their feet, clapping and singing out with full voices. As the lights come down, the Austin East team leads a standing ovation, bringing the cast back for bow after bow. Afterward, the teens describe the play's plot and Lonewolf's crisis to me in minute detail, with obvious enthusiasm.

During the ovations, adult community members watch the young men, smiling, as though something had been confirmed. One woman puts her hand up, bows her head and calls out, "Yes, yes, yes."

How art and culture affect us is an individual matter, of course, and therefore impossible to quantify. We can't know for sure if the Austin East football team was educated, changed or even provoked to reflection by the play, but then again, we can't know exactly what impact the annual observance of Emancipation Day makes either. What is certain, though, is that both provided opportunities for the community to participate in an examination of its culture, obligations and, perhaps most importantly, its story.

—F.L.

Nothin' Nice *is dedicated to John O'Neal,*
who made this work happen; to Lloyd Joseph Martin
and all the stricken angels of New Orleans's "Cancer Alley";
to Adora Dupree and victims of cancer everywhere;
and to all those who struggle for the "Three E's:
Equality, Environmental Justice and Empowerment."

PRODUCTION INFORMATION

Nothin' Nice was commissioned by Junebug Productions' Environmental Justice Project. Co-commissioning partners included the Illusion Theater of Minneapolis and the National Performance Network. It was written by Linda Parris-Bailey, artistic director of The Carpetbag Theatre, and developed by the CBT ensemble company in collaboration with AmeriCorps of New Orleans and other community partners. It is based on stories collected during a multi-year AmeriCorps project.

Nothin' Nice received its premiere in May 1998, as part of the Environmental Justice Festival at the Contemporary Arts Center in New Orleans. It was subsequently performed at Pellissippi State Technical Community College in Knoxville, Tennessee, in February 1999, and at Knoxville College in February 2000, during CBT's four-year term as the resident professional company. In 2001, *Nothin' Nice* was presented at Austin East High School, an arts magnet school in Knoxville, by the Beck Cultural Exchange Center, and at the Alternate ROOTS annual meeting in North Carolina. Excerpts were also performed at the Network of Ensemble Theaters gathering in San Francisco. In February 2002, *Nothin' Nice* was presented by Touchstone Theatre in Bethlehem, Pennsylvania, and in a residency project at Berea College in Berea, Kentucky. The play remains in CBT's repertoire.

The CBT production was directed by Bob Leonard with Nancy Prebilich. Original music was composed by Paula Clarke, Linda Parris-Bailey and Carlton "Starr" Releford. The sets were designed by Jeff Cody, the lighting was designed by Brian Prather, the costumes were designed by Bert Tanner; the production stage manager was Jeff Cody, and the production assistants were Dorothy Bennett and Linda Upton Hill. The CBT cast included: Whitney Blue (Tyra), Quinn Fortune (Tyra), Frank Harp (Lonewolf), Belinda Hicks (Tyra), Angela Higgs (Nicole), Paula Larke (Maylene), Lloyd Joseph Martin (Victor), Zakiyyah Modeste (Nicole), Linda Parris-Bailey (Maylene), Carlton "Starr" Releford (Lonewolf), Keyana Richards (Nicole), Sylvia Rupert (Lil) and Bert Tanner (Victor).

Lyrics: "More Than a Paycheck," Ysaye Maria Barnwell, Barnwell's Notes Publishing, P.O. Box 32164, Washington, D.C. (page 178); "Woke

Up This Morning," words by Reverend Osby and Bob Zeller, from *Sing for Freedom*, 1990, Guy and Candie Carawan, eds., Hal Leonard, Milwaukee (page 184).

CHARACTERS

LONEWOLF, an AmeriCorps worker, twenty-one. He has one daughter, Kesha, who lives with her mother.

VICTOR, Lonewolf's uncle, mid-fifties. He is a Vietnam vet, community organizer and wise man.

LIL, Lonewolf's mother, forty-seven. She is hardworking and honest about her feelings. She and Lonewolf are very close.

NICOLE, Kesha's mother, nineteen. She works and goes to school. She is also an aspiring poet.

KESHA, daughter of Lonewolf and Nicole, a toddler.

TYRA, Nicole's best friend, nineteen.

MAYLENE, a musician who plays the bass guitar and drums. Maylene served in Vietnam as an army nurse and came back a healer and teacher. She sings with neighborhood youth in her courtyard every evening.

SETTING/SET

The play takes place in inner-city New Orleans. The stage is divided into two "home places": the house where Lil and Lonewolf live, and Victor's house and aboveground garden.

In the space that represents Lil and Lonewolf's home, the "shotgun" nature of the house is dominant. The area that serves as kitchen, dining room and family room is dominated by television sets that play continuously, reporting the local news. The multiple televisions provide a backdrop and are programmed to reflect images of "Cancer Alley" and other environmental disasters. Also in the room is Lonewolf's keyboard, which he plays throughout the show.

Victor's home is dominated by an outdoor garden with three large, rectangular, aboveground plots where he grows collard greens and other vegetables. There is a small television in Victor's garden.

Adjacent to Victor's garden is Maylene's backyard, a small courtyard where she and her "pupils," the young people of the neighborhood, play music and visit. She and other members of the ensemble provide the transitional music for the play from this area.

Other locations, such as Louis Armstrong Park and various New Orleans street corners and alleyways, are implied by lighting, simple set pieces and props.

Music is key to the play, and is used to transition from scene to scene. Songs are also used as "teaching tools" by the characters; most of the songs come from the tradition of the Civil Rights movement. Original music has been created to underscore Lonewolf and Nicole's scenes, and Maylene and the "neighbors" (the ensemble) take on the roles of chorus and orchestra. As with all of CBT's original work, *Nothin' Nice* is a play with music.

ACT ONE

Maylene is seated in her courtyard, Victor is tending his garden and Lil is in her home. Maylene begins to sing "Will You Miss Me?" softly, almost to herself. Victor and the other neighbors join her, creating an Appalachian harmony that takes Lil back to her roots.

LIL *(To audience)*: I wasn't born here. I was born in Alcoa. Most people hear "Alcoa" don't even know it's a place. They just think it's another name for aluminum, like Kleenex is a tissue. Then they don't know it's in Tennessee. But that's where I grew up. And I gotta admit, when folks start talkin' about some a those other company towns, I don't know where they are either! My father's people came from Alabama back when Alcoa was recruiting in the Deep South for men to do the work in the pot rooms, stoking the fires and doing whatever else they couldn't get white folks to do. Grandaddy said Alcoa was just another coal camp with jobs and company houses promised to any poor colored man from Alabama or Mississippi. Of course if they moved from down there it was still a big step up, according to Grandaddy. My mother's people were straight out of the mountains. Been there since the days of the Underground Railroad. Her family came out of the mountains when the Tennessee Valley Authority took their land to build dams. They never really were the same off the land my mother

says. They weren't forgiving people. They were some no-nonsense people who did things their own way. My mother stopped talkin' to me
when Jerry and I decided to get married. That hurt doesn't have anything to do with racism. If you knew how I was raised you'd think
I was a lot older than I am. I lived part of my life in the country. I'm
only forty-seven, but I grew up with an outhouse and cooked on a
wood stove at my grandmother's. I grew up in a place where everything that happens, happens ten years after everywhere else. Then I
moved here. And here everything happens with the rest of the country,
but then it happens again ten years later.

(Lil's music plays.)

MAYLENE AND ENSEMBLE:
> Will you miss me? Will you miss me?
> Will you miss me when I'm gone?

*(Victor's music begins. It is a funky, up-tempo, sampled rhythm. May-
lene and her pupils are playing and dancing in her courtyard.)*

VICTOR: Maylene! Hey, Maylene! How come you gotta share everything
you do with the whole neighborhood? Ain't no use in you tryin' to
play that HIP-HOP shit! It ain't part a nothin' we understand. Them
kids know you too damn old to play with them!
MAYLENE: You don't understand nothing after 1975! I'm sampling, fool.
VICTOR: Samplin'? Well, whyn't you sample something that means something and stop messing up my environment. You better start samplin'
some old school: Curtis Mayfield, Donny Hathaway, Sly, War. *(Starts
to sing)* "War—HOO, what is it good for, absolutely nothin'!" You
better put somethin' on these kids. Out here on the streets, no job, no
money, trashin' everything in sight . . . Hey, whyn't you sample this:

> We bring more than a paycheck to our loved ones and families
> We bring more than a paycheck to our loved ones and families . . .

*(He continues to sing. The bass picks up the melody as Victor addresses
the audience:)*

When I was young, back before the war started takin' things from me,
back before the first freedom songs, I fished the Bayous. Walked out my
back door and down the road whenever I got ready. Free, open space.
Then they brought storage tanks and put them between us and the

water. Then they went from house to house buying us out block by block. Finally all of our neighbors were gone and we were left there with the tanks. I couldn't even see the water. So I left. When I came home, I didn't recognize that water. Water would shimmer blue metallic like in a Dalí painting. My dog drank that water one afternoon . . . he died.

(Lonewolf steps away from Maylene's courtyard to address the audience:)

LONEWOLF: First you gotta know whose environment you talkin' about. My environment is my kitchen, 'cause that's where I spend my time. I eat there, I listen to music and my mamma there. My baby gets fed there. Now Kesha, that's my heart right there. She's the only thing that I worry about when it comes to my environment. She's the only thing I see when I look into the future. She wasn't what I'd call the product of family planning, but she came just at the right time to get my head together. I don't know what I was doin' out there. My moms was like, "Get a job! You ain't in school and you ain't doin' nothin' 'round here!" Yeah right, Mom. Hey, I'm young, I got time. I had six months to get ready for Kesha! Her mamma was sixteen. I was only eighteen! I was thinkin' about sex, like the survey says, twenty-seven times or more a day. My mamma was shocked when she heard that. You know, that men think about sex somewhere on average of about twenty-seven times a day. Frankly, I thought that was a low estimate. She said that she understood the term "dickhead" after that.

(Lights come up on Lil.)

LIL: And every dickhead should be blessed with a daughter so he can think about the "dog in me"!
LONEWOLF: That's a low blow, Moms.
LIL: That's the truth, Wolfee. I swear, I don't know how y'all get anything done at all! If it wasn't for birth control . . .
LONEWOLF: Awright Moms. Point made, point taken.
  (Resumes his conversation with audience; lights down on Lil) There ain't nothin' toxic about my kitchen. No, only thing toxic in my kitchen is my mamma's chitlins on New Year's. When I walk out my door goin' to work in the morning, I see my environment: neighbor didn't pick up his trash, wino left his calling card right under my bike tire, and I got to tread through five inches of damn water before I can get to the curb to take the damn bus.

(Lights come up again on Lil as Lonewolf enters his home.)

LIL: Wolfee! Wolfee! Joycelyn Elders is going to be in town! I haven't seen her since she left Washington. I saw her at this luncheon and the moderator was talkin' about how she resigned her position. She stood up in front a all those suits and thanked the moderator for her kindness, but she said that she didn't resign her position, she was FIRED! Because she spoke her mind and said what she believed! I hollered! 'Course she's a doctor and she could go home and find her a job that paid more money anyway. Education is a wonderful thing. You can tell people to kiss your behind and still feed your children. I told you, you better go back to school! That's the only reason I let you take the AmeriCorps job, 'cause you said you'd get money for school.

LONEWOLF: Mom, how'd we get to talkin' about school? And who is Joycelyn Elders?

LIL: Boy, read the paper sometime. Turn off the soap operas and *Ricki Lake* and *Jerry Springer* and listen to some folks who got some sense.

LONEWOLF: I listen to Uncle Victor. The man's read every book in the library! He knows something about everything.

LIL: Now that is education gone to seed! The big weed spreadin' spores and makin' folks sick like ragweed!

LONEWOLF: Why he gotta be all that?

LIL: That man is a walkin' contradiction. Who ever heard of a hippie, Vietnam vet, alcoholic, gardener, vegetarian, who smokes and wears leather clothes? The man spends half his life recycling his own beer cans! Ya know he's the one that talked your father into naming you Lonewolf. Everybody in the neighborhood thought it was a nickname until you went to school. Principal thought I didn't know the difference. Kept saying, "Yes, but what's his real name?"

LONEWOLF: Moms, Uncle Victor taught me to be a man.

LIL: What kinda man, Mr. twenty-seven times a day? What did he teach you to have on your mind? What you doin' for Kesha?

LONEWOLF: What's her mamma doin' for her?

LIL: Goin' to school!

LONEWOLF: And workin' at Mickey D's for minimum wage while I take care of Kesha. I'm doin' my part, Mom.

LIL: Right up to the time you take her home to her exhausted mamma at the end of a twelve-hour day!

LONEWOLF: Why you always on her side? You women always be gangin' up on us. When we try and do good, you just dog us anyway! You think takin' care of a baby by yourself all day is so easy? It ain't like I'm not workin'.

LIL: That little piece of a job at Saint Luke's ain't nothin'. What's it goin' ta do for you next year? You got benefits? You got enough money to put clothes on that baby's back?

LONEWOLF: When I leave there I'll have some carpentry skills. I can rehab a house or paint. I got more skills now than I ever had.

LIL: But what you gonna do with those skills? Only thing a man can do with a little bit a carpentry skills is go to one a those "job" places where they send you out for day labor. What they call that place that opened up down the street?

LONEWOLF: Labor World is down the street, Labor Ready is down on Biscayne.

LIL: It's just like bein' a day worker in the white folks' houses, waitin' on the corner for somebody to pick you out for a day job.

LONEWOLF: Mom, I won't be sittin' at no Labor World lookin' for work. I know people now who will hire me after the program.

LIL: We'll see. —You better check on Kesha, she probably needs another diaper change.

LONEWOLF: I sure will be glad when she's toilet-trained.

LIL: Everybody's always in such a hurry ta get they kids grown and out the way.

LONEWOLF: Well I'm grown, but I ain't out your way yet!

LIL: Brother, how I know that!

(Lonewolf starts to leave.)

Where you goin'?

LONEWOLF: I gotta catch up with Victor.

LIL: Did you forget something?

LONEWOLF: What?

LIL: Kesha!

LONEWOLF: I thought you could watch her while I was gone.

LIL: Then I guess you shoulda asked me! I got a hair appointment in fifteen minutes.

LONEWOLF: Can't you take her with you?

LIL: Wait a minute, I'm going to the hairdresser where some sister's gonna have my head under water, then a dryer, then the curling iron, and you're going to *talk* to your uncle Victor, but she should go with me?

LONEWOLF: You're her grandmother.

LIL: And you're her father. Like LL Cool J says, "All I ever wanted was a father." That man said a father, not a grandmother. That's what Kesha needs—a father—or you think that only applies to boys? As my mamma told me, "I raised mine!" I'll see ya when I get back.

LONEWOLF: Thanks Mom. Come on, Kesha, you goin' with Daddy. *(Exits with Kesha)*

LIL *(To audience)*: I just love Joycelyn Elders! She said that the biggest problem in the country today is the three P's: Poverty, Population and

Pollution. That's my girl! She had it ALL right. You remember what she said about masturbation? It bein' a natural part of life? If Wolfee had been "pleasuring" himself, even twenty-seven times a day, he wouldn't be strugglin' with Kesha now. Abstinence might not have sounded so bad if they had listened to her. Joycelyn Elders knew what had to be done for young folks . . . be real. That's why they fired her.

(Lights down on Lil.)

Scene 2

Lonewolf and Kesha visit with Victor in his garden.

VICTOR: Whose baby are you? You Daddy's baby? Or you my baby? If you was my baby, I'd take you everywhere I went.

(Maylene and the ensemble begin to sing "Keep Your Eyes on the Prize.")

LONEWOLF: You say that now, but if you had her every day, you'd be lookin' for anybody you could find to watch her just for a little while. Men ain't made for this, man.

VICTOR: Men are made for whatever they need to do. My grandfather raised seven children after his wife died.

LONEWOLF: That ain't the way I heard it. Grandma told me that she raised six children after her mother died. She said Great-Grandpa worked the fields, came home and ate and gave out whuppins when they wouldn't mind her!

VICTOR: That might be true, but still, if I had my daughter with me I wouldn't lose her again. Only family I got is in Vietnam somewhere. Or maybe they got out. But I'll never know. That's an old hurt, man. It doesn't go away, the pain just eases up a little. Protect your baby, man.

LONEWOLF: She here, ain't she? She's with me.

VICTOR: That ain't what I said. I said protect her! These knuckleheads around here dress they kids up in little Nike shoes and miniature hip-hop clothes and think that they doin' something. Got dat hat to the back on a little year-old head but can't protect 'em from licking the cocaine off the dining room table or eatin' that old paint, or gettin' shot ridin' in the gang mobile with they daddy! Protecting her is your job, man. Right now you control her environment, so you better protect her.

LONEWOLF: What is this—pick on Wolfee day? First Moms, now you.

VICTOR: This ain't about you, it's about Kesha. She got a right to everything good in life. Speakin' a good, I got some mean greens, come on and get some for my baby. Your mamma'll cook 'em even if they did come outta my garden. That rat in my apartment looks at me with more love than she does. But I got nothin' but love for her.

LONEWOLF: Maybe that's y'all's problem. You were secretly in love with her before Daddy died and after he died you was so guilty about it that she has to keep her distance because she loves you too.

VICTOR: Wolfee, that wasn't even original, man. I saw *Legends of the Fall*! That ain't it, brother. She thinks that I don't know what I'm talkin' about when I talk about what the system is doin' to us. When I start talkin' about Cancer Alley or the Ninth Ward she goes cold on me man, like I just threatened her life or something. She starts that "ain't nobody leavin' here alive" stuff.

LONEWOLF: She's just scared.

VICTOR: Yeah, well me too. But I ain't gonna be scared with my mouth shut. When I get scared I scream! I found out in 'Nam that it helps you get outta bad trouble, brother. Bad trouble.

LONEWOLF: I wish I could scream sometimes. I go out my house every day. I know what I want, but I don't know how to get it, man.

VICTOR: You gotta be like water, Wolfee. You gotta find the source. Find the formula. You need H-2-O. Heart, a partner who believes in you— that's the 2 part—and the ability to overcome whatever obstacles come your way.

LONEWOLF: Sounds good, Unc, but I don't have none a' that. No partner, no . . .

VICTOR: Hold up, brother. I know you got heart, your old man gave you that. I know you got a partner 'cause you got me. And your mamma gave you the ability to overcome. She's been doin' it all her life. So everything you need you got. *("Keep Your Eyes on the Prize" ends)*

LONEWOLF: In three months I won't have no job, then what? I gotta take care a Little Bit, and Mamma's goin' ta throw my ass outta the house if I don't pull my weight.

VICTOR: I got a job for you, youngblood. I need a community organizer. The pay ain't great, but it comes with room and board.

LONEWOLF: Yeah, vegetables outta the garden three times a day. A man needs meat. I'm a carnivore, I can't be livin' off no weeds for the rest of my life.

VICTOR: You haven't even asked what the organizer would do for me.

LONEWOLF: I haven't asked you about the pay neither! 'Cause it ain't hap-penin', Unc! I've seen what you live like and it ain't for me. I don't want ta walk for the rest of my life, make fires in the winter with wood I hauled from some swamp. I don't want ta spend weeks in the country trying ta organize some poor-ass group in Appaloosas so they can get some buses or books or toilet paper for their children's schools. That don't bring me no joy, man. I got my own troubles and when I get to be your age, I wanna be able to put my baby in a good Catholic school so she can go to Dillard.

VICTOR: Well, I hope you find what you're lookin' for, Wolfee, 'cause if Little Bit winds up in that little poor-ass public school around the corner, she goin' ta be up a creek if she thinks you gonna get her some toilet paper! I gotta go. I'll see you later.

LONEWOLF: Unc, don't go away mad.

VICTOR: I know, just go away. I'll see ya, man.

(Victor teases Lonewolf, singing as he goes into his house:)

> Walk, walk . . . Walk, walk
> I'm walkin' and talkin' with my mind (my mind it was)
> Stayed on freedom
> I'm walkin' and talkin' with my mind
> Stayed on freedom
> I'm walkin' and talkin' with my mind (my mind it was)
> Stayed on freedom
> Hallelu, hallelu, hallelujah . . .

(Maylene and ensemble join Victor from the courtyard, taking the song into transition:)

ALL:

> I woke up this morning with my mind
> Stayed on freedom
> I woke up this morning with my mind
> Stayed on freedom
> I woke up this morning with my mind
> Stayed on freedom
> Hallelu, hallelu, hallelujah!

LONEWOLF: That did not go well. Come on baby, let's see if we can find your mamma.

(Music continues. Lonewolf leaves his Uncle Victor's house, heading down a darkened New Orleans street. The sound of sirens. Flashing lights. Lonewolf ignores this and continues to walk with Kesha in her stroller. He finally realizes that the police are stopping him when there is a bullhorn announcement:)

POLICE *(Voice-over)*: Now. I want you to spread-eagle on the ground. *(Lonewolf stops pushing the stroller and lies down a few feet away)* Don't move, don't even breathe. *(Lonewolf tries to move on the ground toward Kesha)* What part of "don't move" do you not understand! Spread-eagle on the ground or this will be the last sound you hear!

(The scene dissolves into sirens and humiliation: a strobe light flashes, and we see Lonewolf following the police orders in slow motion as the lights fade to black.)

SCENE 3

Back at his home, Lonewolf calls Nicole at McDonald's.

LONEWOLF: Nicole, what time you get off tonight? . . . I'll bring Kesha over at 9:30 . . . What you mean you going out? . . . Yeah I went out Friday . . . and Saturday and Sunday of last week, so? I didn't tell you I would definitely keep her this weekend, I said I might! . . . I am not lying! What I look like draggin' her out at midnight ta bring her home to you? I'll be there at 10:30 so you better take care of whatever business you got by then . . . That is a compromise. I'll see you at 10:30. *(Hangs up)* Damn! Something gotta change! Between Moms and Nicole, you women 'bout to drive me crazy! Let me call Unc . . . *(Dials)* Unc? Hey man, I'm sorry. What ya doin'? . . . Whyn't you come over. No, I don't want a babysitter. I just wanna talk to you. OK, so maybe you could babysit after we talk. I really wasn't thinkin' about that . . . Why is everybody callin' me a liar? . . . What does: "If the foo shits wear it" mean? No, tell me when you get here . . . I put the baby down for a nap so we could talk . . . Fifteen minutes, man. *(Hangs up)*

   (To audience) I can't stand this, man! I cannot do this! Protect your baby?! I can't even protect myself. She coulda been hurt out there. Run over in the street. Hell, they weren't watchin' her! They were too busy holdin' a brother facedown! Then they wanna say that they didn't know it was a real baby. What did they think it was? A brother's gonna walk around in the middle of the night with an empty stroller? . . . I can't do this, man! You don' ever stop bein' somebody's father.

(Lights down on Lonewolf.)

Scene 4

Nicole waits for Tyra on a street corner in a low-income New Orleans neighborhood. Tyra enters.

NICOLE: Hey! So we goin' or not?

TYRA: Not through rehearsing yet. I gotta go back.

NICOLE: Tyra, why you make me come all the way over here if you wasn't goin'?

TYRA: I thought we'd be finished! Why you so edgy?

NICOLE: I'm tired!

TYRA: It's no big deal. We can look at the place tomorrow.

NICOLE: Yeah, well next time you need to come up with a place to crash in the middle of the night, don't call me! You're no better than Wolfee. He calls me at work and tells me that he didn't promise to keep Kesha this weekend and he's bringing her over at 10:30.

TYRA: I shoulda known it was Wolfee trouble. That boy still rocks your world.

NICOLE: That is not true! And you ain't the one to talk about what rocks somebody's world. Your world gets rocked every time a little boat cruises by! I swear. You go through life doin' whatever the person next to you does. I'm not gonna let folk around me keep me from doin' what I have to do for Kesha.

TYRA: Well some of us don't think we control everything that happens.

NICOLE: No, you don't control everything, but you can control what you do! You're the one that decides to go or stay. You can decide to get a real job and pay your share of the rent!

TYRA: Nicole, you and me grew up together right in Desire. We went to the same raggedy schools, played in the same vacant houses with the windows broken out. Wolfee comes along and everything changes. He took you away from all that. My stepfather took us away from all that, too, and I owe him something, so let's not act like I'm some irresponsible bitch. I have a "real job"! I'm a singer, or did you forget that?

NICOLE: I didn't forget anything. You know, you let your stepfather take you out of the hood, but he keeps you in the same environment. You aren't any better off than you were before.

TYRA: It's not my fault, Nicole.

NICOLE: It's your fault if you don't do something about it!

TYRA: I'm working on it. Did you bring the poems you want me to use?

NICOLE: I'm on my way from work, girl! But I have one that I just finished. I started it about a year ago and it's finally done.

TYRA: Give it to me. We'll work on it tonight.

NICOLE: Awright, but don't get all freaky with it, OK. It's from the heart.

TYRA: Freaky is as freaky does. I gotta get back. Bye.

NICOLE: Yeah right. And you better be ready to go look at that place that we saw in the paper tomorrow. You the one that really needs to move.

(Lights fade out as they exit.)

SCENE 5

Lonewolf is at home, seated at his keyboard. Victor enters and sits across from him.

VICTOR: So what was so urgent?

LONEWOLF: I'm gonna take you up on your offer.

VICTOR: Why the quick change of heart?

LONEWOLF: Something happened to me on the way home that made me think about what you said. I don't want to talk about it now because I don't want you callin' up "the soldiers" and headin' down to the police station in your battle fatigues, 'cause there's nothing you can do about it, but it made me think about a lot of things. What you said about protectin' Kesha, about never seein' your kids again. How anybody: man, woman, even little kids not old enough to talk, can be picked off without anybody knowing about it. Last week, when I was dropping Kesha off at the day care program at Nicole's high school, there were these little Vietnamese kids and nobody could talk to them so they just lined them up like little sheep and dragged them down the hallways from one place to another. They couldn't even defend themselves because they couldn't speak enough English to tell the teachers to quit! So I start thinking about your little Vietnamese kid and "toilet paper" . . . I just made up my mind. When can I move in?

VICTOR: You're serious?

LONEWOLF: Yeah. We'll try it for like three months and see what happens. Mom will love the idea of me bein' up outta here. And Kesha will have to spend more time with her mamma 'cause I'll be down with the brothers in the struggle.

VICTOR: Hold up, youngblood. This is a new day. You can't be pushin' all the child-rearing off on the sisters 'cause you "in the struggle." Baby girl needs to learn how to struggle, too! You can't start teaching them too early. So if you think you're coming with me to get rid a that baby, you got another thing comin'.

LONEWOLF: You ain't got no faith. Just let me pack my things awright. And by the way, what does this job pay?

VICTOR: You see that movie *Hoodlum*?

LONEWOLF: Yeah.

VICTOR: You remember what they said about Harlem in 1934?

LONEWOLF: No man, what did they say?

VICTOR: That number houses made a fortune in pennies, nickels and dimes.

LONEWOLF: Cut to the chase, Unc.

VICTOR: You gonna be a Harlem millionaire! 'Cause I'm gonna pay you in pennies, nickels and dimes!

LONEWOLF: Oh well, I guess I'm gonna be one a those "happy vegetarian" types whether I like it or not!

VICTOR: You got that right! Let's get your stuff. Your moms maybe happy about you goin', but she's not going to be happy about who you're going with.

LONEWOLF: OK, Unc, but I gotta drop Kesha off at 10:30 so I probably just meet you back at your place.

(Maylene plays djimbe "Rite of Passage" rhythm as Lonewolf packs his bags, going back and forth between rooms.)

SCENE 6

Lil enters and sees Lonewolf packing.

LIL: What's all this?

LONEWOLF: Well you finally getting your wish. I'm leaving home.

LIL: What are you talking about?

LONEWOLF: I'm moving in with Uncle Vic.

LIL: What the hell for?

LONEWOLF: Do you know that the only time you get ta cussin' is when I talk about Unc? There is something really deep between you two.

LIL: Stop stallin'. What's goin' on?

LONEWOLF: Unc offered me a job as an organizer. He said it doesn't pay much but he'd include room and board.

LIL: And you fell for that? You see a future in that?

LONEWOLF: Mamma, make up your mind! First you say get a job! Get outta the house! Now I'm doin' just that and you mad again!

LIL: I said get a job with a future! What's this "job" leading to? You getting any benefits? You getting insurance, health benefits for you and Kesha? What you thinkin' about?

LONEWOLF: I'm thinkin' about Kesha. I'm thinkin' about making her world better than mine is!

LIL: Where is she gonna stay—at Victor's?

LONEWOLF: She'll stay in the room with me. I'll have my own space. You know Unc is crazy about Kesha. He'll probably help me with her more than you do!

LIL: That why you're leaving? So you can pawn your daughter off on your crazy-ass uncle?

LONEWOLF: Mom, I know you think that I'm a little boy, but I'm a man and I gotta start making decisions for myself and my baby. I'm moving in with Uncle Victor because I need some help that you can't give me. Not help with Kesha, but help getting to be the man I wanna be. Unc lives a hard life, I know that. But he doesn't bend over for nobody. He's righteous and he's strong. That's who I wanna be. No, I don't wanna be poor all my life and he knows that. But I gotta figure out how to be successful in my own eyes. You remember that movie about the Million Man March?

LIL: *Get on the Bus?*

LONEWOLF: Yeah. All the brothers on that bus knew that something had to be done. They didn't know what it was, but they knew being together would at least acknowledge that something had to be done. This is my little Million Man March. This is what I'm doing. Now, some a the sisters were mad at the brothers, just like you are, but most of 'em looked at the sea of African American manhood and were proud. I want you to be proud.

LIL: I am proud. And I know you gotta go sometime. I just wish you'd find somebody else to follow, that's all. Your uncle is never gonna be able to take care of himself any better than he does now, and I want you to have something that will support you and your family.

LONEWOLF: I didn't say I wanted to be him. I just want to have some of what he has on the inside. *(Smiling)* Can you imagine me having to dress like that late-sixties fugitive? No, Mom, I ain't even with that. I love ya, baby, but I gotta go. I have to drop Kesha at her mother's before I head out ta Unc's. I'll be back on Thursday to pick up some more stuff.

LIL: Leave Kesha here with me until you get everything moved. I don't want that old man spending all his time spoiling my granddaughter. That's my job.

LONEWOLF: I love you, Mamma. *(Tries to kiss her)*

LIL: Get on outta here, man. An' don't forget to take those thug posters you got on my wall with you. Yeah—all them Big Daddy, Snoopy Dog, Lil whoevers you got, better leave here or they'll be in that music video being shot outside in the alley!

LONEWOLF: I still love ya, baby! As y'all old folks say, skinny legs and all!

LIL: I ain't studyin' you, Wolfee, now go on. *(He exits. She speaks to herself)* If Victor lets anything happen to my son I'm gonna kill him! I raised him in the middle of all this mess and I'm not gonna give him up to somebody else's trouble!

(Lights down on Lil.)

Scene 7

Maylene plays the "Call Tyrone" bass line. Lonewolf goes to meet Nicole, who is walking alone.

LONEWOLF: Thought you had a date tonight?

NICOLE: I thought so, too. But it wasn't the kind of date you talking about. I was supposed to meet Tyra and look at this house we're talking about sharing. Tyra was still rehearsing so she canceled. I was coming to get Kesha.

LONEWOLF: You movin' outta your mother's house?

NICOLE: Yeah, my mother is trying to get me to give up my job and go back to school full time. She wants me to have to get everything from her or Child and Family, and I don't want anybody having that much control over my life.

LONEWOLF: I'm moving out, too. My uncle Victor wants me to live with him and work as an organizer in the community. I just told my moms and she went off. She's okay about it now. Dag, if I'd a known about your movin' out, we coulda got a place together.

NICOLE: Oh no, my brother. I ain't lookin' for no male roommate. I've heard all the patter of little feet I want to, thank you!

LONEWOLF: I wasn't talkin' about "being" together, I was talkin' about sharing space.

NICOLE: Let's be honest. Do you think that you and I could live in a house together, day in and night in, and not "be" together?

LONEWOLF: You think that I have no self-control?

NICOLE: Baby, I know you, shall we say . . . intimately. I know you don't have any self-control! Speaking of which, where is my baby?

LONEWOLF: My moms is gonna keep her while I move to Unc's house. I guess you got the night to yourself.

NICOLE: I guess I do.

LONEWOLF: I guess you could come help me unpack my stuff before you go back to your mom's house. We could both pretend we got dates.

NICOLE: I guess I could come and see where my daughter's daddy is going to be living. I might have to come up here and get my child support or something.

LONEWOLF: Now was that nice? Come on, girl, we got a long way to go.

NICOLE: We walkin'?

LONEWOLF: You don't want me to spend up your child support money on no bus do you. You'd be real mad if I spent all that money on a date!

NICOLE: Oh, you real funny. You wanna walk? We'll walk. As a matter of fact, I been missing the cross country team a whole lot! We'll just start with a little jog.

LONEWOLF: Girl, are you crazy? You think this black man is gonna run through the streets at this time of night? You must be mad. I love ya honey, but I ain't takin' a bullet for ya.

NICOLE *(Laughing)*: All right, we walk. But I'm takin' a cab from your uncle's house.

(Nicole and Lonewolf exit, as Maylene and ensemble sing "Call Him!" in the background.
Lights up on Lil, typing on her laptop at home.)

LIL: I got this damn computer so I could look up things. They don't tell you that the first thing you have to look up is how to look up things. I might as well just go back to the library. I thought it'd be easier. Wouldn't have to go out when I got tired. Wolfee useta help me find what I want. I guess I better learn how to do it myself. I guess we both better learn to do it ourselves.

(Lights down on Lil.)

SCENE 8

Victor is at home sorting glass, plastics and cans when Lonewolf and Nicole arrive.

LONEWOLF: What up, Unc? Your new organizer has arrived.

VICTOR: And he brought troops, too.

NICOLE: Just a lowly poet.

VICTOR: A cultural worker! Now we're ready for the struggle!

LONEWOLF: Since when are you a poet?

NICOLE: Since before you met me.

LONEWOLF: How come I didn't know anything about it?

NICOLE: How come you never asked?

VICTOR: 'Cause the boy wasn't interested in talkin' back then. See how much he's grown? You might have to give him another chance!

NICOLE: Mr. Victor, you're not matchmaking are you?

VICTOR: No sweetheart, just making sure that my grandniece's parents are communicating. Whether you two need each other or not, she needs both of you. So I just wanna make sure that you two understand what's important in each other's lives.

LONEWOLF: Thanks, Unc. I think we got the communication thing down.

NICOLE: Un-huh. Like your knowledge of my poetry?

LONEWOLF: OK, so improvement is possible. Where do you want me to put my stuff?

VICTOR: Front room's probably best for you and the baby. Lotsa light, warm, big enough for two people . . . or three if need be.

LONEWOLF: Knock if off, Unc. Come on, Nicole, help me unpack.

(Nicole crosses to Lonewolf's makeshift bedroom.)

Unc, just be cool, brother. Don't make me sorry already.

VICTOR: You be cool, youngblood. And whatever you do, you won't be sorry if you use a condom! *(Tosses a condom at Lonewolf)* I'm goin' to bed myself. *(Exits)*

(Lonewolf takes the condom and crosses to his makeshift bedroom.)

LONEWOLF: You got to forgive my uncle. He still believes men only got one thing on their minds.

NICOLE *(Taking the condom)*: What would make him think that?

LONEWOLF: See, you got it all wrong. Unc just handed this to me after we got here.

NICOLE: What made him think that you needed it?

LONEWOLF: Wishful thinking.

NICOLE: His or yours?

LONEWOLF: His . . . but you know what they say, like uncle like nephew!

NICOLE: I'm sorry, where is our daughter now?

LONEWOLF: He gave me a condom!

NICOLE: As I recall you had one the night our daughter was conceived! Look, we were havin' a nice night, let's not go there OK? Let's be friends. Just treat me like one a the fellas.

LONEWOLF: "Awright, homes." *(With exaggerated toughness, he tosses a duffel bag at Nicole)* Put that shit away for me, man. I gotta piss.

NICOLE *(Falling on the bed, laughing, also in an exaggerated voice)*: Damn man! Why it got to be all that!

LONEWOLF: And when I get back I wanna hear some a that poetry shit, man!

NICOLE: Damn, man! I didn't bring my shit wid me! I left it at my bitch's house.

LONEWOLF: You callin' your mamma a bitch? Oooh, I'm gonna tell . . .

(She chases him out of the room. Lights fade.)

Scene 9

Several weeks later. Victor is picking up Kesha at Lil's house.

LIL *(Opening door)*: Well, if it isn't brother mentor himself! I haven't seen you or Malcolm X Junior all week. What can I do for you?

VICTOR: I just came over to pick up Kesha.

LIL: Kesha is with her mother and will be for the rest of the week.

VICTOR: Why are you always ridin' my ass?

LIL: 'Cause you cost me too much, Victor. Every man in my house follows you and it costs me too much. Your brother followed you to Vietnam because he wanted to be a man like you. I know you wish that you coulda told him the truth before he enlisted, but you didn't. So he followed you right to hell! He came home and lived in that hell till the day he died. Now Wolfee wants to follow you. He wants to be an organizer, or at least for now he does. What you gonna kill him with?

VICTOR: I'm not tryin' ta kill him. But if he wants to be a responsible man, then I'm not going to stop him, I'm going to help him. What do you want him to be?

LIL: Alive past his twenty-fifth birthday!

VICTOR: Yeah! Then why didn't you protect him when you had the chance? Why didn't you make them move you away from the plant when you had the chance. Why'd you take money for letting them kill everybody in the neighborhood without telling the world what was happenin' and makin' them stop? That's what's been between you and me for years!

LIL: What did you want me to do? You wanted me to tell my neighbors, "Don't take that ten thousand dollars and send your kids to school!" or, "I know it's not enough money to buy a house, but you had better move or your children who've already been exposed might get sick!" Or maybe you'd like me to leave nothing to my son when I die. You think I wanted this cancer . . .

(There is a long silence.)

VICTOR: What kind?

LIL: What? . . . I was just talkin' about all the people that have gotten it . . .

VICTOR: What KIND? And how long have you known about it?

LIL: I don't have to talk to you about this.

VICTOR: Who you gonna talk to? You gonna tell Wolfee? You gonna tell your friends? I'm the only family you got. You got a man? Hell, you got a lover of any kind? Who's close to you that's still living? Wolfee and me is all you got. How could you not tell us? How could you not think about us?

LIL: I've thought about nothing else since the whole thing started! After the explosion, I felt like there was a time bomb ticking in my head. Every time Wolfee got sick I knew it was something serious. I watched every health special that ever came on TV. I took him to the doctor more than anyone else I knew. I stopped sleeping for three years and drank too much and hid from all my friends. Then, all I could do was pray, but I couldn't do that because I knew that God was either punishing me or that he couldn't be trusted. Finally, all I could do was wait for the cancer to find me. When it did, I thanked God for taking me before he took Wolfee.

VICTOR: You're not taken yet. I told Wolfee that I learned to scream in Vietnam. I told him that it could save your life. I want you to scream now. I want you to holler and howl at all the people who have betrayed you, including me. I want you to scream at the companies and the government and the city and the inspectors and the contractors and the experts. I want you to fight! Fight loud and hard!

LIL: Victor . . . I'm tired. It's too late. Now go home. And promise me that you won't tell Wolfee. You have to do what I ask you to do, I'm a dying woman.

VICTOR: You're a living woman and I won't promise you nothing like that. He deserves to know what's happening in his own family. I'm going home. I'll call you tomorrow.

LIL: Victor, please!

VICTOR: I'll call you tomorrow.

(Lights fade on Lil's house as Victor exits. He stands outside her door in a pool of light and screams.
Maylene and ensemble sing:)

MAYLENE AND ENSEMBLE:
> I been in the storm so long
> I been in the storm so long, children
> I been in the storm so long, Lord
> Give me 'little time to pray.

ACT TWO

Nicole and Lonewolf are at a rally in Louis Armstrong Park. Lonewolf is speaking into a microphone on a makeshift stage, addressing the crowd. High-energy rally music plays in the background: something modern and popular, but revolutionary.

LONEWOLF: Some of you may look at me and think, "What's that hoodlum know about organizing? What's he gonna tell me about what the pesticide company has planned for this neighborhood. He don't even live here!" I don't live here, but I grew up in the Ninth Ward. I know what they put in the ground there. I know what they put in the river and in the Bayous and I know, like my grandma useta say it, "Wadn't nothin' nice!" Now if I know anything, I know how bad people need jobs and money. I'm poor myself! I got a daughter to raise. I got a mother who raised me in one of the most polluted areas of the city. I know from firsthand experience what is in store for you. I know that if you "fight the powers that be" it's gonna be a long fight! Long past some of our lives. What I don't want is for it to be going on when my daughter is a grown woman! If you want to know what you can do to stop the dumping of poisons in this community, all we ask is that you simply show up. Just come to the next community empowerment meeting at Saint Mark's Church. Next Thursday at 7:00 P.M. Transportation will be available for those who are not able to get there on their own. Now I'm through talkin'. Everybody say, "Thank the Lord!" *(Crowd responds)* Just one more thing. Any a y'all see Spike Lee's movie *Four Little Girls*? Well just remember, the movement didn't really move until the young people got involved. When students left the classroom and went into the streets, things began to happen. So y'all know, the history of the struggle says you can count on us!

(Lonewolf steps down. Nicole meets him as he begins to walk away.)

NICOLE: Can I count on you?

LONEWOLF: You been countin' on me so why you buggin'? Come on, Nicole, don't try and spoil this for me. *(Changing the mood)* That was a rush. Bein' in front of all those people. I felt strong, you know, like, "I am somebody." *(Beginning to preach)* I am—

NICOLE: Don't go there!

LONEWOLF: Awright. But I'm glad Unc was late. He talks about me developing leadership, but then he won't let any of us talk. Sometimes he treats us like grunts or "errand boys for the struggle."

NICOLE: What held him up?

LONEWOLF: I don't know. He was supposed to pick up Kesha and bring her here.

NICOLE: She's not at your mother's house. She's with my mom.

LONEWOLF: So where is the brother? And how come you didn't tell me she was at your mother's?

NICOLE: For the same reason you didn't tell me that your uncle was gonna pick her up! Because most of the time we don't plan things out together. You go your way and I go mine and sometimes we wind up in the same place. But you are not the world's greatest planner, which means, when it comes to Kesha, I have to be. So let's not question me about why you didn't know something. If you'd called your mother before you sent your uncle out there, you woulda known.

LONEWOLF: Nicole, what is your problem? I just asked you a question. Why are you workin' so hard to make me mad?

NICOLE: I wasn't tryin' to make you mad! It ain't about you.

LONEWOLF: What's the matter?

NICOLE: This apartment thing with Tyra is not workin' out. She keeps takin' me to places that we can't afford and wantin' me to sign the lease because I work full-time and she doesn't have a credit rating because she's never had any credit. She's my pardner and all, but she is out of touch with reality. She has to move though, 'cause there is stuff goin' on in her house that is dangerous.

LONEWOLF: What's goin' on?

NICOLE: She finally figured out why her stepfather always has so much money to spend on her and her mother. He's been dealin' cocaine to his rich buddies in the district. Nobody knew it because he wasn't dealin' crack in the neighborhood. The brother is very upscale with his stuff. But some real strange stuff has been happenin', like folks breakin' into their house and vandalizing her stepfather's car. The police have even taken to pulling him over on a regular basis. Tyra thinks it's because he cheated somebody out of their share of the money. She's afraid of her stepfather's friends, especially the one that keeps coming over when her stepfather isn't home and hittin' on her.

LONEWOLF: That's messed up. But you know you can't get involved in all that. You probably wanna find your own place or stay with your mom.

NICOLE: What about Tyra? She's been my best friend since first grade! I'm supposed to just let her be out there by herself?

LONEWOLF: What about Kesha? You gonna take her into a situation where you know folks are hooked up with drug dealers? I ain't gonna let that happen. You can come and stay with me and Unc.

NICOLE: And Tyra can stay in that house, or be on the streets. Either way she's in danger! Tyra's still a damn virgin. Do you know what could happen to her without somebody helpin' her? She could stay home and be raped or killed by one of her father's so-called friends, or she could wind up on the street getting raped or killed by some cop with gloves and a condom!

LONEWOLF: Stop bein' so damn dramatic. This ain't a life or death issue. She's been livin' there for all these years, and ain't nothin' happened yet.

NICOLE: Wolfee, sometimes things change so quickly that we miss it. And people wind up dead and we realize that we didn't pay enough attention to the signs. We saw what was goin' on, but started to accept it as normal. We've gotten to the point where we think that everything is acceptable because we see it every day. If you want to help, see if you can find a place for me and Tyra. If your family situation is screwed up, the only thing you've got is friends. *(Exits)*

LONEWOLF: Nicole . . .

(Victor enters.)

Why black women so hardheaded?

VICTOR: Because the world keeps slamming 'em in the head.

LONEWOLF: So what's the matter with you? I finally get to feelin' really good about myself and everybody around me is like messengers for the angel of death!

VICTOR: We're all gonna die Wolfee . . .

LONEWOLF: Now you sound like my mother! Where you been anyway? Nicole told me that Kesha's not at the house. You and Mamma been doin' "a little something something"?

VICTOR: Don't disrespect your mother, boy, or I'll do a little something on your skull.

LONEWOLF: What is wrong with everybody? I just asked what you were doin' at the house, that's all.

VICTOR: I gotta talk to you, Wolfee.

LONEWOLF: I'm listening, Unc.

VICTOR: Not here man, at home.

LONEWOLF: Your house or Mamma's?

VICTOR *(Thinks a minute)*: At your mother's house.

LONEWOLF: OK, Unc. I'll meet you there later, about six?

VICTOR: Yeah.

LONEWOLF: Unc?

VICTOR: What, Wolfee?

LONEWOLF: Ain't nothin' we can't handle, man!

VICTOR: That's right, Wolfee. See you at six. *(Exits)*

LONEWOLF *(Sings as he exits)*:
> If you miss me at the church a Saint Mark's
> You can't find me nowhere
> Come on up to Louie Armstrong Park
> I'll be flowing down there
>
> If you miss me at the pool hall
> You can't find me nowhere
> Come on up to city hall
> I'll be speakin' out there

(Lights fade.)

SCENE 2

Lights up on Lil's house. Lil is at her laptop, typing furiously. She is still upset by her conversation with Victor, but tries to hide it. Lonewolf enters.

LIL: What you doin' here this time a day?

LONEWOLF: Uncle Victor wanted me to meet him here. He got to the rally all late and then wanted to jump on my case. I knew something was wrong with him but he wouldn't talk to me then. He said to meet him here.

LIL: He didn't tell you anything?

LONEWOLF: I just said that. What is wrong with everybody? I made a joke about you and him like I always do and he got pissed.

LIL: Why don't you go ahead and wait for him at home, you know how late he can be. Usually if he's not here ten minutes after he says, then he's gonna be a couple of hours. Besides, don't y'all live in the same house?

LONEWOLF: . . . Why you tryin' ta get rid of me?

LIL: I am not tryin' ta get rid of you! I just don't want to get into some big argument with you and your uncle about what I should and should not do!

LONEWOLF: About what? Something is goin' on here and it looks like I'm gonna be the last person to know what it is.

LIL: All right, you go on and wait for him. I'm goin' to the store. I don't have nothin' to drink in the house.

LONEWOLF: Bring me a forty when you come back.

LIL: Man, if you don't stop messin' with me! . . . I'll bring you a Coke and peanuts if you promise to be a good little fella.

(She moves to exit, but Victor is at the door.)

VICTOR: Where you goin', Lil?

LIL: To the store, Vic, you want a forty, too?

VICTOR: I don't want nothin' except for you to stay here.

LIL: I'm going to the store, Vic. I'll be back.

VICTOR: We are going to talk to Wolfee now. You can go to the store later.

LIL: Victor, you ain't none a my daddy and I will go to the store whenever I damn well please!

LONEWOLF: What's goin' on here?

VICTOR: We got something to tell you.

LIL: "We" don't have nothin' to say. You got something you want to talk about, go on home and do it.

VICTOR: And who's gonna hug him and tell him it's gonna be all right? Isn't that what a mother does for her son when he's hurtin'? You just gonna let me take him home and tell him because you're too scared to talk to him? You gonna let him waste time runnin' behind me when he needs time with you? You gonna be a selfish bitch or you gonna be his mother?

LONEWOLF *(Challenging Victor)*: What did you say to my mother?

VICTOR: Don't come at me like you a man! Talk to your mother like you're a man. Your mother has cancer. She won't tell me what kind or what kind of treatment she's having done, but her not tellin' all of us has me worried. I wanna know if she's dyin'.

LIL: We are all dying.

LONEWOLF: Shut up, Ma.

VICTOR: Lil, if we are all dying then why can't we talk about it? Stop suffering alone.

LIL: And let you suffer with me? And let my child suffer with me? That's just what I don't want, Victor. I'm tired of all the suffering. That's all black folk seem to have plenty of and I'm tired of it. Kids are killing themselves because they don't know how to handle the suffering anymore. We've finally lost the talent for it. I don't blame them. I'm tired of having to teach each generation how to suffer. How to hold on.

VICTOR: Do you think that we're the only people who have been suffering long, Lil? I've seen some suffering in the world, Lil, and I know we can handle our share. We have to teach our young people about suffering, not because they're black, but because it's life. You live the life you're given and you shape it the best way you can. But you shape it, Lil. You fight to keep the battle on your own terms as much as possible.

LONEWOLF: Ma, tell me what you're living with and we can talk about dying later.

LIL: I'm living with cancer, Wolfee . . . I'm dying of cancer. I'm telling you now 'cause I don't know how much "later" there's gonna be. I don't want to say this to you and I wouldn't be if Victor would've minded his own damn business. You're too young to have your mother die on you. I'm too young to leave my grandbaby. I don't want to, but nobody asked me. I have to accept this and so do you. Like the old folks useta say, "All I gotta do is stay black . . . and die." *(Pause)* Wolfee, I love you . . . talk to me.

LONEWOLF: My chest hurts . . . Grandma useta tell me that something could hurt so bad to hear that it brought pain to your body. *(Sits holding his chest, his mother wraps her arms around him)* Mamma, I can't breathe! My chest hurts!

LIL: Wolfee, when you were a little boy I took you to see *E.T.* and when E.T. was put into that incubator and everybody said he was dead, do you remember what you told me?

LONEWOLF: No, Mom.

LIL: You looked at me with water running down your cheeks and you said, "My throat hurts," and I said, "It's all right, son, you're just sad," and you said, "NO! My throat really hurts!" I knew from that day on that your heart could be touched by people's pain and I tried to protect you. But I didn't do enough. I didn't take you out of here when I found out it was dangerous. When folks asked me to sign that paper for the class action suit, I did. We needed the money and everybody figured that was all they could get out of the situation. But I didn't think that I would get sick. I worried about you every day, but somehow I never thought that I'd get sick. I thought I'd die of cancer at seventy, not forty-seven. I'm sorry, son, I'm so sorry.

LONEWOLF: This is not about me. Most of my life it's been you and me and Uncle Victor working things out. Whatever I got myself into, the two of you got me out. Why you tryin' to change the formula? We got a good team, don't go changing the rules on us. We got to live together till we die. You, me, Unc, Kesha. Nicole loves you, too, Ma. She says from the time you found out she was pregnant, you treated her like your daughter. You respected her. We have to let her help. We got things to do, Ma. I want you to start by telling me the whole truth. I want you to tell me how sick the doctors say you are.

VICTOR: I'm gonna leave you two alone. You've got a lot to talk about.

LONEWOLF: Where you going, man? Didn't you hear what I just said? We are one family that handles things together. You two may not love each other like lovers, but you love each other. I can't figure out if it's sister-brother love, friend love or what, but you two are connected like . . . like those pictures of DNA. All twisted up together, like a long chain.

VICTOR: I'll stay if your mother wants me to.

LIL: Victor, I want you to stay. I need you—whoever you are in my DNA chain.

(Lights fade.)

SCENE 3

Maylene and ensemble sing as Victor enters and begins pruning the trees in his garden.

MAYLENE AND ENSEMBLE;

> Good-bye, good-bye,
> If I never ever see you anymore
> Good-bye, good-bye,
> I will meet you on the other shore.
>
> Fare thee well, fare thee well,
> If I never ever see you anymore
> Fare thee well, fare thee well,
> I will meet you on the other shore.

(Lonewolf enters.)

VICTOR: I'm making some greens. I'm gonna take them over to your mother. You want some?

LONEWOLF: I'm not ready, Unc.

VICTOR: They won't be ready for another couple a hours. You got time.

LONEWOLF: I'm not talking about the damn greens, Unc, I'm talking about losing my mother.

VICTOR: Nobody is ever ready to lose their mother, Wolfee. You want her to be there forever. The only end to life is death.

LONEWOLF: But we didn't have to be helped along by something in the water or in the air. You ever think about what you might be growin' those greens in? You think that we know half a what's goin' on around us? I'm out there organizing folks all over the state, just like you taught me to, and do you think that I know what I'm talking about? I don't know shit, Unc! Just like she didn't know shit when she signed those papers. Now I know why she was always scared—why she busted my head if I ate something off the ground or played in the water built up around the house. Why do we always walk around thinking it happens to somebody else's mother?

VICTOR: You can know, Wolfee. You can find out. I asked you a while back about protectin' Kesha.

LONEWOLF: Why are you talkin' about Kesha? I'm talking about my mother.

VICTOR: Because your mother has cancer. She thinks it's her fault, but it isn't. She just chose what she thought was the lesser of two evils, but there was no less evil. Kesha is your daughter, just like you're Lil's son. You have to make choices for yourself and her, just like your mother did. You can't go back, you go forward. You find out what happened and you stop it from happening again. That's what's possible. You protect Kesha. Now, I grow my greens in beds above ground with soil I bring back from the country with that wood you always complaining about. There ain't nothin' in them greens that will hurt your mother. Do you want some greens?!

LONEWOLF: Yes sir. I'll have 'em as soon as they're ready. I'm gonna pick Nicole up and take her over to Mom's house this afternoon. I can take the greens when I go. I told Nicole I had to talk to her, but I didn't tell her what was goin' on over the phone.

(Lights down on Victor and Lonewolf. Maylene plays "I Will Meet You on the Other Shore.")

SCENE 4

Lonewolf and Nicole arrive at Lil's house.

LIL: Hello babies. Wolfee, are you all right?

LONEWOLF: Ma, how come you always ask me if I'm all right? Are you all right?

LIL: Baby, I'm fine. Nicole, where's my grandbaby?

NICOLE: I left her with my mamma. I wanted to talk to you. I wanted to know how you really are. I love you, Lil, and I gotta know what's goin' on.

LIL: Wolfee, you go get Kesha from Nikki's mother. We need to do a little girl talk for a minute.

LONEWOLF: I just got here. I wanna spend time with you.

LIL: We'll have time, Wolfee. I have some things that I have to tell Nicole. When you get back I won't talk to anybody but you.

LONEWOLF: Yeah, right. You know and I know if I bring Kesha back you'll spend the whole night with her on your lap.

LIL: I'll put her on one knee and you on the other. Now get going so you can get back.

(Lonewolf kisses Lil and exits.)

NICOLE: Are you in pain?

LIL: Not now. But I don't want to talk about what's goin' on with me. I want to talk about Wolfee and Kesha. Wolfee needs women in his life and I'm not going to be around. I don't know what you see for the two of you. I'm not asking you to marry him if that's not what you want. I'm asking you to be his friend for life. What I want you to promise me is that you will help him get through this. I'm asking you to make sure he always has his daughter. Men can slip away from their children and have nothing but regrets. They don't intend to live their lives that way, it's just that everything around them says that they can. It's not your responsibility to mother Wolfee. Wolfee's never had death around him. He doesn't know what to expect. Victor will stand by him, be a man for him, but he'll need the closeness of a woman.

NICOLE: Lil, I love Wolfee. I don't know if we'll ever even live together, but he'll always be Kesha's father even when he doesn't want to be. I won't lose him and he won't lose me. We'll be connected . . .

LIL: Like DNA chains.

NICOLE: What?

LIL: It's how Wolfee described my relationship with Victor. That we were connected in some strange way. Bound together like pictures he saw of DNA chains. I guess you two are like that, too. Victor and I are not in love, we simply love each other.

NICOLE: Lil, I promise I'll be there for Wolfee whatever happens. Now, is there going to be chemo? Surgery? Natural remedies?

LIL: We're doing some radiation right now.

NICOLE: I spent a lot of time with my grandmother when she was suffering. She told me a lot about what gave her strength. Did you know that she was in the Civil Rights movement?

LIL: I seem to remember someone saying something about Selma or Montgomery.

NICOLE: She told me that the work she did with Civil Rights—goin' to jail, getting' beat—scared her, but that nothin' scared her like the cancer. She knew that there was a chance she would be killed in the movement, but she knew she was gonna die of the cancer. So when she needed strength—when the pain got to her—she would sing these movement songs. She taught them to me. When she got to the point that she couldn't sing them herself, she would ask me to sing them. *(Sings:)*

> We are soldiers in the army,
> We have to fight although we have to cry,
> We have to hold up the bloodstained banner,
> We have to hold it up until we die . . .

We would change the words sometimes to fit what she was feeling, 'cause she told me that was part of the tradition. Maybe sometime we could share some songs.

LIL: Of all the girls Wolfee has been with, you were always my favorite. You were always the one who was about doing something. When you got pregnant, I was upset because I saw so much in you both. I knew if you hadn't had a baby, you probably would have gone on to school and done something with your lives. I hoped that, maybe some day, when you were older, you'd have a life together. I knew a baby would change all that. You couldn't see each other without blaming each other. I care about you, Nicole, and I want you to sing to me just like you did with your grandmother. Victor likes to sing those "movement songs," too. Maybe you can make him sing some new words 'cause I sure am tired of him singing about Ross Barnett.

NICOLE: I'll work on him. Did I tell you about my poetry?

LIL: No.

NICOLE: My grandmother useta listen to my poetry and sometimes we would write together. We could do that, too.

LIL: I am not a writer, Nicole.

NICOLE: That doesn't matter. It's just thoughts that we pass back and forth. We can do it or not do it.

LIL: I'll try it one time. Then we'll see.

NICOLE: OK, Lil.

LIL: When Wolfee comes back, I don't want you to tell him that I asked you to take care of him. Men don't like to think that they need women.

NICOLE: Lil, you gotta treat Wolfee more like a man. Stop keeping things from him or he won't have time to say all the things he needs to say to you.

LIL: I'll try. He's my only child and he'll always be my baby.

(Victor enters.)

VICTOR: Well, how are my second and third most favorite women in the world doing today?

LIL: Second and third? Who's number one?

VICTOR: Kesha of course! Which is who I've been looking for all day. I have a little present for her.

LIL: What is it?

VICTOR: A T-shirt from the "Undoing Racism" workshop. I brought you a book, too.

LIL: Victor, racism ain't gonna be undone in our lifetime.

NICOLE: My grandmamma useta say the same thing. She'd say, "Not in my lifetime, but surely to God you'll see it in yours."

VICTOR: Maybe it will be in Kesha's. Besides, I didn't bring you a T-shirt, I brought you a book. I want you to read it. It could help you understand more about what's happening to you. I want you to understand that you didn't do anything wrong.

LIL: Victor, I don't need a book to tell me what I did or did not do.

VICTOR: You don't have to read it. I just brought it over so you could if you wanted to. You old stubborn black woman you.

LIL: What has racism got to do with what's happening to me?

VICTOR: Racism has to do with everything that happens in this country.

LIL: Victor, I don't wanna spend the rest of my life talkin' about what the white man has done to me. Whatever time I have left will not be spent on negative things. There are good and bad people of all colors, shapes, sexes and anything else you wanna talk about.

VICTOR: But there are people who will put things in our community because they have no regard for black life. They don't think twice about putting dangerous chemicals here because they think we can't do a thing about it!

LIL: Do you know who you are talking to? Do you remember what I've been through? I'm the one who had to go through all that time with the lawyers! I'm the one who had to hear about the effects of this chemical or that chemical! I'm the one who took money for my life and maybe Wolfee's too. Don't talk to me about what some people will do!

VICTOR: What are you going to do with that knowledge, Lil? Who are you going to tell? You gonna take that information to the grave with you, or are you going to give it to those people who need it to save their own lives?

NICOLE: Give it to me, Lil. I wouldn't want to go to my grave without doing everything I could to save someone else. I promise I'll use it to protect Wolfee and Kesha.

LIL: Nicole, this is not your fight, baby. You'll have your hands full with what we talked about. *(To Victor)* Maybe I should give it to you so you can carry that burden with you for the rest of your life.

VICTOR: It's not a burden, Lil, it's a weapon. And I can use it to fight the white sons a bitches who put it inside the community and inside you!

(Lonewolf enters with Kesha.)

LONEWOLF: For people who ain't married y'all sure can find a lotta time to fight with each other. What's goin' on now?

LIL: Your uncle is pissing me off real bad right now.

VICTOR: The truth always did piss you off!

LONEWOLF: What great truth are we talkin' about now?

VICTOR: About racism and chemicals and . . . dying.

LONEWOLF: We don't need to talk about all that right now.

VICTOR: When do we talk about it, Wolfee? When you get sick? When Kesha does?

LIL: Get out! Get the hell out of my house! You say another word about my son and my granddaughter and I will kill you myself!

LONEWOLF: Ma, calm down. Unc was just makin' a point.

LIL: Point be damned!

VICTOR: Lil, that's just what I'm talking about. You have no reason to kill me, I didn't do nothing wrong! Neither did you. But something wrong was done and I want somebody to keep it from happening again. I want someone to stand up and say, "They put poison in my home and asked me to take money for my life and this is the result!"

NICOLE: Please stop. I can't stand it when all we can do is turn on each other. We're all tired. Doesn't all this madness make you just feel tired?

VICTOR: I feel tired . . .

LONEWOLF: I feel hungry! I need some food! Unc, warm those greens up for everybody. And I'll take whatever animal flesh Mom has out of the refrigerator.

VICTOR: Nicole, your mamma teach you how to make cornbread?

NICOLE: I been making cornbread since I was four! From scratch, no Jiffy mix in my house. Mom, you got eggs and baking soda?

LIL: I got whatever Wolfee didn't eat up. That is the egg-eatin'-est man I have ever seen in my life!

LONEWOLF: We got eggs here, Ma. I eat Unc's eggs now. *(To Kesha)* Come on, baby, your mamma's gonna show you how to make real cornbread!

(Lonewolf and Nicole exit with Kesha.)

VICTOR: You can't hold an important study like yours in, Lil. You have ta tell people how and why they need to fight. It'll make you stronger. It'll make you live forever.

LIL: Victor, I swear to God if you don't give it a rest . . .

VICTOR: What you gonna do? You can't whup me! Besides—you a lover, not a fighter.

LIL: I love you, Victor.

VICTOR *(Smiling)*: I love you too, Hillbilly. I always did hear it was hard to love a black woman from the mountains.

LIL: Yeah, but the blessing is that they love you hard back.

SCENE 5

Later, after dinner. Victor and Lil are alone. Lil, who has been napping in a chair, awakes with a start.

LIL: I was dreamin' about water.

VICTOR: What kind of water? Blue, clear, Caribbean water?

LIL: No, river water. I was crossing the Little Pigeon River in a paper boat, and the river was foaming like soap suds.

VICTOR: That's the way it useta look.

LIL: Stop interrupting me. The suds was just rolling through the rocks scooping up everything in their path: trees, houses, dogs . . . It just kept rolling along until everything was connected: cities, towns . . . Alcoa ran into Oak Ridge, New Orleans ran into Knoxville. All the buildings were connected by the river. And the foam just kept coming. There were people standing on the shores and they were glowing. You know at home we useta joke about folks from Oak Ridge glowing. We were just jealous 'cause they all made more money than we did, but we figured that they paid the price 'cause they all lived down water from the nuclear waste, especially the black folks. Anyway, everybody had on company clothes, TVA overalls, Alcoa hats, and they were all dancin'. And some big ol' man was callin' the dance—you know, like square dancing. That's the way it is in a company town anyway, big man calls the shots. People were all over the place, but as they danced they kept dividing into smaller and smaller groups. Then I noticed that all the white people were over to one side and all the other folks froze up! And you were running around tryin' to force their jaws open with one a those big walkin' sticks. I guess we don't have ta call the psychic network to understand this dream, so I guess I'm gonna do what you asked me.

VICTOR: Exactly what part of what I asked you to do are you going to do?

LIL: I'm gonna pry my mouth open and tell anyone who'll listen what's happening here.

(Lights down on Lil and Victor.)

SCENE 6

Maylene plays a Nina Simone song, "I Want a Little Sugar in My Bowl." Lonewolf and Nicole enter and sit in Victor's garden.

LONEWOLF: Ya know, I never saw how it all fits together before. The work at Saint Mark's, the work with Unc. My mom's situation. You, your mom, Kesha. You know your mother still doesn't really like me.

NICOLE: That's because she blames you for ruining my life.

LONEWOLF: I didn't ruin your life, did I?

NICOLE: No, we both just changed courses . . . I want to help with your mother.

LONEWOLF: I can take care of my mother. I'm gonna move back home.

NICOLE: She's not gonna let you do that.

LONEWOLF: What are you talking about?

NICOLE: She wants to take care of herself. The whole reason she didn't tell you what was happening with her was because she knew you wouldn't move forward if she told you. She wants you to live your life. She wants to know that you can make it without her.

LONEWOLF: What makes you such an expert on what my mother wants?

NICOLE: Experience, being a mother, and listening. Do you listen to her? I'm not talking about what she tells you to do, I'm talking about what she needs and wants. Do you listen to what she says when she's not speaking?

LONEWOLF: Nicole, I know her.

NICOLE: Then you know she doesn't want you to watch her die.

LONEWOLF: She's gonna need help.

NICOLE: I know. Let me help her. I want to move in with her. I think I can help her and I think Kesha should spend as much time with her as possible. I was gonna move out anyway, and now it just seems that I can do something useful. I know your mother thinks we ruined our lives, too. But she never blamed me. I know she loves Kesha and me and I can't let her go without letting her know how much we love her. You need to continue the stuff you're doing with Victor. I'm not asking you not to take care of your mother, I'm asking you to let me share that care with you. Whether we ever live together or get married or anything, we're connected.

LONEWOLF: We'll try it for a while. But you better know I'm gonna be up under you women all the time. You're gonna think we're married.

NICOLE: As long as you're not tryin' to father no more children, that'll be all right.

LONEWOLF: Twenty-seven times a day.

NICOLE: What?

LONEWOLF: Nothin'. I love you.

NICOLE: Did you tell me that before?

LONEWOLF: Only in bed. You might not remember. I said a lotta things but they were a little jumbled up.

NICOLE: No, I remember something about, "I love it." Nothing personal like a "you" in there.

LONEWOLF: You the wordsmith. What did you say?

NICOLE: I wrote you a poem that night.

LONEWOLF: How come I never heard it?

NICOLE: 'Cause it was too personal. I hide the things that are important to me in my grandmother's cedar chest. My mother won't go in it, too many pieces of her left there, she says. But I go into it all the time, because my grandmother taught me to value my own words. I visit her there through my words.

LONEWOLF: I take it you keep the trunk next to your bed.

NICOLE: Right at the foot.

LONEWOLF: Maybe you can show it to me some night when your mother's not at home. We can crawl into it together.

NICOLE: Wolfee, if you don't quit . . . I'll read you all my poems one day, and maybe you'll know who I am and who you are to me.

(She begins to exit.)

LONEWOLF: Where you goin'?

NICOLE: I'm goin' to check on Tyra.

LONEWOLF: I thought you were stayin' with me?

NICOLE: Not tonight. I gotta figure out what to do about Tyra if I'm gonna move in with your mom.

LONEWOLF: Can't you do that tomorrow?

NICOLE: Ain't nobody promised tomorrow. That's what my grandmother always said.

LONEWOLF: OK, I'll go with you.

NICOLE: Wolfee, you ain't getting none a this tonight if you follow me to the end of the world! Go see about your mamma! I'll talk to you in the mornin'.

LONEWOLF: I don't want you travelin' alone.

NICOLE: Then you better start takin' me to and from work every day, 'cause I do that alone too! Good night, Wolfee. *(As she's leaving)* Oh, and I love you, too.

LONEWOLF: What? What you say? *(Shouting)* I heard you! Girl can't even say it facing me . . .

(Lights fade.)

SCENE 7

A bass line, similar to the Neville Brothers' song "The Ballad of Hollis Brown," plays in the background. Nicole arrives at Tyra's house. A loud argument is taking place. Nicole stands at an outside courtyard gate. She is frightened and disturbed by the sounds inside.

TYRA *(Offstage)*: Get your hands off me, you son of a bitch!

NICOLE: Hey, Tyra? Tyra . . . come open the gate.

TYRA *(Offstage)*: Don't tell me to stop screaming, I don't give . . .

NICOLE: Hey, Tyra, come out here or I'm gonna call the cops . . .

TYRA: *(Offstage; overlapping)*: I told you to take your hands off me!

NICOLE: Damn it! Let me in there!

TYRA *(Offstage)*: He ain't my father and you better hope he doesn't find your ass here!

NICOLE: Tyra, stop arguing and get your ass out here!

TYRA *(Offstage)*: I don't have his shit, OK!

NICOLE: You can't fix what's goin' on there . . .

TYRA *(Offstage)*: I can't tell you where it is . . .

NICOLE: Stop with your stepfather and his thugs and get outta there . . .

(Shots are fired. Nicole falls.)

Oh shit! Oh God! Tyra, call an ambulance! Tyra, help me! Somebody HELP ME! Damn it. Mamma . . . Wolfee . . . Kesha . . . Grandma, please help me.

(Blackout.)

SCENE 8

The next day. Victor and Lonewolf are at Victor's house.

LONEWOLF: I ain't goin' to no goddamn funeral! I ain't takin' Kesha anywhere near that place!

VICTOR: It's not just your decision, Wolfee. Nicole has a mother, too.

LONEWOLF: No. Nicole *had* a mother—and Kesha *had* a mother, too! And she's not going to see her in a goddamn box with cheap satin cloth and horse track wreaths all around her! I told her! I told her she had to stop trying to save her damn worthless-ass friends! I told her to stay away from that house. I should've gone with her! I told her not to be roaming the streets by herself. And I was right there! I was tryin' to get her in bed not one hour before she died. I want her, Unc. I want her back with me. I want to touch her. I want to touch her soul and her body. I'll never be with her again. Do you understand that, Unc? . . . I won't touch her cardboard, cold body in no box! I ain't goin' to no church, no funeral parlor, no cemetery.

VICTOR: What about her mother? What about your mother? Do you think they're going to stay away? Who picks them up when they fall out? Who tells Kesha about her mother, who she needs to see one last time, at rest? Get your head out ya' ass, boy, and see what you have to do! Good people are going to die. That's just a fact. But we don't have to accept black-on-black murder. A bullet took the mother of your child away from here. But people need to grieve and people need to know. We've got to expose Tyra's stepfather to the rest of the community, and they will be coming to the funeral. You've got to make sure Nicole's death brings something to life.

LONEWOLF: You'd use anybody or anything to promote a cause wouldn't you? You don't actually give a shit about the way I feel or who I lose!

VICTOR: I'm just trying to find the message in it, Wolfee. We keep lookin' for the reason in what happens in our lives when the only thing that will ever be clear is in the message. When we lose all understanding of what is going on in the world, the only question we can ask is, "What am I supposed to learn and who am I supposed to teach it to?" Come here, Wolfee . . .

LONEWOLF: Don't touch me, man.

VICTOR: You need touching, man. Everybody needs touching. You need your father to hold you and teach you. But he's not here, I am.

LONEWOLF: I'm not changing my mind, Unc.

VICTOR: I ain't askin' you to change your mind, not right now. I just want you to let me help you.

LONEWOLF: That's one of the last things she told me, Unc. She told me that she wanted me to let her help with Mom . . . she also told me that she loved me.

VICTOR: She did, Wolfee. You could see that. You're my son, Wolfee, even if I'm not your father, and I love you, too. Now come here. I've seen a lot of death, Wolfee, and I know that when death comes people need to hold each other. I learned how to cry in Vietnam. Men cried together in 'Nam. We need to cry together for Kesha's sake.

(Lonewolf crosses to Victor, who embraces him. Lonewolf begins to cry. The lights fade.)

SCENE 9

Music that sounds like violent cussing and screaming begins the scene. Lil is at home. She has heard about Nicole and reacts violently.

LIL: I'm gonna kill that mother fucka! I ain't got a damn thing to loose. I'm the only one who can do it and not have to worry about jail time! I'm gonna take my .38 and insert it in his nostril and blow his fuckin' head off! *(She breaks down)* He killed my only daughter. He killed my grandbaby's mamma. What did he do to my child? How many graves does he have to cry into?! Where is my damn gun! I'll kill 'em all, I'll start with Tyra's stepdaddy, and no I don't care that we can't prove that he pulled the trigger. Then I'll get around to all his crackhead . . . No, his cocaine-addicted buddies. But I'm not gonna stop there. I'm gonna go up to Jake Tindale's office at the chemical plant and shoot him in the nuts for spoiling our generations. Now that's only fair considering what he did to ours! Then I'm gonna get everyone who didn't protect us against the poison and the drugs, 'cause you one and the same and I know you! I know where you live! I'll borrow somebody's car and get there . . . Where is my damn gun!

(She looks for her gun. She finds it, just as Victor enters, and accidentally points it at him.)

VICTOR: What the hell are you doing? Is everybody in the whole damn family goin' crazy? Give me that thing.
LIL: You gonna use it?
VICTOR: On who?
LIL: Tyra's stepfather first, and then the other drug dealers, and then the petrochemical and pesticide company men, and then . . .
VICTOR: And then?
LIL: And then on me, 'cause I can't take any more of this shit! Victor, I can't take any more of this shit! It's too much.
VICTOR: Then let me take a little off your shoulders. Come here.
LIL: Don't touch me, Victor. I'm mad enough to kill somebody.
VICTOR: Boy, you sure can tell Wolfee's your son. You ain't gonna kill nobody. And you ain't gonna be here that much longer yourself, so you might as well wait. You've got a baby to raise, so you better start trying to stay well. Now come here—I need you. I want you to hold my

neck and tell me it's gonna be all right, 'cause I haven't had that in a long time. Come here . . . Bring me the gun. *(She is startled by his honesty. She walks to him and hugs him. He removes the gun from her hand. He checks it)* And the damn thing was loaded! How long have you had this thing?

LIL: Since your brother died.

VICTOR: You haven't unloaded it or cleaned it since then?

LIL: Never had a reason to. I never wanted to kill anybody before.

VICTOR: And you don't now. You've got to come with me.

LIL: Where are we going?

VICTOR: We're going to Nicole's mother's house.

LIL: I can't look that woman in the eye.

VICTOR: We have to talk with her about the funeral. I told her my ideas about what we could do to teach with the funeral and how we could make some good come out of her death and she wanted to talk to us about it.

LIL: Can any good come out of the death of a nineteen-year-old woman?

VICTOR: Only if we make it. Let's go.

(Lights fade.)

SCENE 10

A traditional New Orleans "second line" funeral—a solemn parade to the gravesite—is about to begin. People are gathered in Louis Armstrong Park. Victor is dressed as the funeral marshal and carries an umbrella. The ensemble sings "This May Be the Last Time." Victor begins the ceremony.

VICTOR: When we lost folks in the Civil Rights movement, we knew we'd made a choice. Each of us who went to the battlefield knew that it might be the day to die. But we made a choice, we made a commitment. Now these days it seems as if people don't make a choice. I don't think Nicole made a choice to be in the battlefield. I think the choice was made for her. When I think of Lil's cancer, I don't think she made a choice, the choice was made for her. But when I look around at all of you today, I know that we must, once again, choose to fight. We must choose to struggle. We must fight the pesticide companies, the petroleum companies, the companies who put poisons in our community and the people who bring violence to our community. We must fight them.

(Tyra steps up to sing "Nicole's Song," lyrics in hand. She breaks down, and Maylene takes over:)

MAYLENE:

> To know and be known in the world carries responsibility
> It's clear to me
> To be known to reveal to lay bare
> Is to conquer fear
> To call a thing a simple name
> Clear and direct is claiming its possibilities.
>
> If we are human we may touch each other
> Fearless and undamaged we touch each other
> Or we may wound and wear each other down
> Until the earth swallows us
> The only thing that can contain
> The grief of not being known or remembered
> Of someone we allowed to enter
> Some truth we were allowed to see.
>
> I know that it's the power of committing our lives
> The witnessing is the very thing that brought us together
> I saw in you a hope
> For more or less
> For all the things that life held in store and I wanted it all.
> The future is in our hearts tonight
> But it's in your hands tomorrow.
>
> I want to walk there with you
> In fresh flowing waters and open seas
> No danger for you and me
> And others living from the giving tree.
>
> I want to walk there with you
> I call your name,
> In fresh flowing waters and open seas
> So simple and plain
> Your name is possibility
> 'Cause I know you
> Your name is possibility
> I know you
> Your name is possibility
> Your name is love
> I know your love
> I know your love
> I know your love
> I know your love.

LIL: This is my only daughter. She is not my blood, but she is my child. I asked her to look after my son after I died of the cancer that is in my body. But the violence that surrounds us in our own communities took her life before the cancer took mine, and I want to know why. I wanna know who keeps the drugs and the guns here, because I'm going to battle today. I may be a casualty of the war against chemical companies that continue to put poison in our groundwater and air, but I won't be a victim anymore. This is fair warning. If you come at me, my son, my granddaughter or anyone else in my community, I'm coming back at you! And I won't be alone! I may have cancer, but I'm far from dead.

LONEWOLF: In this box is the mother of my child. Next to me is my mother and on my right is my daughter. My mother is dying. My daughter and I are trying to live without our mothers. We want to know why. We want to know why poisons and bullets roll freely through our neighborhoods. We want to know why the media over there doesn't tell our stories. But you know, that's not quite true. The day after the mother of my daughter died, the headlines read: WOMAN KILLED IN COCAINE HOUSE SHOOT-OUT. It did not read: BRAVE, YOUNG BLACK WOMAN DESPERATELY TRIES TO SAVE HER BEST FRIEND FROM THUG IN HER OWN HOME. In the article it says that she is survived by her mother and one daughter. But I survived, too. When my mother dies, from chemically induced cancer, they will say that she died after receiving a ten-thousand-dollar settlement in a class action suit. And white people all over the city will say: "At least she had something to leave her son." They will forget that ten thousand dollars that they spend on one year of private school. They will forget that it was ten thousand dollars that they spent to remodel the slave quarters at their bed and breakfast. They will forget how little ten thousand dollars really is. And they will forget that the waste products are still in the ground. They will forget that areas of this city are not part of a super-fund cleanup. They will forget that in certain parts of this and other parishes, you cannot plant food to eat because the soil is too contaminated! They will forget that people will put poisons in places where they assume people won't, can't or don't fight back. That drugs thrive where people are already dying and in despair. They know that people who are taught to think nothing of themselves, who have internalized racism, who have no respect for themselves left, cannot protect the land that they walk on, the air that they breathe or the water that they drink. It is so hard to think of ways to make a safer world for our children when the man's boot is so far up your behind that it rattles your brains! . . . But there is the mother of my child. I now have to raise my daughter. My mother can't help me. I have to protect my daughter. I have to fight corporations, government, dealers, thugs, pimps or anybody else who wants to rob my daughter of her family and her future. My uncle once told me, "You gotta protect that baby." I thought if I dragged her through the streets behind me while her mother was workin' her ass off, I was doin' my job. I didn't know what he was talkin' about. Today I know. And I'm asking all the youngbloods out there to make a pledge today. I'm asking you to protect your children for the future. I'm asking all the brothers and sisters to remember the Movement, but make it our own. Make your own strategies against racism and pollution and poverty. Make our own "Movement." Make our own music and poetry and theater. Let us make our message clear that we, young people, are the ones who are mad as hell and not goin' to take it anymore. Let the powers that be know that we are ready to protect the generations to come.

(Lil begins to sing "Soldiers in the Army." The ensemble joins in, singing a medley of civil rights songs. The audience is encouraged to sing along.)

END

The Carpetbag Theatre

The Carpetbag Theatre (CBT) is a professional, multigenerational ensemble company dedicated to the production of new works. Its mission is to give artistic voice to the issues and dreams of people who have been silenced by racism, classism, sexism, ageism, homophobia and other forms of oppression. CBT serves communities by returning their stories to them with honesty, dignity and concern for the aesthetic of that particular community, helping culturally specific communities re-define how they organize. The company works in partnership with community artists, activists, cultural workers, storytellers, leaders and people who are simply concerned, creating original works through collaboration in a style based in storytelling and song. For more than thirty years, CBT has told stories of empowerment, celebrated African American culture and revealed hidden histories.

MAD LOVE

Dell'Arte International

Donald Forrest (left) and Joan Schirle.

BRANDI EASTER

INTRODUCTION

One irony about Dell'Arte International is the sheer volume of creative output that it generates from its tiny hometown of Blue Lake, California (population 1,400). Each year, ten new original works will appear on Dell'Arte's stages, while thirty-five students are trained at the Dell'Arte School of Physical Theatre, and 2,500 locals are visited by the company's outreach programs. Meanwhile, Dell'Arte tours the U.S., Europe and South America. And, for one month each summer, its annual Mad River Festival imports the finest ensemble performers from around the world, alongside local talent. Here, for instance, a weekend's bill might include a Brazilian street theater troupe, storytellers from the local Yurok tribe, a lounge-style hypnotist and the company's adaptation of *Paradise Lost*.

Dell'Arte's founders came to the northern California woods more than thirty years ago looking for a context that would enable intense collaboration. Since then, the company has mastered a variety of styles, created dozens of original works from diverse sources, and nurtured a strong relationship with the community. (One community collaboration included the mayor and hundreds of enthusiastic locals in a vast staging that encompassed the entire town.) Blue Lake has recently begun to grow in population and complexity, challenging Dell'Arte to consider anew its relationship to the local community.

Mad Love was developed by Dell'Arte's resident company, and is a testament to the high level of artistry made possible by its collaboration over many years. The script was adapted from the 1930s film of the same name, a German-British collaboration starring Peter Lorre as Doctor Gogol.

Although Dell'Arte's *Mad Love* is set in South America at the turn of the twentieth century, it is not without its community context. Dell'Arte's original attraction to the material was sparked by the Blue Lake parent-teacher organization's banning of an annual Halloween event. The celebration, they said, promoted "witchcraft and the dark side." Reflecting on this, Dell'Arte found itself considering the means by which populations are coerced and controlled. "We were fascinated by both the style and the theme," Joan Schirle, Dell'Arte's co-artistic director, said. "Particularly given the highly manipulative means of suggestion developed in the twentieth century. Masses of people can be convinced to buy, to support or oppose, to hate, and even to kill."

Using a stark black-and-white palette from designer Giulio Cesare Perrone, the original production was staged with elements of German Expressionism in mind, as well as melodrama, and especially Grand Guignol, the nineteenth-century French theater phenomenon, which staged the day's real-life crimes and horrors as spectacles of violence, sado-masochism and mutilation.

—F.L.

Production Information

Mad Love received its premiere in 1997 at the Dell'Arte Mad River Festival in Blue Lake, California. It was adapted by the company from *The Hands of Orlac* by Maurice Renard. It was written by Michael Fields, Donald Forrest, Joan Schirle and Jael Weisman, and directed by Jael Weisman. The original music and sound design were by Tim Gray, with additional music by Valerie Moseley; the sets and costumes were designed by Giulio Cesare Perrone; the lighting design was by Michael Foster; the special effects were designed by Donald Forrest and constructed by Donald Forrest and Dennie Beeson; the stage manager was Bridget Banber McCracken. It was produced with support from the Flintridge Foundation and the National Endowment for the Arts. The cast included Sharon Bayly (Stagehand), Michael Fields (Gogol, the Ripper), Donald Forrest (Orlac, Stagehand, the Duke, Second Assistant), Bridget B. McCracken (Maria, Mariela, Assistant) and Joan Schirle (Yvonne, Prostitute, Child).

In 1998 and 1999, the production toured to the Festival of Five Continents in Venezuela, the Aarhus Festival in Denmark, the Noorderzon Festival in Holland, the Carmel Festival in California and the Network of Ensemble Theatres Festival at the Yerba Buena Center for the Arts in San Francisco. The touring cast included Joan Mankin and Sayada Trujillo (Mariela) and Guillermo Calderon, Anthony Courser, Greg Lojko and Brian Samsboe (Stagehands).

Setting/Set

The action takes place in Montevideo, Uruguay, in 1937. Pianist Stephan Orlac, born to a German father and a French mother, has left Germany in the face of the rising Fascist tide. His French wife, Yvonne, is an actress in the Theater of Horrors, a very popular boulevard theater presenting performances in the Grand Guignol style.

Giulio Cesare Perrone's set for *Mad Love*, designed to tour, consisted of white hanging drops, which frame the stage, and a center white drop rigged to assume various positions, from a shadow screen to a low ceiling to a tortuously dancing fabric display. Upstage is a black scrim, creating a playing area between the scrim and the back wall, which is hung with black drapes. A pinrail at stage right holds the rigging for the center drop and the hanging hand manacles that are used throughout the show. There is a standing guillotine at far stage right. Throughout the play, two rolling black carts become, variously, a piano, an organ, an operating table, a gurney, a Victrola stand and a dressing table.

AUTHORS' NOTE

Created in France at the end of the nineteenth century, Grand Guignol— "the theater of terror and laughter"—preceded and influenced Gothic horror movies, splatter films and film noir. To the basic elements of melodrama were added graphic depictions of violent acts. The style of acting was in the melodramatic tradition; however, the actors were required not only to act, but to execute tricks of illusion to make the spectators imagine they were seeing real decapitations, eye gouging, blood spurting and burns.

A number of the special effects in *Mad Love* require the construction of specific props: for example, a cutout of the statue of Galatea, which is seen only in silhouette; the appearance of smoke rising from the burning dagger; the decapitation of the Ripper by guillotine; metal prosthetic hands for Gogol when he is disguised as the Ripper; and a specially prepared gurney to create the illusion in the final scene, when the Ripper's disembodied head and Orlac's disembodied hands appear to come to life.

The poetry extract on page 232 is from "Sonnets from the Portuguese," VII, Elizabeth Barrett Browning.

ACT ONE

SCENE 1: THEATER OF HORRORS 1

Scene 1A

GALATEA 1: BUYING THE STATUE

Gogol enters, wearing a long, flowing overcoat. He sees a statue of Yvonne advertising a show.

GOGOL: Beautiful, beautiful. It's Galatea. *(Starts to explore the statue)*

(A Stagehand enters and begins to take the statue away.)

    Where are you taking her?
STAGEHAND: To the melting pot.
GOGOL: Melting pot?
STAGEHAND: Sure, the Theater of Horrors is dead. People want to be entertained. They don't want to be frightened out of their wits. There's fifty pesos of wax in this.
GOGOL: No doubt you'd take seventy-five.
STAGEHAND: What's the idea?
GOGOL: Did you ever hear of Galatea?
STAGEHAND: Gala-who?

GOGOL: Galatea. You see, she was a statue. Pygmalion formed her out of ivory, not wax . . . Then she came to life in his arms. Here are one hundred pesos if you deliver the statue to my house.

STAGEHAND: It's a go, Dr. Gogol. I'll have her over there tonight.

(He starts to carry her off.)

GOGOL: Please, be careful. That's very precious.

(The Stagehand exits with the statue.)

That idiot didn't know what he was carrying; he handled her so brutally. I will serve you better. Galatea, Galatea, you are mine now . . .

(Gogol crosses to sit in the Theater of Horrors. Center drop falls.)

Scene 1B

BACKSTAGE

Maria rolls on a cart with a radio, a makeup box with brushes, a mirror and a powder puff, and a bouquet of flowers with a card. Yvonne enters, adjusting her costume of white surgical gauze. Her midriff is bare, and she wears long bandage-like gauntlets on her arms. She carries a gauze headpiece that will cover her head like post-operation bandaging.
Maria hands Yvonne the card.

YVONNE: Flowers again? A gentleman of the old school, Maria.

MARIA: Old and new, they all try the same things, Señora.

YVONNE *(Reading card)*: "Tonight I am sad, for I will no longer be able to watch you from my lonely, shadowed box." And no signature.

MARIA: A man can't take the same box for forty-seven nights in a row without the whole theater knowing who he is: Dr. Googol.

YVONNE *(Correcting her)*: Gogol!

MARIA: Gogol. The man gives me the creeps, Señora, with his autopsies and surgeries.

YVONNE: That's very mean of you. You ought to be ashamed of yourself. Dr. Gogol is a very famous man.

MARIA: If he's so famous what's he doing hanging around here all the time?

YVONNE: Why Maria—my public! But seriously, Dr. Gogol is a brilliant surgeon. He helps deformed children and mutilated soldiers.

MARIA: Soldiers. I wish he'd fix one up for me. Do you remember this, Señora?

YVONNE: Oh yes, the little thumbscrews from last season.

MARIA: That had them screaming. *(Puts various objects into a suitcase)*

YVONNE: Do you remember these?

MARIA: Oh, the fake eyeballs. It had them fainting.

YVONNE: I remember it well.

(Maria accidentally catches her fingers in the thumbscrews.)

MARIA: Owww!

YVONNE: Maria! These are not toys, you know. *(Releases her from the thumbscrews)*

MARIA: I'm just so nervous.

YVONNE: We'll finish packing tonight after the performance. What time is it?

MARIA: Just on the hour.

YVONNE: What number's the station?

MARIA: Twelve-fifty.

(Yvonne turns on the radio and applies her stage makeup.)

I only told you four times tonight, Señora Orlac. After I was married a year, I remembered things like radio stations and forgot my husband.

RADIO ANNOUNCER'S VOICE: Continuing our concert from Montevideo, we shall hear one of South America's most brilliant pianists. An immigrant from Eastern Europe, Señor Orlac is an artist with an unlimited future here in Uruguay and in the world at large.

MARIA *(Powdering Yvonne)*: How about mentioning he's married to a brilliant artist with—

YVONNE: Louder Maria. He can't hear you.

RADIO ANNOUNCER'S VOICE: Señor Orlac, known for his brilliance of tone and purity of technique, will play Chopin's Ballade in G-minor . . . Señor Orlac is just now come out on the stage.

MARIA: You'll miss your entrance, Señora. *(Starts to exit with cart)*

YVONNE: If he coughs twice . . .

MARIA AND YVONNE: . . . it means, "I love you."

(Yvonne exits.)

Scene 1C

ORLAC IN CONCERT

Maria rolls away the cart. Center drop rises. The sound of applause is heard, as if through the radio, and the lights come up on Orlac seated at the piano behind the scrim. He is dressed in a tuxedo. He quietly coughs twice and begins to play. The music, still coming through the radio, plays as the lights fade.

Scene 1D

A Performance of the Grand Guignol

Yvonne enters, wearing her head covering and iron maiden manacles on her hands. They are attached to ropes that are rigged to pulleys overhead, and controlled by a Stagehand at a pinrail visible to the audience at right. As she walks downstage, the ropes are pulled up, so that she arrives in place with her hands strung up over her head. A metal brazier is set at left, with a dagger in it. As she looks about fearfully, the Duke enters, masked as an inquisitor.

YVONNE: Sir! How dare you threaten your duchess!

(The Duke snaps his fingers and the ropes jerk, causing Yvonne pain. She screams.)

Upon what charge am I held? Show your face, sir! *(He snaps his fingers and the ropes jerk again)*
DUKE: You have but one question to answer, Duchess. Name the man seen fleeing your quarters, this night.
YVONNE: I do not believe in your authority. I answer only to the duke.
DUKE *(Reveals his face)*: Believe. I will know his name.
YVONNE: The duke! My husband! But you love me . . . *(He snaps. The ropes tighten, raising her arms higher)* The pain! How can you think me unfaithful?
DUKE: I don't think you unfaithful—I know your treachery—in my heart! How you must love him. Perhaps you'll find this music more soothing.

(The sound of tortured screams.)

YVONNE: YES! YES! . . . There was a man—my lover! And I love him! Do you think I would betray him to your revenge?
DUKE: How unfortunate . . . for you. The steel . . . *(Takes dagger from burning brazier)* The name.
I'll have my revenge.
YVONNE: I would die first.

(The Duke laughs.)

I'll never tell. *(He pokes her)* I'd never give you the satisfaction.

(The Duke places the dagger to her breast and bears down. Smoke rises and Yvonne screams.)

It was Roland! His name was Roland! *(Faints)*

(The lights dim and come up on the curtain call featuring Yvonne and the Duke. Manacles fly out. The sound of applause. The Duke bows and exits. Yvonne continues to bow to applause. Gogol throws a rose to her. She exits. The center drop falls.)

Scene 1E

BACKSTAGE: THE KISS

The sound of applause continues. Yvonne enters, downstage of the center drop. Maria enters and takes her headpiece.

YVONNE: Did he cough?
MARIA: But of course: six . . . eight . . . ten times. I lost count.
YVONNE: Oh! Maybe he has a cold . . .
MARIA: If he doesn't cough he doesn't love you . . . If he coughs too much, he has a cold . . . What a system.
YVONNE: From now on we won't need any more systems.
MARIA: Maybe we'll miss all this—the curtain calls, greasepaint . . . an audience . . .

(The applause stops.)

YVONNE: Stephan will be my audience.
MARIA: It's a waste. One person.
YVONNE: No, no, Maria . . . Stephan will be the toast of New York! But I will miss you. Go on now, Maria—they need help with the party. Go. I can dress myself. And Maria, don't get too near the punch bowl!

(Maria exits. Yvonne moves to the radio, turns it up, and listens intently.)

RADIO ANNOUNCER'S VOICE: The last number of Señor Orlac's farewell concert will be his own composition, *The Morini*, based on Uruguayan folk motifs.

(Through the radio, Orlac coughs twice.)

YVONNE: Moi aussi, cheri. Je t'aime.

(Radio music begins. Yvonne goes behind a screen to pursue her toilette. Gogol enters the dressing room. He observes Yvonne behind the screen. The piano music continues under the scene.

Yvonne emerges from behind the screen, wearing a fur stole. She is surprised to see Gogol.)

Doctor Gogol . . . You frightened me.

GOGOL: You know me?

YVONNE: Everyone in this theater knows you. You've kept the theater in business by buying that box every night. Won't you come in? Thank you so much for the lovely flowers.

(Yvonne extends her hand. Gogol kisses it.)

GOGOL: Every night I've watched you, and tonight . . . the last night . . . I felt I must come and thank you for . . . for everything you've given me.

YVONNE: Oh, I'm very flattered, Doctor.

GOGOL: When the theater reopens, I shall be in my box again. Every night!

YVONNE: I do hope you will, for the theater's sake. I won't be here, I'm afraid.

GOGOL: You . . . You are playing somewhere else?

YVONNE: Never again.

GOGOL: Never again?

YVONNE: No. I'm going to the United States with my husband.

GOGOL: Your . . . husband?

YVONNE: Yes. That's him playing now at Teatro Solis, Stephan Orlac.

GOGOL: Stephan Orlac . . .

(Yvonne puts on her wedding ring.)

YVONNE: How do you think he plays? That's his own composition.

GOGOL: Very modern music.

YVONNE: Stephan's been on tour and my life has been the theater. So this is going to be our honeymoon.

GOGOL *(Taking Yvonne's hand)*: I have come to depend on seeing you every night.

YVONNE: But I'm going to New York.

GOGOL: But I must see you again, I must! *(Moves close to her)*

MARIA *(Entering)*: Señora Orlac! Hurry! They're all waiting! *(Sees Gogol)* Doctor Googol!

YVONNE: Gogol!

MARIA: Gogol. Why not join our party? Have some champagne and cake. And the leading lady gives a kiss with every piece of cake. You might even be first . . .

(Maria exits. As Yvonne starts to go, Gogol stands in front of her.)

GOGOL: Please, may I have the first kiss?

YVONNE: Well, I . . . *(Hesitates)*

(Gogol grabs Yvonne and kisses her. She is repulsed. Maria returns.)

MARIA: Señora Orlac! We can't cut the cake without you! *(Yvonne exits)* Come on, Doctor. We can't forget our public. There's even a miniature guillotine on the cake.

GOGOL: Thank you.

(They exit.)

SCENE 2: THE RIPPER 1

The center drop falls, leaving a space of two feet beneath it. The Ripper and a Prostitute are visible only from the knees down. Then the Prostitute enters, in high heels and rolled-down nylons. She paces, looking for a john. The Ripper enters, wearing white oxfords and shabby pants. He stops. She comes toward him. She starts to caress him, and he pulls her toward him. His hand reaches down and he pulls out a knife from his sock. He stabs her. Her bloody slip falls to the ground. He eviscerates her, her "guts" fall to the ground. He drags her off. We hear sirens and police whistles. The center drop falls to the floor.

SCENE 3: GALATEA 2

Lights come up behind the center drop to reveal the Galatea statue in silhouette. Mariela, Gogol's housekeeper, enters, pushing the "piano" cart. Her face is deformed from several of Gogol's experimental operations; she is superstitious, and she is slightly drunk.

MARIELA *(To the statue)*: Whatever made him bring you here? There has never been any woman in this house but me. If he must have 'em here, I prefer live ones to dead ones. Look at what I've become, a housekeeper to a waxwork.

GOGOL *(Entering)*: Mariela!

MARIELA: Yes, Doctor.

GOGOL: Get out!!!

MARIELA: Yes, Doctor. The police called. They caught that Ripper. *(Mumbles sign of the cross)* They are going to cut off his head tomorrow. The guillotine. *(More sign of the cross)* The police want you to do the autopsy. They said they would bring the body by.

GOGOL: Yes, of course.

MARIELA: Pretty, isn't she?

GOGOL: I said get out!

MARIELA: Sí. I am going, Doctor. *(Exits)*

(Gogol places a strand of pearls around the statue's neck, then drops rose petals around it.)

GOGOL: Galatea, I am no Pygmalion. *(Reads poetry)* "The face of all the world is changed, I think / Since first I heard the footsteps of thy soul." . . . "Guess now who holds the reins of death. 'Death,' said I. 'No. These silver hands hold not death, but love.'"

(Gogol sits down at his organ and plays for Galatea.)

Scene 4: Domestic Bliss 1

Scene 4A

The Kiss

The manacles are lowered, and the center drop rises two feet from the floor. Behind the drop, Orlac and Yvonne embrace and kiss, reminiscent of the Ripper and the Prostitute.

Scene 4B

Backstage: His Hands Are Ruined

The drop rises to reveal Orlac and Yvonne cooing to each other backstage.

ORLAC: How was your farewell party?

YVONNE: It was fabulous.

ORLAC: Fabulous? Then perhaps you change now—or do we do Montevideo in this costume? Oh! Liebling, are you so upset? Gemaha, we go.

(*Indicating macabre assortment of Grand Guignol props*) We're not going to crate all these relics to New York, are we?

YVONNE: No, but I'm a little bit sad to say good-bye to all this . . .

ORLAC: Really!

YVONNE: This theater has supported you very well.

ORLAC: Tut, tut.

YVONNE: That is, until now. Now that you are established as the greatest pianist in all of South America . . .

ORLAC: America . . . South America. What I would not give to play one last time in my beloved Vienna. But it is not possible without a Nazi pedigree. You are now married to an enemy of the Reich. You can no longer return to Paris. Why? Because France will fall. They are weak.

YVONNE: It's a shame they hounded you to leave the Vienna Philharmonic. But I think you are being a little overdramatic . . . We could always live in Paris. But for me these years in Montevideo have been happy.

ORLAC: Really, Yvonne! I'm embarrassed by your having to prostitute yourself in this brothel of a place. No self-respecting artist in Europe would set foot in a theater with seats from a cinema.

YVONNE: I know it isn't the Philharmonic, but this was my family calling. These mementos are dear to me. These little handmaidens . . . (*She handles the manacles expertly*) . . . were a gift from Le Comte Du Bourbon. Authentic, actually used by Torquemada over four hundred years ago.

ORLAC: Really, Yvonne! Who is being overly dramatic now? I think Le Comte took little schoolgirl for a ride. (*Picks up manacles*) These are as authentic as my uncle's rug.

YVONNE: Be careful of those precious pianist hands.

ORLAC: These hands are real. And this is all such artifice. There is no substance here. You said yourself that Grand Guignol is a coarse art form, even for the theater.

YVONNE: Oh, and your concert world is so very sophisticated. Nazi thugs take your home and position in Austria, and here you bribe the same type of people for concert dates. Maria!

ORLAC: Oh, Yvonne. Don't behave so cleverly. It was worth it! We're going to New York where the stage is awarded to merit. I know it!

YVONNE: Be careful!

ORLAC: Oh, I shouldn't worry about that. (*He is now wearing the manacles*) You see! I've learned your silly little trick. You go like this, "Ow! Ow! Ow!" And the audience, they are . . . (*Claps hands*)

YVONNE: Stephan, no! Don't move! The bolts are still operative.

ORLAC: This one is pinching a little.

YVONNE: Be still—let me look at the other one.

ORLAC: Ow. Yes, now they are both pinching.

YVONNE: I'll let you down.

ORLAC: Yes, let me down . . . They're just . . .

YVONNE: Don't move! Don't pull, it only makes them tighter . . . All right, I'll pull you up.

(She goes to the pinrail and starts to pull up the manacles by hauling on the rope attached to the pulley. He screams in pain:)

ORLAC: AHHHHHHHHH!!!!

(Yvonne releases the rope. It goes slack, and the manacles and chains drop to the floor, pulling Orlac down with them. Yvonne rushes to help him, but cannot release the device, which is crushing his hands. Her attempts to help make him scream louder. They begin to move off-stage, his hands still in the manacles, as Yvonne calls for help:)

YVONNE: Maria! Maria! Help!

(Maria runs across the stage. Lights change.)

SCENE 5: THE RIPPER 2

THE GUILLOTINE

The Ripper enters. His arms have been bound to his sides, and his head is hooded.

THE JUSTICE *(Voice-over)*: Señor Rollo! Or, as you are known to the public: The Ripper. You have been tried by the high court of Uruguay and found guilty of the crime of murder. Stalking. Mayhem. In my twenty-five years as justice I have never seen such hideous, unspeakable crimes against mankind!

RIPPER: Womankind! *(Laughs)*

THE JUSTICE *(Voice-over)*: It is by the power invested in this office that I condemn you to death! The sentence of death is to be carried out immediately . . .

(The Ripper continues to laugh.)

Proceed . . .

(The Executioner appears, also hooded, and moves the Ripper to the guillotine. He continues to laugh. The Executioner pushes the Ripper

to a kneeling position upstage of the guillotine. The Ripper's head is placed in the yoke and the blade is raised by a cranky lever on the side of the device. When it reaches the top, it is released. The distant echo of laughter reverberates. The Executioner retrieves the head from the basket and exits.)

SCENE 6: NEW HANDS

THE PLEA

Gogol's operating room. Gogol's Assistant brings in the body of the Ripper on a cart. Only his white shoes are visible.

GOGOL *(Entering)*: So this is Rollo, the famous Ripper. *(The Assistant and Ripper's head nod twice)* I will clamp the spinal column. Electrode. I will implant the electrode. We must begin our work soon.

YVONNE *(Offstage)*: I must see Doctor Gogol.

GOGOL: I cannot be disturbed now.

YVONNE *(Entering)*: Oh, Doctor Gogol.

GOGOL: Madame Orlac.

YVONNE: You must help me. My husband . . . It was an accident.

GOGOL: Bring him in.

(Yvonne sees Ripper's head and screams.)

I'm sorry you had to see that, but it is my scientific duty to find out what makes a man a murderer, a ripper.

(The Assistant brings Orlac in on a gurney.)

(Examining Orlac) Your husband is in no danger.

YVONNE: His hands, Doctor! Can you save them?

GOGOL *(Examining hands)*: There are some things, Madame Orlac, even I cannot do. Prepare for amputation.

YVONNE: But his hands are his life!

GOGOL: There are other things in music besides playing. Is he not also a composer?

YVONNE: I understand. Do what you have to do. I just believed you could save them. I believed you could help me.

GOGOL: If it would help . . . I would gladly give my own two hands. Go now. Rest. And soon it will all be over.

(The Assistant ushers Yvonne out, then returns.)

If only I could help her. If I could only find a way. There must be a way . . .

(Orlac's hand drops. Ripper's hand drops. Gogol gets an idea.)

ASSISTANT: It is impossible, Doctor!

GOGOL: Impossible? That word is not in the German language. Prepare the anesthetic.

(The Assistant starts anesthetic on Orlac.)

(To Orlac) Breathe deeply. Deeper. Deeper. Excellent. *(To Assistant)* Scalpel. Saw.

(The center drop is lowered in front of the two bodies on the carts. Lights come up behind the drop to reveal Gogol, in silhouette, sawing off the hands of the Ripper and then sawing off Orlac's hands. We hear the sound of the saw as he works. Gogol attaches the Ripper's hands to Orlac's arms. Blackout.)

Scene 7: The Examination

The center drop rises on Orlac's home. The piano cart is onstage; Gogol's Assistant brings on the stool. Gogol, Orlac and Yvonne enter. Orlac's hands are bandaged. He sits. Gogol takes a pair of scissors from his medical bag and begins to remove the bandages.

GOGOL: Please do not be shocked by how they first appear. The natural color of the skin will be affected.

ORLAC: I can handle it, Doctor. I just want my hands back.

YVONNE: I'm going to miss having you all to myself like these last two months.

ORLAC: You're a selfish little thing, aren't you. *(He tries an awkward kiss)* I just feel so helpless.

YVONNE: Never mind. The bandages will be off in minutes.

GOGOL: Yes.

(Gogol removes the last of the bandages.)

ORLAC: They look dead.

GOGOL: That's normal. They will for a time. The muscles are atrophied from lack of use.

ORLAC: But they don't look like my hands. They are so large.

GOGOL: That, too, is normal. You forget, they were badly mangled in the accident.

YVONNE: Only you, Doctor Gogol, could have performed this miracle.

GOGOL: I did it because you trusted me.

YVONNE: We can't possibly express our gratitude.

GOGOL: Please . . . *(Touches Orlac's pinky finger with an instrument)* Now I want you to move each finger as I touch it. This one. Excellent. And this one. Good. This one. Please, you must try. And this one. You must move the finger. Move it. YOU MUST MOVE THE FINGER. Splendid. Now the thumb.

(Orlac's thumb moves very easily.)

ORLAC: Yah. No problem.

GOGOL: Now, can you feel this? *(Taps Orlac's hand once with the instrument)*

ORLAC: No.

GOGOL: Hmmm. Can you feel this? *(Taps several times)*

ORLAC: Nein. I feel nothing.

GOGOL: Can you feel this? *(Adjusts instrument and pokes it deep in Orlac's hand)*

ORLAC: Yah!

(Gogol has trouble pulling the instrument out of Orlac's hand.)

GOGOL: Excellent. Now . . . I want you to squeeze my fingers. Harder. Squeeze the fingers. You must try, please. Do it for your lovely wife . . .

(Orlac grasps Gogol's fingers, while taking Yvonne's hand with his other hand. Orlac squeezes both of them hard.)

Splendid!

ORLAC: Well, I began playing the piano with one finger. I can start that way again.

GOGOL: I must caution you, there is still much to be done. You will need graduated exercise. Some ultraviolet treatments, electromagnetic stimulation. It may prove a long and expensive recovery.

ORLAC: Thank you.

(Gogol crosses to his Assistant and gives her silent instructions.)

YVONNE: But Doctor Gogol, how can we ever pay you?

(Gogol dismisses his Assistant.)

GOGOL: I do not operate for money.

YVONNE: No, I insist we must . . .

GOGOL: It would make me so happy to see you on the stage again.

ORLAC: That part of Yvonne's life is over for good . . . Write us out the bill. We'll pay it in full.

YVONNE: But, Stephan . . .

ORLAC: Darling, you are once again the wife of a concert pianist. Thank you for everything, Doctor Gogol. We'll manage.

GOGOL: As you wish.

YVONNE: Let me show you out.

(Yvonne exits with Gogol.)

SCENE 8: DOMESTIC BLISS 2

Scene 8A

PLAYING THE PIANO BADLY

Orlac walks to the piano. He gingerly places a finger on the keys, plays a note. Plays another. Yvonne enters silently and listens. He tries to play a series of notes, but is clumsy—it sounds awful. He bangs on the piano with his hands, pounding out dissonant chords, then collapses in frustration. Yvonne goes to him.

YVONNE: Oh, Stephan!

ORLAC: I can't play anymore. Not with these.

YVONNE: Don't say that, Stephan. Hold me. *(Kisses his hands)* You just got the bandages off.

ORLAC: Forgive me for thinking so much of myself, darling. You know what I want to do with these brand-new hands right now? Practice.

YVONNE: Yes, that's it. More practice. Now, get busy, mister.

(Orlac looks at Yvonne and coughs twice.)

Scene 8B

TIME PASSES

Music plays: the sound of practicing, scales, etc. The center drop falls, creating a shadow screen. We see Orlac at the piano in silhouette, with Yvonne moving in behind him, sometimes listening, sometimes touching his shoul-

der. Calendar pages are projected on the screen, days and months falling away as if blown by the wind. Yvonne removes her rope of pearls and exits as Orlac continues to play. The music suddenly becomes beautiful—it is the music of The Morini, *heard on a Victrola. Blackout.*

Scene 8C

VICTROLA

Music continues as the drop rises. Yvonne enters, thinking Stephan is playing.

YVONNE: Stephan! . . .

> (*She looks around for him. Orlac enters with the Victrola, unveiling it with one hand.*)

ORLAC: I used to play rather well, once. Didn't I?

YVONNE: And you will again, cheri.

ORLAC: No. Not with these hands. Wonderful invention, the phonograph. It keeps a man alive long after he is dead. Sometimes I feel that these records are all that is left of Stephan Orlac.

YVONNE: Stop it.

ORLAC (*Scratches record*): Now all I need is a monkey.

YVONNE: Everything is left of Stephan Orlac. His tenderness . . . his genius . . . his arms that hold me close.

ORLAC: I know what you're doing. Selling everything that belongs to us. Even the pearls that I give you. All these money troubles . . . Yvonne, I'm so sorry. It's all my fault.

YVONNE: We'll be all right.

ORLAC: Yes, of course we will. We'll just cancel the trip to New York and tighten our belts a bit.

YVONNE: Stephan. I must return to the theater.

ORLAC: We've been through this. It's out of the question!

YVONNE: They will repossess the piano!

ORLAC: I'll think of something.

YVONNE: You could play, too . . .

ORLAC: What are you, joking?

YVONNE: It's only a theater, not a concert hall.

ORLAC: These hands are not ready.

YVONNE: You've got to start somewhere or you'll never play again!

ORLAC: No.

YVONNE: Yes.

ORLAC: No!

YVONNE: Yes!

ORLAC: Yes . . . *(Yvonne caresses him)* I'll start now with a little something.

(Orlac bangs viciously on the piano and sends it crashing. Yvonne exits angrily.)

SCENE 9: GOGOL'S LOVE 1

Lights come up behind the black scrim, revealing Gogol. Yvonne enters behind the scrim and crosses to him.

YVONNE: Doctor Gogol, I must speak with you. *(Moves very close to him)*

GOGOL: To be near you like this is more happiness than I have ever known.

YVONNE: But, Doctor Gogol . . .

(Yvonne removes a glove.)

. . . You have been so understanding.

GOGOL: I would do anything for you.

YVONNE: I've come to ask you about Stephan. And you must tell me the truth. Will he ever play again? I mean the way he used to.

GOGOL: Your thoughts are only of him.

YVONNE: He's my husband, I love him.

GOGOL: Is there no room in your heart . . . even pity? . . . for a man who has never known the love of a woman but who has worshipped you since he first walked by that absurd little theater. *(He takes hold of her glove)*

YVONNE: Doctor Gogol . . . Please.

GOGOL: I cannot be silent any longer. You are a woman . . . You must have known.

YVONNE: Yes. Yes! I knew of your feelings for me, and I traded on them. Since you've saved Stephan, I feel deeper friendship for you than for anyone. But I can give you nothing more in return.

(Yvonne's glove ends up in Gogol's hand.)

GOGOL: Nothing? . . .

YVONNE: Even if I didn't love him, there is something about you that . . .

GOGOL: Repulses you?

YVONNE: Frightens me.

GOGOL: You are cruel. But only to be kind.

YVONNE *(As she exits)*: Cruel to be kind . . . Cruel to be kind . . .

SCENE 10: THEATER OF HORRORS 2

THE PLAY WITHIN THE PLAY

A Stagehand sets a chair out for Gogol at his usual place in the Theater of Horrors. Gogol enters.

GOGOL: Thank you. *(He takes out Yvonne's glove and smells it)*

> *(Orlac enters, dressed in his tuxedo and wearing the manacles, which are attached to the ropes overhead. As he comes downstage, the center drop lowers behind him. We hear applause. He makes a fumbled bow, then begins to deliver his lines:)*

ORLAC: No! No! Please stop! Please. Please!

> *(Yvonne enters. She is dressed as the Duke, but wears stockings and high heels. She carries the dagger in her belt.)*

YVONNE: So the duke is not happy? You were pleased enough when you were torturing me . . . *(Prods him with the dagger)* . . . were you not?

ORLAC: Yes . . . Yes!

YVONNE: But now, so to speak, the glove is on the other hand. *(She snaps her fingers. A Stagehand jerks the rope)*

ORLAC *(Weak scream)*: No! Not my hands . . . You must stop!

YVONNE: We can't hear! What about your hands?

ORLAC: You are my wife!

YVONNE: In name only! My true love was murdered! Who killed him? It was you!

ORLAC: Forgive me! I beg of you . . . I'll do anything.

YVONNE *(Musing)*: I am having some friends in this evening for a little diversion . . . the latest shudder. It is well known that the duke is a famous musician. I would like for you to play a little something for us.

ORLAC: I can't.

YVONNE: Did you not say "anything"? What do you mean, "can't"? Can't what?

ORLAC: My hands, they are . . . not right.

YVONNE: Let's have a look at them . . . these famous hands.

(She snaps her fingers, and the manacles are lowered. She releases the latch, and Orlac removes his hands. She snaps again, and the manacles are pulled up to hang above their heads.)

ORLAC: No, not my hands, they're . . .

YVONNE: Big! Yes, very large. They look strong!

ORLAC: These hands are . . . I can't play . . . piano . . . now.

YVONNE: We all know of your trials and tribulations, my liege, but you're a brave man, are you not?

ORLAC: "Brave man . . ."

YVONNE: It would be so uplifting for my guests to hear the famous duke play one last time.

(She picks up a melodica—a small, handheld keyboard with a mouthpiece.)

ORLAC: Please, YVONNE! . . .

YVONNE: Play something . . . anything. Play for us!

(She hands Orlac the melodica. He struggles, then finally plays a sad, halting tune. He stops the music and caresses the keyboard.)

(Whispers) Stephan!

ORLAC: Yvonne!!

YVONNE: You must, my liege! You must!

ORLAC: No! I must not . . .

(He grabs the dagger from her and holds her around the neck, pulling her close to him and holding the dagger to her throat.)

No! I must not . . .

(Orlac throws the knife at Gogol and releases Yvonne. Stagehands enter, wondering what the noise is. The knife sticks in the wall near Gogol's head.)

(Sadly) These are not my hands. You understand, they're not mine.

(Yvonne signals madly to the light booth to cut the lights. Blackout.)

ACT TWO

SCENE 11: PRELUDE TO MADNESS

Scene 11A

GOGOL THE HUMANITARIAN: THE CHILD IS PREPPED

Lights up on the statue of Galatea, in silhouette. Organ music plays. Gogol enters and gives the statue some pearls. As the lights come up full, a Child is rolled in on a gurney by the Assistant. The center drop forms the ceiling of the operating room.

GOGOL *(Stroking Child's head)*: My little one . . . now don't be afraid.
CHILD: Will I be able to walk . . . after?
GOGOL: Yes, my child.
CHILD: Then I'm not afraid.
ASSISTANT: She is ready for operation.
GOGOL: Prepare the anesthetic.
ASSISTANT: Señor Orlac is outside. He says he must see you.
GOGOL: I cannot be interrupted.

Scene 11B

PSYCHOBABBLE

Orlac rushes in.

ORLAC: I must see him! I must! *(Seeing Gogol)* What have you done to me?

GOGOL: Señor Orlac . . .

ORLAC: What have you done to me?!?

GOGOL *(To Assistant)*: Prepare her for operation.

(Assistant begins to exit with Child on gurney.)

ORLAC: You and your black magic!

CHILD: Bye.

GOGOL: Bye bye. *(To Orlac)* What's wrong?

ORLAC: You know very well what's wrong.

GOGOL: You were distraught last night, emotional. I do not hold you responsible for what you did. For your attack, or . . . your performance. It was regrettable, but . . .

ORLAC: Well, whose hands are these??

GOGOL: What's wrong with them? Ten fingers, every muscle, every nerve. Works perfectly.

ORLAC: What's wrong with them? They have a life of their own. They feel for knives. You saw that last night. And that's not the worst. They want to kill. And when I hold . . . *(Stops himself)*

GOGOL: The knife?

ORLAC: Yes.

GOGOL: Hmmm. I think I understand your case. And I think I can help you.

ORLAC: Well, go on please.

GOGOL: I am Gogol and I tell you that these are your hands.

ORLAC: Yes, but why—

GOGOL: Don't interrupt! After the shock of the accident came a second shock—your hands were altered by my knife. You could no longer play. As a result, your disturbed mind was ready for any phobia.

ORLAC: But I have these dreams . . . Another man enters my body, taking my hands, leaving me his—

GOGOL: Yours is a case of arrested wish-fulfillment.

ORLAC: But why should I wish to throw knives?

GOGOL: Perhaps as a little child, some playmate threw a knife cleverly. You wished you could do it like him. Now, that wish was not fulfilled. It festered deep in your subconscious. Your dreams . . . Acting in a play began to activate the phobia. If you could bring that forgotten memory, whatever it is, into consciousness, you would be cured instantly.

ORLAC (*Trying to remember*): Knife . . . Knives . . . no. I remember nothing.

GOGOL: Nothing?

ORLAC: I remember nothing.

GOGOL: Come, you must go now. You need rest. I will tell you what you must do . . .

(Gogol puts his arm around Orlac and escorts him off, speaking quietly to him. The Assistant wheels in the Child, continues prepping her.)

Scene 11C

THE IDEA

Gogol returns.

ASSISTANT: You told him the truth?

GOGOL: I told him a lot of nonsense I don't believe myself. I didn't dare to tell him his hands are those of a murderer. That would probably drive him . . . *(He is suddenly struck by an idea)* . . . completely mad . . .

ASSISTANT: Madame Orlac is in the waiting room.

GOGOL: Have her come in!

ASSISTANT: But the operation!

GOGOL: Leave me!

(The Assistant goes.)

Now I have found the way to have her.

Scene 11D

GOGOL'S LOVE 2

Yvonne runs in.

YVONNE: What's happened? Where is he?

GOGOL: I sent him home. I think if he follows my advice . . .

YVONNE: What advice?

GOGOL: To go away. To lose himself in the country. It's absolutely necessary for his cure that he go alone.

YVONNE: But—do you mean without me?

GOGOL: Yes. You must continue to perform.

YVONNE (*Suspicious*): Why did you give him this advice?

GOGOL: I did what I could for him. I failed. The shock has affected his mind. His life is ruined. Yvonne, you must get away from him before he ruins your life as well.

YVONNE: Now I understand.

GOGOL: No you don't. How could you? I, a poor peasant, I who have conquered science. Why can't I conquer love? Don't you understand? You must be mine, not his. You are mine, Yvonne. Yes, mine.

(He lunges for her. She pushes him back.)

YVONNE: Liar! Hypocrite! *(Lashes at him with her gloves and stole)* You disgust me! *(Exits)*

Scene 11E

OBSESSION: OPERATION ON THE CHILD

Gogol dazedly returns to the Child on the gurney and begins to absently tie his surgical mask.

SECOND ASSISTANT *(Entering)*: She is completely under the anesthetic, Doctor Gogol. Scalpel.

(The Assistant enters with the Victrola and winds the crank. A soft tango begins to play. The Second Assistant dresses Gogol in a surgical gown. He picks up a scalpel to begin the operation. As Gogol begins to operate, his vision starts to swim. The Second Assistant wipes his forehead. Yvonne's voice rings in his ears.)

(Calling after him) Are you all right, Doctor Gogol?

YVONNE *(Voice-over)*: "Liar! Hypocrite! You disgust me!"

(Gogol grows faint, sways, drops the scalpel, then leaves the operating table.)

SECOND ASSISTANT *(Calling after him)*: Doctor Gogol?

SCENE 12: THE MIRROR

As Gogol leaves the operating table, he hears his own voice in his head. The Second Assistant, wearing the same surgical mask and gown, joins Gogol and faces him, mirroring his actions as though Gogol were seeing his own reflection. It is as if we are inside Gogol's mind. The voice-over is enhanced with a reverb effect.

VOICE-OVER: Gogol! They are laughing at you in there. Go back. They are laughing. Go!
>Let them laugh. Nothing matters to you but one thing.
GOGOL: Yvonne. Yvonne. Yvonne.

(Yvonne enters, wearing Gogol's flowing overcoat from Scene 1 and rubber gloves, like the others. She imitates Gogol's walk, joining Gogol and the Assistant so that they become a fantasy trio of Gogols. All three speak simultaneously with the voice-over.)

VOICE-OVER: You can conquer love. Of course you can.
>Think!
GOGOL AND VOICE-OVER: The power of suggestion . . . Already working . . . See how easy it is . . .
GOGOL: Splendid, splendid! Orlac is weak anyway.
VOICE-OVER *(Overlapping)*: Do it! Do it! Do it! Do it! Do it! Do it! . . . And then . . .
GOGOL: She'll be happy . . .
VOICE-OVER: Because of you. *(Echoing and repeating)* Because of you . . . Because of you . . .

(The three "Gogols" exit. The Assistant wheels the cart off. A pulsating organ figure plays, and the center drop, manipulated by a Stagehand at the pinrail, begins a turbulent dance, twisting, turning, flowing and dropping, before finally coming to rest.)

SCENE 13: DESCENT INTO MADNESS

Scene 13A

ORLAC MEETS THE RIPPER

Lights come up behind the scrim. A strange figure descends a ladder. It is Gogol, dressed as the Ripper, with hat, dark glasses, overcoat, white shoes and strange metal prostheses for hands. Orlac enters behind the scrim.

ORLAC: Was it you telephoned me to come here? You said you'd tell me the truth about my hands.
RIPPER: They use knives.

ORLAC: How could you know this?

RIPPER *(Showing metal prostheses)*: I have no hands. Yours, they were mine, once.

ORLAC: I knew it. He lied.

RIPPER: Yes. And so when you threw the knife at Gogol in the theater last night, you tried to kill him with my hands.

ORLAC: Last night . . . Last night . . .

RIPPER: You remember that?

ORLAC: Yes, I . . .

RIPPER: Take it. *(Hands Orlac a knife)* Feel the balance. Use it.

ORLAC: When?

RIPPER: You'll know.

ORLAC: Wait. Who are you?

RIPPER: I am Rollo—the Ripper.

ORLAC: No, no. Rollo is dead. He was guillotined.

RIPPER: Yes, they cut off my head. But that Gogol, he put it back!

(The Ripper reveals grotesque headgear and laughs maniacally. He exits.)

Scene 13B

DOMESTIC BLISS 3

YVONNE *(Entering behind the scrim)*: Stephan, I've been searching for you everywhere. What are you doing in this dark place?

ORLAC: It wasn't I that did it. It was the Ripper's hands . . .

YVONNE: Did what?

ORLAC: Last night when I tried to kill Gogol, it wasn't me. And I . . . *(He looks fixedly at his hands)*

YVONNE: I know, darling. It's all my fault . . .

ORLAC: You remember the Ripper? He was just here. They cut off his head. But Gogol put it back on. The Ripper told me I'll kill.

YVONNE: Oh, Stephan. This is all some wild dream. You're with me now. Everything will be all right.

ORLAC: So, you don't believe these are Rollo's hands? They may not play the piano, but watch how they can use a knife.

(He parries and thrusts expertly with the knife. He appears about to stab her.)

YVONNE: NO, darling, please! It's Gogol. He's trying to drive you mad. *(Tries to hold him)*

ORLAC: Don't touch me.

YVONNE: Stephan . . .

ORLAC: Not you! I can't. I can't go on. I can't go on . . . *(Runs off)*

SCENE 14: DENOUEMENT: GALATEA COMES ALIVE

Scene 14A

ANOTHER FAILED EXPERIMENT

Gogol's home. Darkness. Mariela enters carrying a lantern and a bottle. Lights come up dimly on the Galatea statue, in silhouette. Mariela walks toward the statue. She is tipsy, and takes a few swigs from the bottle.

MARIELA: What he sees in you . . . You couldn't love him like I did . . . you can't even talk . . . but he likes it better that way . . . You'll see. *(Exits, mumbling)*

(Yvonne enters, using a flashlight. She is looking for Orlac and Gogol. Her flashlight illuminates the back wall, where she sees body parts hanging, including hands. She gasps, realizing Gogol's insanity. As she looks for a way out, Mariela returns and sees Yvonne. Mariela drunkenly believes the statue has come to life.)

How did you . . . move??? Get back over there before he comes back and finds you wandering around! Another failed experiment—he's not going to like that.

YVONNE: But I want to see Doctor Gogol.

MARIELA *(Screams)*: Ahhh! It talks! It's come alive! Help!!!

YVONNE: Please, I must see Doctor Gogol!

MARIELA: He made you prettier and now you think you'll be the queen around here. But you'll see—you'll fall in love with him and he'll turn you into a monster. I was supposed to be his Galatea. Look at this . . . *(Points to her deformed face)* I didn't always look like this, Miss Statue. And here, there's something just for you, just wait and see, just wait and see!!! *(Uncovers the gurney, revealing the head of the Ripper and Orlac's hands)*

YVONNE *(Crosses to gurney)*: Stephan's hands!

MARIELA: Now watch this.

(She turns on the device. The head and hands come to life. The hands begin to play the piano in the air.)

The hands of a pianist and the head of Rollo the Ripper!

YVONNE *(Horrified)*: Turn it off! Turn it off!

(Mariela exits, cackling.)

Scene 14B

YVONNE CONFRONTS GALATEA

Realizing she is in a madhouse, Yvonne looks for a way out. She sees the statue of Galatea and is drawn to it. Suddenly, she hears Gogol's mad laughter as he approaches. Thinking fast, she puts out her flashlight and steps into the shadow of the statue.
  Gogol enters, talking to himself. He is now utterly mad. He sheds his Ripper disguise—hat, gloves and headgear.

GOGOL: That fool! He has the mind of a murderer! The power of suggestion!!! How easily it works, my friend. Ha, ha, ha . . .

(He sees Galatea and approaches her.)

Triumph, Galatea! Triumph! He has the mind of a murderer—it's only a matter of time before he goes completely mad. She'll come here now, flesh and blood. Not wax, like you.

(He goes to his organ.)

And he . . . he shall be shut up in the house where they keep the mad. I, Gogol, will do that. Even though it is I who am mad. But nobody knows it, excepting you and me . . . it's our little secret! And now, Galatea, I shall play to you. For the last time.

(He begins to play.)

Scene 14C

MAD LOVE: GALATEA COMES ALIVE

Gogol closes his eyes, lost in his playing. The silhouette of Galatea stirs as Yvonne moves onto the stage. She positions herself at the foot of the organ, standing in the pose of the wax statue, immobile, with eyes closed. Gogol opens his eyes, sees her and stops playing, transfixed.

GOGOL: Galatea . . . *(Goes to her)* It seems that wax can breathe . . .

(Gogol touches Yvonne, and she opens her eyes and looks at him.)

I am Pygmalion!! You were wax, but you came to life! *(Embraces her)*
YVONNE *(Breathlessly)*: My creator . . .
GOGOL: You speak! You speak to me! My love has made you live! Galatea,
    give me your lips! *(Tries to kiss her)*
YVONNE: Not yet!

(She eludes his grasp and tries to exit, but Mariela enters with a tray of surgical equipment, blocking her way.)

Help me!
MARIELA: I'm sorry. *(Reveals a bodkin)*
GOGOL: No. Don't run away from me. I love you . . . I love you . . .
YVONNE: No.
GOGOL: No, you must stay here . . .

(Realizing she is trapped, Yvonne tries another tactic. She turns and advances seductively, a temptress, toward Gogol. He is both suspicious and frightened of her sensual power.)

YVONNE: You are the world's greatest surgeon, now you must show the world
    that you are also the greatest sculptor, and the world's greatest lover.
GOGOL: Your lover?
YVONNE: Yes, only the world's greatest lover can bring Galatea to life in his
    arms. Only the world's greatest lover could breathe life into this inan-
    imate, virginal form.
GOGOL: No. You will run away.
YVONNE: No . . .
GOGOL: You are lying.
YVONNE: You are afraid.
GOGOL: You hate me.
YVONNE: No!
GOGOL: All of the others despised me. You will, too.
YVONNE: No . . .

(Gogol hears Yvonne's earlier words to him.)

(Voice-over) "Liar! Hypocrite! You disgust me!"

(As she reaches for him, he pulls a handkerchief soaked in chloroform from his pocket and puts it to her mouth. She faints, falling onto the organ.)

GOGOL: B-but I love you! . . . You must not leave me, Galatea. You must never leave me. *(Grabs her wrists)* And so I find the thing to do with all her bandages, in one long pure white strand I wind, three times around, and hold her fast. I must blind you. *(Yvonne stirs. She watches as he takes a bodkin off the organ table)* Yes, that is what I must do, so that you can see no one but your Pygmalion. And I must cut out your tongue . . . *(Picks up a scalpel)* so that you can tell no one of your disappointment in me. And I must stop up your ears so you will not hear the compliments of others. Yes. I will show the world my greatest experiment. But I prefer my Galatea to be . . . almost a statue. No pain will she feel . . . no pain. I'm quite sure she will feel no pain. *(Prepares a syringe)*

YVONNE *(Making a last ploy for her life)*: Play for me! Before I can no longer hear you. My creator, my Pygmalion—let me hear you play.

GOGOL: Play? Yes, my Galatea . . . for you . . .

(He waves Mariela off, sits at the organ and begins to play. Yvonne takes the bodkin and plunges it into his hand, fixing it to the keyboard. She then wraps her bandages around his throat and strangles him. He struggles, still playing.)

YVONNE *(As she strangles him)*: You took his hands! You took Stephan's hands! You are a monster! You deserve to die!!

Scene 14D

THE FINAL PLAY WITHIN THE PLAY

ORLAC *(Offstage)*: YVONNE!

YVONNE: STEPHAN!

ORLAC *(Entering)*: Yvonne!

YVONNE *(Releasing Gogol, who slumps onto the organ)*: Stephan! Thank God you've come.

ORLAC: You were all alone with him!

YVONNE: It was Gogol, he tried to, he wanted to . . . it was horrible! *(Falls into his arms.)*

ORLAC: I followed you here . . . I find you here alone with him. What was it you did with Gogol . . . to my hands?

YVONNE: Gogol's dead. I tried to save your hands and instead . . . I unleashed a monster.

ORLAC: A monster, YES!

(Orlac suddenly turns violent, grabbing Yvonne by the wrists and dragging her to the manacles, which drop from above. He forces her hands into them. A Stagehand pulls the rope until her hands are suspended over her head. As this is happening, Gogol revives and staggers downstage, mouth foaming, to take his box seat.)

I have only one question, Duchess . . . Were you and he lovers from the beginning?

YVONNE: No!

GOGOL: Yes!

YVONNE: He's lying!

GOGOL: We've loved each other for all time.

YVONNE: You cannot believe him. You're my husband . . . I love you.

GOGOL: Look at your hands . . . believe . . . We turned you into a joke: a funny, funny joke!

YVONNE: Stephan, we're free now, can't you feel that?

ORLAC: Yvonne! I'm not free! I am trapped in this body with these hands! These hands that know the truth! *(Produces the knife from his sock and starts toward her)*

YVONNE: What are you doing?

(Orlac turns suddenly toward Gogol and kills him by poking his eye out. He then turns and advances on Yvonne, weeping.)

Oh, God! Stephan . . . NO!

(Yvonne manages to free one hand before Orlac stabs her to death. She collapses, still held up by one manacle. He stares at his hands.)

ORLAC: Yvonne, Yvonne, I . . .

(He coughs twice. The hands rebel and kill him.)

END

DELL'ARTE INTERNATIONAL

The mission of Dell'Arte International is to employ and revitalize traditional physical theater forms to explore contemporary concerns. Dell'Arte is internationally recognized for its unique contributions to American theater via its non-urban point of view, its more than thirty-year history of ensemble practice, and its work to push the boundaries of physical theater forms in professional productions and in its MFA and certificate training programs. In 1998, the Wallace Foundation recognized Dell'Arte as one of six "exemplary community-based arts centers in the United States." In 2000, Dell'Arte was honored by the James Irvine Foundation as one of twelve Cornerstone Arts Organizations in California, for "making significant contributions to the cultural and economic life of our state." In 2005, Dell'Arte and its artistic director received the "Prize of Hope" in Denmark for making a "significant contribution to fighting for human hope in a daring, vulgar, loving, sincere, serious and poetic manner, and for fighting with sparkling energy against habitual thinking."

The Dell'Arte company has collaboratively created more than forty-five award-winning original works, and has toured regionally and internationally, performing in rural communities like Forks of Salmon, California, and at international festivals in Colombia, Venezuela, Brazil, Italy, the Netherlands, Denmark, Croatia, Hungary and France. The Dell'Arte School of Physical Theatre, which has an international student body and faculty, is the only full-time professional training program of its kind in the United States, and offers the only accredited MFA in ensemble-based physical theater in the world. The Dell'Arte Youth Academy, now in its twelfth year, is a partnership program between classroom teachers and internationally renowned theater artists.

Dell'Arte produces the Mad River Festival, a six-week summer event that includes Dell'Arte company productions, emerging theatrical artists, a community pageant, and the Humboldt Folklife Festival. In the summer of 2005 Dell'Arte will produce the first National Ensemble Theater Festival at its home base in Blue Lake, California, featuring fourteen companies and eighty artists and ensemble practitioners.

IT'S AN EARTHQUAKE IN MY HEART

Goat Island

Left to right: Bryan Saner, Karen Christopher, Mark Jeffrey and Matthew Goulish.

INTRODUCTION

Obsession with authorship typically haunts those new to artistic collaboration. Entering into an ensemble creation process for the first time, few young artists can shake the unspoken question, "Who owns my original ideas?" Fortunately, the question is easy to answer in its literal sense. The implied underlying conflict, however, is more difficult to resolve.

Original collaborative works question cultural assumptions about sole authorship, the role of the artist and audience, even the value of "genius." These are questions that each ensemble must address head-on, and no group that I have studied does it as aggressively as the Chicago performance ensemble Goat Island.

For the Goats (as they are known by their fans), the erasure of authorship is the keystone of the creative process. The five members of this ensemble bring original ideas to the rehearsal hall as offerings rather than as desires or possessions. In the development process, the members actively work to blur the lines of identity between their ideas, and at the point where sole authorship fails, the real artistic mining—and real collaboration—begins.

In a collaboratively composed paper delivered at the 2000 Association for Theatre in Higher Education (ATHE) conference, the Goats described their approach to authorship this way: "Divisions between individuals and ideas of authorship are blurred. Through this we see that the creative material connects to others, and is completed by them."

They go on to describe a "decentering expansion" that "divests the work of an absolute author. Instead, the precarious structure takes shape from the absence of a master builder." They have found that because of this precariousness "the responsibility is on the group to listen for the still small voice, and a genuine respect for different types of creativity and intelligence emerges. This multiple-voice process (and product) has a better chance of survival over the years. As if it had more legs to stand on . . . more dimensions to view."

Since its founding in 1987, Goat Island's director and four performers have devoted three nights a week, year-round, to the development of new works. Each project takes approximately two years to complete.

Although their work displays a level of physical precision usually associated with dance companies, as well as the de-centered self-awareness and irony of postmodern studio art, the theatrical nature of Goat Island's work is unmistakable. Their singular combination of choreographic precision, visual clarity and raw energy creates poetic images that invite us into our most fragile, and therefore human, dimensions. They tell us that exploring "the moment when things fall apart" ultimately brings us to the point "where ownership counts least and collaboration counts most."

As with collaboration, so with life. The Goats say, "We try to respect each other with a sense of dignity, without judgment or prejudice, with the knowing that each contribution has its place."

—F.L.

Dedication

With thanks to Litó Walkey and Rebecca Groves

Production Information

It's an Earthquake in My Heart was a commission of the Wiener Fest-wochen (Vienna Festival), Arnolfini Live (Bristol), Kampnagel (Hamburg; the artistic director from 2001–2002 was Gordana Vnuk) and Podewil (Berlin). Goat Island's work is partly supported by The Illinois Arts Council, a state agency; and by a CityArts 1 Program grant from the City of Chicago Department of Cultural Affairs.

It's an Earthquake in My Heart was created by Goat Island: Lin Hixson, director; CJ Mitchell, company manager; Karen Christopher; Matthew Goulish; Mark Jeffery and Bryan Saner. The technical director was Margaret Nelson, the lighting designer was Scott Halvorsen Gillette and Goat Island, the clothing designer was Cynthia J. Ashby; the woodshoes were by Dan Mackessy, the small chairs were by Dionicio Portillo and the fans were by Taro Hattori.

AUTHORS' GUIDE

Starting

Every process overflows its description. *It's an Earthquake in My Heart* premiered at the Vienna Festival in June 2001, and toured until November of that year. We had begun to make the piece in May 1999, and we continued to make changes to it until the end of the tour. This Authors' Guide, The Performance text and The Process, which follows the text, attempt to document the piece in its November 2001 form, while also attempting to describe the processes engaged over the two-plus years.

Please use the Authors' Guide and The Process to attempt a re-creation of the performance itself, or to attempt a re-creation of aspects of the process. Either approach, we expect, will result in the creation of a new work, one you may call your own.

Continuing

We sometimes think of our creative process as a series of directives and responses.

Lin may start by producing a directive: a phrase or sentence, a question, a collage of images, a specific task.

The performers/collaborative members of the group (Karen, Matthew, Mark, Bryan) then produce and present performative responses to the directive. These responses, often fragmentary, may take the form of individual or group presentations, composed for oneself or for another member of the company, or for some combination of people, to perform. While many responses take entirely imaginative forms, others involve extensive research. Many responses for *It's an Earthquake in My Heart*, often because of the nature of the directives themselves, involved material appropriated, imitated or copied from video sources. (See The Process for details about the Directives/Responses process.)

In response to these responses, Lin may then (1) produce more directives, (2) combine and organize the presented material into sequences, (3) submit performative material of her own or (4) present some combination of all three.

The performers in turn may present new material in response to the new directives, the old directives, the sequences or the other responses, which also serve a secondary function as indirect directives themselves.

Before we know it, we have a performance in its early stage, and we need to look at it and ask ourselves, "What is it?" Meanings arise retroactively (and in unexpected ways) related to or unrelated to the directives.

During the course of the long creative process, we work toward small deadlines: usually public work-in-progress presentations. These may involve delivering short context talks, as well as presenting performance sequences, followed by conversation with the audience about what we think we did, and what they think they saw. We think of communication less as a transmission of knowledge and more as a coordination of behavior. The performance itself, in addition to the conversations about it, reflect this coordination, this harmonizing of actions and reactions.

Finally, we finish the piece and present it. We do not understand everything in it. Sometimes we arrive at increased understanding over repeated performances. Sometimes we don't. We live with *not understanding* in our everyday lives. We don't think of the performance as necessarily reflecting everyday life, but we do think of understanding as a limited process. We try to learn how to continue with *not understanding*, as well as with understanding, and how at the same time to love the world.

We then continue working on the piece after presenting it. The changes, adjustments and shifts in emphasis become smaller and smaller as we go.

The text of *It's an Earthquake* documents only the material that found its way into the finished performance. In a sense, this approach does a disservice to all the material that we edited out or abandoned. The rejected material remains present, like last year's gardening. It fertilizes the whole endeavor.

This approach to documentation also reduces and refocuses the successful material, by assessing it in a trans-temporal way. In reality, one may present a response nearly a year after its corresponding directive. A first sequence may start to take shape, then lie untouched for months while a second sequence takes shape. The company then revisits the first sequence, and makes changes to it based on the differences observed by its proximity to the second sequence. Furthermore, *forgetting* plays an important role in the creative process, as does misunderstanding, and the occasional accident. This text cannot document or make sense of those subtleties in any comprehensive way. Instead, it simply tries to align the steps in the process in their most sensible shape, to emphasize their investigatory aspects without misrepresenting them (too much).

Similarly, this text cannot document the entire finished performance. Given the peculiar shape of our playing area, outlined by the audience configuration, an audience member's choice of seat determines in many ways the performance that audience member will experience. Audience members who return often comment on the difference of experiences in the different seats. Seat choice represents a basic form of audience participation.

Can one see the same performance twice? As Zeno of Heraclitus said: One cannot step in the same river twice. Furthermore, stepping twice into the Chicago River in Illinois produces two different experiences, which then differ radically from the two different experiences produced by stepping twice into the River Rheidol in Wales. Seeing the same performance twice, we believe, produces two different experiences that share the same neighborhood. So this text attempts to document the neighborhood, as specifically as possible, in order to allow repeated visits.

Also, what we are able to document here cannot trace the network of connections between the process and the performance, or within the performance itself, with any accurate degree of complexity. We often assess the strength of a particular moment in the performance in terms of its connections to other moments. The more complex the pattern of interconnections, we think, the more resilient the work. These interconnections remain at least in part outside of our control. Audience members often point out connections that they make within the work, or that they feel the work makes to their points of view, which we may never have observed. With this in mind, we hope we've presented the material in enough detail to render a sense of dynamic interconnection legible to the reader.

THE
PERFORMANCE

Texts, Structures and Images

PROLOGUE

Matthew enters carrying four small chairs. He arranges them around an
imaginary table. Karen, Mark and Bryan enter. All sit.

Text: Insurance Sales Training Dialogue #1

MATTHEW: What would your family do if you did not come home last night?
Let us articulate clearly, what it is we wish to take from the client. Yes?
MARK: Fear?
MATTHEW: Exactly, fear. For when we say: Imagine you won't come home
tomorrow, we are making them afraid. We have a profession where we
have to point out the risks involved. Many people have no idea what
risks there are, nor do they know how to insure themselves. That is our
job. And therefore we must ask such questions, putting them in the
past tense, thus removing the client's fear. Mr. Kopchinsky, you wanted
to say something?
BRYAN: Above all what is important is—one puts an idea in the client's
head, so that he begins to think: What would have happened yester-
day, what would the situation be today? And I think it's important that
the client confronts himself with the question.
MATTHEW: Yes, Miss Ritmer?

KAREN: I would like to add that by consulting the client we wish to create a positive future for them, and therefore it is not favorable to put the "what-would-happen-if" question in the future.

MATTHEW: I think with this basic attitude, that, with the consultation, we want to make the customer's future secure and positive, I think we can take a break, you have earned it. We will continue in fifteen minutes. OK.

(Bryan flips sideways off the chair and holds a semi-collapsed position on the floor. Karen stands abruptly. Mark exits. Matthew collects chairs and exits. Karen moves to center. She begins a hand movement sequence: hands fluttering like falling leaves—she traces patterns on her head while turning slowly in a circle.)

Movement Sequence: Bryan on Floor, Karen Circling with Hand Movement

Text: Statement of Three Parts

MATTHEW *(On microphone, at edge of space):*
  It's raining.
  Raining in my heart.

  Merry Christmas.
  Merry Christmas in my heart.

  It's an earthquake.
  An earthquake in my heart.

PART I:
TUESDAY MORNING.
TRAFFIC JAM.

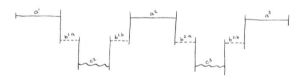

a: Car Chase ——
  a^1: #1
  a^2: #2 (fans on)
  a^3: #3 Wences Hand

b: Driving Commands ------
  $b^{1.a}$: We Drivers 1-6
  $b^{1.b}$: We Drivers 7-10
  $b^{2.a}$: The Italian Job 1-4
  $b^{2.b}$: The Italian Job 5-10

c: Insurance Sales Training Dialogue ～～

(Matthew removes and discards his shirt, revealing an identical shirt beneath it with words on the back: "Part 1: Tuesday Morning." He exits. Mark enters and begins the Movement Sequence to "Car Chase #1," quickly walking the length of the space, then slowly walking back to his starting place. Matthew enters carrying a battery-operated car horn.)

PART 1

TUESDAY MORNING. TRAFFIC JAM.

Text: First Announcement

MATTHEW:
> Part 1.
> Tuesday morning.
> Traffic jam.

Movement Sequence: Car Chase #1

Text: Driving Commands #1a/Insurance Sales Training Dialogue #2/Driving Commands #1b

(Matthew moves to position. Bryan joins Mark on his second slow walk back during "Car Chase #1," paralleling his movement, then bumping into him. On Mark's third slow walk back, Karen stops her "Circling Hand" Movement Sequence, and joins Matthew. Mark must now walk between Karen and Matthew. On Mark's sixth fast walk, Matthew honks the car horn; Mark falls, stands, then performs the "Lost Keys" Movement Sequence. Then he begins the "Driving Commands" Movement Sequence. Matthew, Karen and Bryan sprint to position and perform fragments of the "Bausch" Movement Sequence. Matthew resets the four chairs around the imaginary table, as at the beginning of the piece. Matthew, Bryan and Karen sit).

MARK:
> 1
> Always be courteous!
> 2
> Know how to drive!

3
Both hands on wheel!
4
Watch traffic signs!
5
Keep a safety margin!
6 . . .

(Mark sits.)

MATTHEW *(As if "calling on" Bryan and Mark)*: Mr. Kopchinsky, Mr. Pohl-Jordan.

(Bryan and Mark stand, as if to begin an improvisation.)

BRYAN: Which door shall I knock on?

(Matthew indicates an imaginary door.)

Brief mental preparation.

(Brian knocks on a door.)

MARK: Yes?
BRYAN: Mr. Pohl-Jordan? Good morning, my name is Kopchinsky, we had an appointment today. May I come in?
MARK: Please do.
BRYAN: Hello, Mr. Pohl-Jordan.
MARK: Take a seat.

(Bryan and Mark sit.)

BRYAN: How does this weather affect you?
MARK: Badly, when one has to work. I'd prefer to be on holiday.
BRYAN: You're no better off than I.
    Tell me, Mr. Pohl-Jordan . . . eh . . . What would happen if you had not come home last night? Have you ever thought about that?
MARK: Never, one can't think about such things. *(Stands)*

(On Mark's "driving commands," Matthew, Karen and Bryan sprint to remove chairs, and repeat the "Bausch" Movement Sequence.)

7
Keep right!

8

Keep sober!

9

Stop when angry!

10

Obey all laws!

(Mark ends commands, then he, Karen and Bryan move to position for the "Car Chase #2" Movement Sequence.)

Movement Sequence: Car Chase #2 (Fans On)

Text: Driving Commands #2a/Insurance Sales Training Dialogue #3/Driving Commands #2b

(Mark, Bryan and Karen begin the "Car Chase #2" Movement Sequence, a repetition of the "Car Chase #1" Movement Sequence but at a reverse orientation. On Mark's first slow walk back to start, Matthew switches on a battery-operated fan, which is attached to Mark's shirt, level with his heart. On Mark's third slow walk back, Matthew backs up into position and switches on Karen's fan, worn on her dress, also near her heart. On Mark's fourth slow walk back, Matthew switches on Bryan's fan, at heart level of his shirt as well. On Mark's fifth slow walk back, Matthew honks the car horn twice. Mark performs the "Lost Keys" Movement Sequence, then again begins the "driving commands." Matthew, Karen and Bryan sprint to position and perform the "Bausch" Movement Sequence. Matthew again resets the four chairs, as at the beginning. Then he, Bryan and Karen sit.)

MARK:

1

Take your flowers, and get in the car!

2

You are not gonna be sick, you are not gonna have your migraine, and you're all sitting in the back of the motor!

3

Keep calm!

4

Get yourselves sorted out and shut up! *(Sits)*

MATTHEW *(As if "calling on" Karen and Mark)*: Miss Ritmer, Mr. Pohl-Jordan.

(Karen and Mark stand, as if to begin an improvisation.)

KAREN: Mr. Pohl-Jordan? Good morning. A nice place you have here.

MARK: Not very tidy, didn't get 'round to it, but . . .

KAREN: That's atmosphere.

Mr. Pohl-Jordan, let's begin right away. Have you ever thought about what would happen if you had not come home last night?

MARK: I've never really thought about it.

MATTHEW: Yes, that was good. Now you must pay attention! *(Karen and Mark sit)* The hand, these three fingers, you don't need them. Sometimes they move a bit, due to concentration, and then the fingers become a distraction. You must watch that the hand does not move.

(On Mark's "driving commands," Matthew, Karen and Bryan sprint to remove chairs They move into position for the "Car Chase #3: Wences Hand" Movement Sequence.)

MARK *(Standing)*:

> 5
>
> Don't talk like that! And apologize to the lady!
>
> 6
>
> No one talks anymore except me!
>
> 7
>
> Put your foot down!
>
> 8
>
> Get the wheels in line!

9

Leave the beer!

10

Hold still! Don't move! Don't move at all! Don't no one get out the door neither!

(Mark ends his "driving commands" and takes his position.)

Movement Sequence: Car Chase #3: Wences Hand, Concluding with Car Collision and Confetti

(Mark and Karen are at opposite ends of the length of the space; Bryan and Matthew are at the opposite widths of the space. All raise his/her right hand into "Wences" position. Mark and Karen slowly walk the width of the space. Matthew and Bryan quickly walk the length of the space, curving sharply to avoid colliding with Karen and Mark. On the fourth repetition of the movement, Matthew drops out. He brings on a micro-phone and pignose speaker, which he positions for Bryan's upcoming monologue, then moves into position for a confetti throw. On the fifth repetition, Bryan drops out and waits at the edge of the space, leaving Mark and Karen to walk the pattern as a duet. On the ninth repetition, Mark and Karen collide. Matthew throws confetti into the air above them.

Bryan moves into position near the audience. He bends over the microphone.)

PART I:
TUESDAY MORNING.
RAINING.

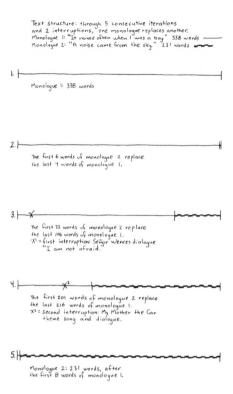

Text structure: through 5 consecutive iterations
and 2 interruptions, one monologue replaces another.
Monologue 1: "It rained often when I was a boy." 338 words
Monologue 2: "A noise came from the sky." 231 words

1.
Monologue 1: 338 words

2.
The first 6 words of monologue 2 replace
the last 7 words of monologue 1.

3. x^1
The first 73 words of monologue 2 replace
the last 106 words of monologue 1.
x^1 = first interruption: Señor Wences dialogue
"I am not afraid."

4. x^2
The first 201 words of monologue 2 replace
the last 216 words of monologue 1.
x^2 = second interruption: My Mother the Car
theme song and dialogue.

5.
Monologue 2: 231 words, after
the first 8 words of monologue 1.

PART 1

Tuesday Morning. Raining.

Text: Bryan's Monologue, Second Announcement

BRYAN: Now let's talk about something that is easy to understand.

MATTHEW:
Part 1.
Tuesday morning.
Raining.

(Bryan reads a variation of this monologue five times. He begins with "Monologue #1," then starting with the first repetition, he begins to replace the words with those of "Monologue #2." This replacement begins at the end of the monologue, moving further and further toward the beginning with each repetition. By the fifth reading, he speaks the entirety of "Monologue #2.")

Action in first reading: Bryan speaks bending over microphone without moving. Karen and Mark remain in place after their collision. Matthew throws two more handfuls of confetti after his announcement, rotating slowly in place, then exits. Karen and Mark repeat "Car Chase #3: Wences Hand" Movement Sequence four times. Mark moves to position beside Bryan. Karen moves to position at the edge of the space. Matthew brings Mark a wooden hand on a short stick, then exits. Mark holds the wooden hand over Bryan's head. After Bryan says, "Now let's talk about something that is easy to understand . . ." Bryan and Mark jump in unison three times in place.

Action in second reading: Matthew enters, switches off Karen's fan and removes it from her dress, then exits. Mark moves to a new position. Matthew enters with an extension for the handstick. He screws it into the bottom of the handstick, doubling its length. Bryan faces opposite. Mark lowers the handstick over Bryan's head. After Bryan says, "Now let's talk about something that is easy to understand . . ." Bryan jumps twice in place, while Mark raises the handstick. Matthew enters and gives Karen woodshoes and exits. Karen buckles the woodshoes to her feet.

Action in third reading: Matthew enters and gives Karen birdfeet sticks. Karen walks across the space in her woodshoes with her birdfeet sticks. Mark raises the handstick, and he, Karen and Bryan perform "First Interruption—Señor Wences Dialogue." Mark moves to a new position. Matthew enters with another extension, which he screws onto the bottom of the handstick. Bryan moves to the opposite side of the space. Matthew switches off Mark's fan, removes it from his shirt, and exits. Mark lowers the handstick over Bryan's head. Matthew takes the birdfeet sticks from Karen. Karen unbuckles her woodshoes. Matthew removes them and exits across the space. After Bryan says, "Now let's talk about something that is easy to understand . . ." Bryan jumps once in place, while Mark raises the handstick.

Action in fourth reading: Bryan bends over the microphone, speaking without moving. Matthew enters carrying a Walkman and pignose speaker. Mark raises the handstick. Matthew and Bryan perform "Second Interruption—My Mother the Car Dialogue." Matthew exits.

Action in fifth reading: Mark exits with the handstick. Matthew crosses to Karen and gives her the Walkman and pignose speaker. Mark enters holding a small artificial spruce tree. He circles. Karen carries the pignose speaker, which plays piano music and the voices of children. She circles. Bryan turns opposite the group. Matthew circles, remaining with Bryan. Mark and Karen exit. Matthew removes Bryan's fan, then removes the microphone and its speaker. Bryan speaks the last words of the monologue without the microphone.)

BRYAN *(Monologue #1):* It rained often, when I was a boy. I sat on the veranda and watched the rain fall into the cabbage patch. How important the veranda is to me, I would think. The rain falls without beginning or end. As it falls, time and space become mixed and entwined, until no distinction remains between the two. And then I too deteriorate from the center, like rotting cabbage.

My heart was always racing like a dog's—"thump, thump, thump" it would pound. I was possessed by the thought that if I didn't break the world apart, if I left it alone, somehow disaster would strike. I paced around and around and around. Hail would fall, and it would make no difference to me.

So various things went on like this . . . events that occurred and those that didn't . . . they were all there. When I think about them, I get carried away by the image of myself in grammar school, pattering down the long corridors like a sperm. Though I don't let anyone see, tears pour down my face when I recall my youth.

The rain, the cabbage patch, the school, the movements of the next-door neighbor's dog. They are like so many broken boats, drifting inside me in bits and pieces. From time to time, the boats gather, speak and consume the darkness.

Now let's talk about something that is easy to understand: An expert carpenter is more accurate than a weather report. Rather than predicting the weather he "feels" the weather. Every day he studies the humidity in his wood shavings. When we watch the expert carpenter, we may think of him as a weather station. After strenuous work, he takes a break. He rests his hands on the table. At a casual glance, we think they look like hooks, or carpenter tools. And yet, they are living things. If we watch long enough, we might even see an expert carpenter try to feed an entire sandwich to his own hand. Then we know it will rain soon.

(Monologue #2:)

A noise came from the sky.
It was like the rush of a mighty wind.
It filled the house where we were sitting, and tongues of fire
    appeared to us.
A distribution of tongues, as of fire, resting on each of us.
We began to speak.
Each one of us heard the words spoken in our own language.
We came from many nations.
But each one of us understood.
I'll begin again.

The wind flung the door open.
It knocked over my water cup.
I went outside.
I looked at the sky.
This event appeared to confuse the birds.
But I was not afraid.
I saw a cloud in the shape of a country church.
The country church from my hometown.
Two smaller clouds in the shape of my parents.
A car-shaped cloud with a "just married" sign hanging on it.
The clouds showed me my parents' wedding day.
It was very nice for nature to imitate reality this way.
My father wore blue, and my mother wore white.
They got in the car cloud and drove away.
Other clouds threw rice, as was the custom in those days, long before
    I was born.
Then it started to rain.
I held out my hand.
I caught a raindrop in my hand.
These things are miracles.
And not only miracles.
They are improbable miracles.
I never stopped loving the world.

Text: First Interruption—Señor Wences Dialogue

Movement Sequence: Karen's Woodshoes and Birdfeet Walk

MARK: Don't talk.
KAREN: How long?
MARK: "How long?"
KAREN: Yes.
MARK: Three months.
BRYAN: Too long.
MARK: Listen to me OK. If I say don't talk, don't talk.
    Don't talk.
    Don't talk.
KAREN: "Don't talk."
MARK: Don't talk, please.
BRYAN: Sorry.
    S'arright.
MARK: Are you afraid?

KAREN: Yes.

MARK: You're not afraid.

KAREN: No, I am not afraid. *(Singing)* I am not afraid.

MARK: I like your voice.

KAREN: Yes?

MARK: Yes, so beautiful.
Are you afraid?

BRYAN: No. Not yet.

KAREN: I am not afraid.
I am not afraid.

BRYAN: Close the door.

Text: Second Interruption—My Mother the Car Dialogue

(My Mother the Car theme song plays twice. On the second round, Bryan sings along. Then Matthew takes over, singing at first, then speaking the text.)

MATTHEW: Randy. I want you to brace yourself. This car, this car right here, did talk to me and pleaded and begged me to take her home. Now I say her because this car . . . is my mother. Now I know you find it hard to believe, only I did too. Gosh, when this car first talked to me, I didn't believe it would be my own mother. I asked her all sorts of questions, things that only my mother would know—like what year I broke my collarbone, and she knew, and she answered, man. And only then did I realize that this car is Mother. So, how'd you like to go for a spin around the block?

BRYAN: Sorry, Dad, I have to do my homework.

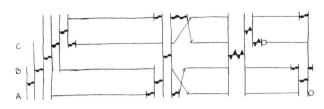

Movement structure: 2 sections, with varying transitions.
First section: solos/duets partly derived from Bausch.
Second section: repetition of first section with roles traded.
Etherboom walk (unison) at start, midpoint, and end.
Bake a Cake dance (unison) interrupts second section.

$\times$ — role trade
O — change into wet clothing
A — Karen
B — Mark
C — Bryan
D — Matthew

PART 2

53 Years Earlier.

Text: Third Announcement

MATTHEW:

> Part 2.
> 53 years earlier.
> Merry Christmas.

(Matthew removes and discards his shirt, revealing an identical shirt beneath it with words on the back: "Part 2: 53 Years Earlier.")

Movement Sequence: Ether Boom Walk/Bausch Part 1/Ether Boom Walk/Bausch Part 2/Ether Boom Walk

(This twenty-minute central section repeats a densely choreographed series of movements derived primarily from imitations of fragments from various works by Pina Bausch's Wuppertaler Tanztheater. These movements are woven together with original movements developed by the group. The movements engage the small chairs, the woodshoes and a pair of woodshoes with artificial spruce trees attached to them. "Bausch Part 2" echoes the choreography of "Bausch Part 1," with Mark and Karen trading roles, and Bryan and Matthew trading roles. "Bausch Part 2" includes an interruption of a unison dance quartet performed to "If I Knew You Were Comin' I'd've Baked a Cake," sung

by Eileen Barton with The New Yorkers. During each "Bausch" section, the Brass Suite, Sarabande, by Johann Christoph Pezel, plays near the conclusion. At the end of "Bausch Part 2," Bryan changes into a dress similar to the one worn by Karen, only soaking wet and dripping water, and with a damaged fan attached to it. He wears the dress for his final dance solo in "Bausch Part 2," and for the remainder of the performance.

Matthew drops out of the last slow "Ether Boom Walk" to set up the microphone and pignose speaker for Karen's "Radio Speech." Bryan and Mark conclude this section lying motionless on the floor.)

PART 3:
TUESDAY EVENING.

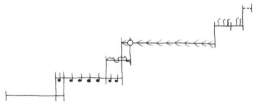

PART 3

Text: Fourth Announcement (Series)

> Radio Speech
> Hymn
> Civil War/Phantom Child Dialogues
> Last Speech

Movement Sequence: Lost Keys

> Woodshoes and Birdfeet Walk

MATTHEW:
> Part 3.

(He removes and discards his shirt, revealing an identical shirt beneath it with words on the back: "Part 3: Tuesday Evening.")

> Tuesday evening.
> 7:01.

KAREN *(Bending over microphone, holding wet clothes similar to those previously worn by Bryan):*
> Are we brave.
> Are we true.
> Have we the national color.
> Can we stand ditches.
> Can we mean well.
> Do we talk together.
> Have we Red Cross.
> A great many people speak of feet.
> And socks.

(Karen moves to a new position and changes into a wet shirt, with damaged fan attached to it, and trousers. Matthew assists and brings her the woodshoes. Mark stands and performs a slow "Lost Keys" Movement Sequence. Matthew brings the microphone to Karen's new position. Karen straps on the woodshoes, which she wears for the rest of the performance. Mark falls to floor.)

MATTHEW:
>   Part 3.
>   Tuesday Evening.
>   7:02.
>   Earthquake.

(He tosses confetti into the air over Karen and exits.)

KAREN *(Raising the microphone, no longer bending over)*:
>   Did we do something to cause this?
>   I was in the grass beside the road.
>   I heard voices and I waited for them to come.
>   My father was still in the fire.
>   A flame that shot from the carburetor, down to the creek bed, and
>   through the valley.
>   I ran through three walls of fire down this road we came in on.
>   A leak in a gas company supply line, they told me later, and propane
>   had settled all around in that land that that morning my father
>   had agreed was a good buy.
>   We had talked together.
>   No sense in not going along for the ride and not enjoying the games
>   when that's what the trip seemed to be about.
>   If the goals didn't seem serious for moments, then certainly nothing
>   more serious could happen.
>   Maybe there even would be a trip to Blue Hawaii. I certainly didn't
>   want to stop it.

MATTHEW *(Lifting Bryan to his feet)*:
>   Part 3.
>   Tuesday evening.
>   7:03.
>   It's an emergency. *(Exits)*

KAREN *(Into microphone)*:
>   But in the Fun House, how do you know what's really crazy? How
>   do you know that it's supposed to be you that stops it.
>   Right now.
>   And that you don't know how to stop it.
>   The morning clear and vanishing.

*(Bryan interrupts by nailing a white paper stripe into the floor at one
end of the space, stretching it across the length of the playing area,
then nailing the other end into the floor opposite.)*

The night's approach unnoticed.
Nobody will touch you anywhere on your body ever again.
I asked the farmer to bring me a gun.
Can't you see I'm a dead man?
But the gun was always with the water pistols.
And in the best United States way there is a pistol hanging low to
   shoot man and the sky in the best United States way, and the pis-
   tol is I know a dark steel-blue pistol.
And so I know everything I know.

(Piano accompaniment to the hymn, "My Life Flows On," begins.)

(Off microphone) Are you out of your mind?
BRYAN: I'm sorry, David, the guy said it was an emergency.
KAREN: I don't care what the story is, I'm on the air.
BRYAN: Anything you say, I'm sorry.

KAREN *(Into microphone)*:
   That was not my story.
   There was no part in it that was my part.
   But the first time I heard, it moved my liver three inches to the left.
   And I have never recovered.
   I'm told that we are experiencing some difficulties.
   We appreciate your patience.
   We may even need to go off the air for a little while.
   So enough talk.
   Let's hear our theme all the way through tonight.
   Until Wednesday then
   I will try again
   If not then
   What matters is that it could have happened.

(Matthew enters singing. During the first verse and refrain he removes the microphone and speaker. Mark rises from the floor, and Matthew tackles him, returning him to the floor.)

MATTHEW *(Singing)*:
   My life flows on in endless song,
   Above earth's lamentation.
   I catch the sweet, though far-off hymn
   That hails a new creation.

   No storm can shake my inmost calm
   While to that rock I'm clinging.

Since love is Lord of heaven and earth,
How can I keep from singing?

(Singing into a prop telephone:)

Hi how are you?
I'm fine. How's Dad?
And how's the new car running?
What though the darkness gather 'round?
Songs in the night I'm singing . . .

(During the following refrain, verse and refrain, Bryan, Karen and Mark rotate slowly in place. Bryan and Karen repeatedly begin to fall and Matthew returns them to a standing position. Mark repeatedly tries to stand, and Matthew returns him to the floor.)

ALL *(Singing)*:
No storm can shake my inmost calm
While to that rock I'm clinging.
Since love is Lord of heaven and earth,
How can I keep from singing?

I stood alone among the crowd.
I felt the earthquake coming.
What though I die? With my last sigh,
How can I keep from singing?

No storm can shake my inmost calm
While to that rock I'm clinging.
Since love is Lord of heaven and earth,
How can I keep from singing?

MATTHEW *(Spoken into prop telephone, while the group hums the hymn's melody and continues to rotate in place)*:
I'm standing here in the phone booth.
Tell me, do you also find parking a problem here?
I've been driving around for half an hour.
The weather on top of it. Not a good day.

This heat is unbearable, but we all have to live with it.
Air-conditioning—that's the best investment.
You certainly have achieved a good standard of living.
And you want to hold onto that for your family.

We haven't met personally.
But tell me, we'll get right down to it.
What would happen if
you had not come home last night?

Do you know what your family's financial situation would be?
I'm here to help you to think about that.
Protection. Protection. Certainty. Assurance. Security. You want
    confidence. A pledge. Safety. Guarantee.
Promises. Expectation. Consideration. Sincerity. Selflessness. Inti-
    macy. Attraction. Gentleness.

Understanding. An understanding without words. Dependence with-
    out resentment.
Affection. To belong. Possession. Loss.
If you prepare yourself with the appropriate policy, there is nothing
    to fear.

Part 3.
Tuesday evening.
7:04.
Honk if you've lost your keys.
Part 3.
Tuesday evening.
7:05.
How's my driving?

(Matthew brings car horns to Mark and Karen.)

ALL *(Singing)*:
    Through all the tumult and the strife,
    I hear the music ringing.
    It finds an echo in my soul.
    How can I keep from singing?

    No storm can shake my inmost calm
    While to that rock I'm clinging.
    Since love is Lord of heaven and earth,
    How can I keep from singing?

*(Piano accompaniment stops. All continue singing a cappella, repeat-
ing verses one through four and refrains. Mark and Karen perform the
"Lost Keys" Movement Sequence in mirror reflection on opposite sides*

MARK:

> I know about death.
> I'm not afraid.

BRYAN:

> Don't you think you will get well?

MARK:

> I may.
> But probably not.
> Do you enjoy religion?

BRYAN:

> No.
> Not in the way you mean.

MARK:

> It is my chief reliance.

BRYAN:

> I think those people are going to sing a hymn.
> Would you like to see them?

MARK:

> Yes.

(Bryan and Matthew reposition Mark so that he is facing out. Matthew exits.)

BRYAN:

> Oak.
> Cedar.
> Tulip, the lumbermen call it yellow poplar.

(Matthew enters, bringing the birdfeet sticks to Karen, then exits. Karen takes four steps with the woodshoes and birdfeet sticks as in Part 1, heading toward the edge of the space.)

> Sycamore.
> Gum, both sweet and sour.
> Beech.

(Karen takes two steps with the woodshoes and birdfeet sticks.)

Black walnut.
Sassafras.
Willow.
Catalpa.

(Matthew enters. He and Bryan lift Karen to the other side of the white stripe, so that she is facing the opposite direction. Matthew exits.)

Persimmon.

(Karen takes two more steps with the woodshoes and birdfeet sticks, heading toward Mark. She continues walking, reaching her new position on "Locust" below.)

MARK:
    Slowly please.

BRYAN *(More slowly)*:
    Mountain ash.
    Hickory.
    Maple, many kinds.
    Locust.

(Karen ends her woodshoes and birdfeet stick walk. Matthew enters with a fourth small chair.)

MATTHEW:
    Part 3.
    Tuesday evening.
    7:07.
    Tell me about the man with the phantom child.

(He places the chair near the space's edge, then exits.)

MARK:
    The man is standing in water.
    The water comes to the level of his heart.

BRYAN:
    Birch.
    Dogwood.
    Elm.

MARK:

It is not deep for him, but it is deep for the child.
She stands at the water's edge.
She is afraid.

BRYAN:

Chestnut.

MARK:

He fears that if he touches her, he will discover she is not there.
Don't be afraid.
I'll catch you.
Jump.

KAREN:

I am not afraid.
She has begun to cry.

MARK:

Don't cry, he says.

BRYAN:

Linden.
Aspen.
Spruce.
Hornbeam.
Laurel.
Holly.

MARK *(Lowering his right arm)*:
He reaches out his arms.
That's the end.
It is a phantom moment.
It never happened, and it never will happen.

KAREN:

But there are real children by the water.

MARK:

There are real children.
And there are phantom children.
And the man reaches out his arms to both of them.

BRYAN:
> Pine.

(Matthew enters carrying a gift box. He stands near Mark.)

MATTHEW:
> Part 3.
> Tuesday evening.
> 7:08.
> Merry Christmas.

(Matthew opens the box and removes one of the three fans with red ribbon flames. He switches it on, then hands it to Mark.)

BRYAN:
> I think those people are going to sing a hymn.
> Would you like to see them?

MARK:
> Yes.

(Music begins: "Variation on a Theme by Pezel #1": "Sarabande of Doom" by Smokey Hormel. Mark removes the chairs. Bryan and Matthew remove the trees. Mark removes the white paper stripe. Bryan and Matthew carry Karen to the center of the space. Karen crouches and holds position with the birdfeet sticks. The lights dim. Mark, Matthew and Bryan place the three flame fans on Karen's back, hand and foot. The music ends. Lights slowly come up on the following:)

MATTHEW *(On microphone at the edge of the space, in near darkness)*:
> Did they remember who we were?
> Did they remember what we said?
> Maybe somebody else came along and said pretty much the same thing.
> Did anybody notice?
>
> Part 3.
> Tuesday evening.
> 7:09.
> The end.

(Music begins: "Variation on a Theme by Pezel #5": "Sara's Band" by Smokey Hormel.)

Did we have to go to work every morning.
What kind of cars did we drive?
What sort of houses did we live in? Cities. I remember.
What did we wear?

Did we speak the same language?
Did it rain?
Was there a wedding?
Did we have parents?

Did we mean well?
Did we think that life was sacred?
Did it matter?
Do we matter?

*(As the music builds, Mark, Matthew and Bryan remove the three flame
fans from Karen. Karen unbuckles and steps out of the woodshoes.
All bow and exit as the music ends.)*

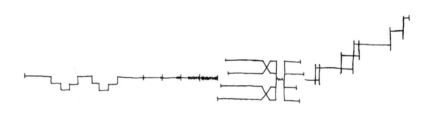

It's an Earthquake in My Heart - 1 hour 33 minutes

END

THE PROCESS

Directives and Responses

The Process documents "the process" in Directives/Responses. Read this, taking elements of it for your own use in regards to creating processes of your own, creatively and collaboratively.

The Performance documents the performance in Texts, Structures and Images. You may look at this in order to re-create a similar performance. *Or* read The Performance without reading The Process, and try to work in reverse, guessing at what the process may have been that produced this piece, then make that process your own. *Or* read The Process without reading The Performance, and try to re-create our performance using our process, with no knowledge of what our actual performance was. *Or* attempt something else.

Directives (1)

Lin extracted this first group of directives from the poetry of Marina Tsvetaeva (*Selected Poems*, New York: Penguin Classics, 1994) and Jeff Clark (*The Little Door Slides Back*, New York: Farrar, Straus and Giroux, 2004), and from the theoretical writing of Paul Virilio. She juxtaposed diagram images and added tasks of her own devising.

Using your body, create a chase
Using your body, create a path

*

Create a circulatory chase
or a circulatory lullaby
with your body

> war and blood are at the door

[vein head image]

> What a fine thing it was to walk that autumn out of one's body
> and into a death filled
> with ether boom and no more

> To make a motor isolated from being

> *

Construct a chase-lullaby

> no   arms no   legs
> now, only the bone of my side is alive
> where it presses directly against you

[bird track image]

Responses (1)

Movement

Car Chases and Bumps

"Matthew recorded 'The World's Most Amazing Videos' one night in order to see the detonation of a beached whale on the Oregon coast. He accidentally recorded a police car chase through a traffic jam on the same program, and brought these movements into the piece, where we are cars chasing and contacting while weaving through traffic. From this material we leaped into the world of the automobile.

The directive: 'Create a circulatory chase or a circulatory lullaby with your body' included the diagram of veins in a head. This resulted in the fingers tracing on the head movement combining the reminiscent automobile chase pattern with the ideas of nanotechnological widgets cruising the highways of our vascular system."

Bryan Saner, work-in-progress lecture, Chicago, November 13, 1999.

[Car chases 1 and 2]

"My childhood family lived through a series of old cars. The axle broke on the old Ford at high speed on the expressway, the wheel came off, metal sparked the road, the gas tank on the Edsel dropped to the pavement and the fire department used their hoses on the street to stop the fire that might have started."

Karen Christopher, Goat Island's "Lecture in a Stair Shape Diminishing—366 Sentences for Vienna," It's an Earthquake in My Heart—A Reading Companion, *Goat Island, 2001.*

[car chase 3]

WENCES AND HAND

The directive to create a lullaby with your body inspired research into the Spanish ventriloquist and puppeteer Señor Wences, specifically in relation to the puppet Johnny, which Wences formed out of his hand. This research produced several approaches to movement, including walking and jumping, while holding the right hand still in the "Wences Hand" position.

[Wences Johnny image]

ETHER BOOM WALK

Jeff Clark's line, ". . . to walk that autumn out of one's body and into a death filled with ether boom and no more" prompted the development of a walk: the lower body stepping in a slow metronomic rhythm, while the upper body oscillates from a crouching position up to a standing position, and then down again. We retained only the crouching part of this walk, eventually naming it the "Ether Boom Walk."

[Ether Boom diagram]

Music

"We are, at times, reporters of artificial experience.
    We like to summon a feeling or a memory by false means.
    Recorded sounds of children's voices. Not real. Recorded sounds of children's voices on a fall day and someone is practicing the piano. Soft notes play alongside the children's voices.
    These recorded sounds play through a speaker Karen holds while Mark stands in the performance space with a pinecone in his hands.

It is important to us that you see how this moment is made while watching it. The wires. The machine. The speaker. The audiotape. You too can do it yourself. This exposure is done not to destroy the memory or the emotion but to enhance it. And if an emotion arises, it comes from the mind as well as the heart."

Lin Hixson, work-in-progress lecture, Chicago, November 13, 1999.

Bryan produced several mini disc recordings, including the one described above of children's voices and a piano rehearsal. The playing of this recording became a simultaneous event during his monologue.

Structures

PERFORMANCE SPACE

"For those who haven't seen Goat Island's work before, each piece has a different audience configuration—the audience sits on two, three or four sides of the performance area, which itself changes size and shape with each piece. The group, in an attempt to create intimacy and community between the performers and the audience, work away from the proscenium arch used in most theaters. The seating configurations in past Goat Island pieces have been broadly symmetrical, around a center point or center line, which might imply hierarchy, order or stability. With this new piece, one side of the performance space has been skewed outwards. The shift suggests that movement has taken place—the space has been altered—it is not only imbalanced, it marks intervention. Does it require to be corrected? Is the performance an attempt to reconcile the space?"

CJ Mitchell, work-in-progress lecture, Chicago, November 13, 1999.

[before and after space diagram]

"But then we went to Berlin, where the architect Daniel Libeskind has designed the Jewish Museum along three obtuse axes, each representing an aspect of the history of German Jews: exile, extermination, continuation.

Public forms, as we have inherited them at the end of the twentieth century, will not suffice to express the events of that same century.

Those ruptures, brutalities, sufferings and beauties must provoke equally radical designs if we want to keep up with ourselves, if we want to remember.

When we return to Chicago, we look at our performance space.

We have devised a symmetrical area, which when seen from above, resembles the logo for Chevrolet.

The heartbeat of America.

But now this seems inadequate.

We push one side out to a peculiar angle.

With this simple change, it seems to us, our performance space no longer reflects the world of public space and theater.

It seems to dictate its own world.

This wide axis leading out may be the axis of remembrance.

Along this, one could say, the phantoms dwell."

Matthew Goulish, "Memory is this," Performance Research: 5(3), Taylor & Francis Ltd, 2000.

3 Parts

"Use one cloud form structure for structure of the piece. Moving from cold and light to heavier darker and warmer. We didn't get the residency that would have allowed us to study clouds in the way we had proposed and because of this (as well as other things) we went off clouds and didn't really look back. Now we are looking at cars. Now there's no proposal. We'll just do it ourselves, but not with clouds—with cars."

Karen Christopher, work-in-progress lecture, Chicago, November 13, 1999.

The creative process for the piece had begun with the proposal for a residency to study cloud formations, which the presenting organization rejected. A certain amount of research had already transpired simply to conceive of the proposal, and a structure presented itself based on the life of a raindrop: start at a high, cold, slow, gaseous atmospheric environment, and accelerate to a low, warm, liquid condition. Lin engaged this scheme to organize early material into three sections: (1) standing; (2) stooping and (3) bottom. The finished piece retained aspects of these postures, as well as a three-part structure, and references to clouds and precipitation.

Objects and Clothing

Fans (1)

The directive from the writing of Paul Virilio: "To make a motor isolated from being" prompted a discussion of pacemaker mechanisms. The group discussed the possibility of installing small battery-operated fans (purchased from Walgreens) on the performers' shirts over the heart area. These took many forms, finally resolving in a design by the artist Taro Hattori in collaboration with Cynthia J. Ashby's clothing.

Handstick and Birdfeet

An oversized, prosthetic version of "Wences Hand" appears in the form of a long stick with a wooden hand on the end. Mark suspends this over Bryan's head while Bryan speaks most of his monologue. In response to a bird-track directive, Bryan built a pair of life-size wooden raven feet to which he attached long, thin wooden sticks. These echoed both the handstick and the woodshoes. Karen, while wearing the woodshoes in Parts 1 and 3, walks with these birdfeet in a way that interrupts the spoken texts.

Pinecone into Tree

Mark displayed a pinecone during the playing of the mini disc recording of children's voices and piano practice, near the end of Bryan's monologue. The pinecone, suggesting a kind of childhood object and relation to nature, was eventually replaced by one of many small artificial trees.

Texts

The directives suggested spoken texts for individual performers, derived from various sources, often collaged with original writing. A speech titled *Kazedaruma* by Butoh dancer Tatsumi Hijikata, specifically the parts of that speech describing childhood and rain, provided the material for a monologue for Bryan. He spoke this into a microphone in a bent-over posture, echoing the Ether Boom Walk. This monologue took on a cyclical form, repeating itself five times. Eventually, a second monologue of approximately the same length (derived from Michel Serres's description of the Pentecost flames and original writing describing the clouds in the sky reenacting the wedding of the speaker's parents) merged with the Hijikata text in a replacement canon. A series of ten numbered driving safety statements from a 1936 industrial film titled *We Drivers* seemed appropriate for Mark to perform. A second list of ten driving commands, almost a parody of the first list, was assembled from orders shouted or spoken by ringleader Michael Caine in the film *The Italian Job*. A radio voice was developed for Karen from a speech by Jack Nicholson near the end of the film *The King of Marvin Gardens*. This speech grew to absorb war-related material from Gertrude Stein, and the description of a fire survived by Dax Cowart from the documentary film *Concern for Dying*. A transcription of a Señor Wences performance dialogue ("I am not afraid.") found its way into the piece. Ideas of phantomness and childhood suggested a monologue for Matthew from the failed 1960s TV sitcom *My Mother the Car*, as well as a dialogue about the man with the phantom child. This derived some phrases from the novel *My Phantom Husband* by Marie Darrieussecq, which eventually combined with texts relating to the American Civil War.

DIRECTIVES (2)

Lin edited together five-minute video segments from several different sources for each performer. Since each video contained a large amount of material, she asked the performers to learn or interpret selectively. Sources for the videos included *How to Live in the German Federal Republic*, a film by Harun Farocki; and different performances of the Wuppertal Tanztheater directed by Pina Bausch, including *Café Muller* and *Walzer*.

[Pina Bausch/*Café Muller* image]

"I watch a German documentary on TV. The filmmaker has taken fragments of thirty-two scenes from German instructional/training films and compiled them into one film.

How to sell insurance.

How to wash patients in nursing.

How to test beds for longevity with rolling metal bars.

How to test washing machines by repeated shakings.

How to test toilet seats by lifting them up and down over long periods of time.

How to do a striptease.

How to be sensitive to a senior citizen who has lost her keys.

How to resuscitate a victim.

How to live.

How to rehearse to live.

How to live the rehearsed, taught by the professionally living.

I decide to edit together my version of the 'How to's' taken from the German version of the 'How to's.' It is two minutes. I give separate videos of these minutes to each member of the group to watch in order for them to perform and reenact the instructional enactments of the people and the machines in the film. In one part of this edit, an elderly actress in a community theater is being directed to perform the act of a woman who has discovered she has lost her keys. She moves to the wall, over to the door, catches her breath, and retraces her steps. This becomes the 'Lost Keys' dance in our performance."

Lin Hixson, Goat Island's "Lecture in a Stair Shape Diminishing—366 Sentences for Vienna," It's an Earthquake in My Heart—A Reading Companion, Goat Island, 2001.

Objects and Clothing

SMALL CHAIRS, BIG SHOES, TREE SHOES

"A TV is turned on and a video cassette is placed into the VCR. A person takes hold of the remote control and presses play. A man falls off his chair. He begins to run along a line back and forth. He falls, he runs, he pauses for breath, he runs. A man chases him, over and over again, following his pattern, creating a pathway. Chairs are constantly removed, thrown to the side away from the man who is running. A woman with red hair and high-heeled shoes paces along with the man who is clearing the pathway for the other man who is running and falling."

Mark Jeffery, work-in-progress lecture, Chicago, November 13, 1999.

The video footage of Bausch's *Café Muller* showed a stage full of chairs. A dancer repeatedly danced a very fast and somewhat athletic solo in a single-minded state resembling sleepwalking. A kind of attendant hurriedly moved the chairs out of the dancer's way, and then replaced them behind him in an orderly fashion. We liked this activity, but knew we could never afford to travel with that many chairs in our performance, so we reenacted a version using only one miniature chair, a kind of doll's chair, from a thrift store. Lin liked the little chair, and wanted to engage it throughout the piece. We commissioned Dionicio Portillo to construct four sturdy under-sized chairs out of oak. We sit in the little chairs in the Insurance Sales Dialogues in Part 1. They return in Part 2, used in a way resembling the chairs in Bausch's *Café Muller*. They then remain on stage for Part 3's Hymn/Lost Keys and the Civil War/Phantom Child dialogues.

We also took turns imitating the part of the red-haired woman in high-heeled shoes, and asked Dan Mackessy to make a pair of shoes out of wood that we could easily trade during the performance. To our surprise, he gave us massive wooden wedges with leather straps on top. (After chiropractic consultation, we revised these "shoes" into square blocks.)

These blocks resembled the wood bases for the artificial miniature Chinese Cedar trees which we used to build a small forest in Part 3. At the suggestion of an artist friend (Mark Booth) we exploited this resemblance by attaching leather straps to two of the tree bases to create a pair of "Tree Shoes." Matthew wears these in Part 2 when he does his imitation of Pina Bausch's solo from *Café Muller*, dragging two trees behind his feet.

COLOR

Cynthia J. Ashby approached the clothing design, after discussions with the group, through the idea of two-tone color of the type seen in 1947 automobiles. The clothing cut and style also drew loosely on that period. She designed brown (earth) trousers and blue (sky) jackets for the men and a green dress for Karen. The dress design had to suit Bryan, as the jacket and trousers design had to suit Karen, because they needed to appear to exchange clothing. The design remained simple enough for the clothing to receive the changes applied to it during the performance with a degree of legibility: the removal of the heart fans revealed a small red cross shape sewn beneath, and the water and confetti to signify damage.

WATER AND CONFETTI

At about this time in the process, Lin and Matthew witnessed a minor car accident at the corner of Columbus Drive and Jackson Boulevard in Chicago. Matthew attempted to diagram this from memory in order to produce more choreography. This became the basis for the "bump" which concludes the third Car Chase as a transition into the start of Bryan's monologue.

Many conversations took place about altering the performance clothing in a way to signify damage and the survival of disaster resulted in the simple solution of using water and confetti. At various points after the midpoint of the performance, Bryan, Karen and Mark change into costumes identical to their previous costumes except that the new costumes have been soaked in water. Bryan also puts on a wet version of Karen's costume, and Karen a wet version of Bryan's, reflecting a choreographic trade that takes place at the midpoint of Part 2. Matthew tosses white confetti in the air at moments that refer to disaster, and the confetti sticks to the wet clothes.

[car accident diagram]

FANS (2)

As the piece progressed to concern images of flames and destruction, the shirt fans underwent a similar transformation. In the end, Taro Hattori designed three versions of the fans: the original version operated in Car Chase #2 and Bryan's monologue, a second "destroyed" version attached to the wet clothing, and a third "flame" version used to conclude the piece. In this third version, the fans, blowing upward, billow small strips of red fabric which they also light with a small flashlight bulb. The image derived from artificial flame-lamps popular at the time in party stores. It rendered a theatrical image which echoed the Pentecost "tongues of fire" in Bryan's monologue. At the piece's conclusion, Karen stands still in the woodshoes and birdfeet with the three flame fans on her back, foot and hand, like a burning monument.

Movement

[lost keys space diagram]

Mark suggested dividing the space down a middle diagonal with a white line at one point, to make it appear more roadlike. In the performance, Bryan interrupts Karen's radio speech by stretching a white paper line into place and hammering the ends to the floor, just before the start of the hymn.

The Lost Keys dance, which Karen diagrammed from Harun Farocki's film, overlaps the second half of the hymn, and repeats three times, primarily as a duet between Mark and Karen, who echo one another as kind of mirror images across the white line. Bryan and Matthew set up the playing area—one half full of artificial trees, and the other with the small chairs, setting the stage for the piece's conclusion.

Structures

Movement material that remained from the first series of directives combined with the appropriations of the Wuppertal Tanztheater videos to form the material of Part 2, a wordless section composed of physical movements, actions and dances in mostly solo and duet form. Part 2 is itself in two parts. In the first part, performers dance the parts they learned and created. The second part repeats the first part, with performers trading roles. This meant that each had to learn the partner's part.

The overall three-part structure of the piece became clarified with the idea that Parts 1 and 3 occurred on the morning and evening of the same day (Tuesday), and Part 2 occurred in the somewhat distant past (fifty-three years earlier). This gave the dance sections a quality of pastness. In the performance, Matthew announces the transitions by giving the parts names, such as, "Part 2. Fifty-three years earlier. Merry Christmas." Part 1 divided into two subparts: the Car Chases (Traffic Jam) and Bryan's monologue (Raining). Part 3 appeared to expand through repeated announcements such as, "Part 3. Tuesday evening. 7:06. Civil War." And six minutes later, "Part 3. Tuesday evening. 7:07. Tell me about the man with the phantom child."

In order to articulate the structure visually, the group had fabric signs printed, which they sewed to the backs of Matthew's shirts (a different shirt for each part), with each part's title in red lettering. These acted as constant structural reminders.

Texts

The group transcribed a series of training dialogues for life insurance salespeople from Harun Farocki's film. These alternated with the Car Chases in Part 1, notably with the repetition of some version of the question, "What would your family do if you did not come home last night?"

Señor Wences prompted a second phase of research into the hand as a performative theme. This research led to the discovery of a remarkable series of journal entries from August 1863 by Walt Whitman in his book *Specimen Days*. Whitman describes his life as a volunteer at the Civil War field hospitals. He relates a dialogue with a wounded soldier who says he relies on religion, and does not fear death, and who dies a few days later. Whitman also encounters a soldier, wounded in the hand, whom he helps to watch an amateur choir sing a hymn. In the midst of these episodes, Whitman lists the trees that he has observed in the region. All of this material found its way into the performance's closing scene, and inspired the use of a hymn.

Once the hymn had been more or less learned, many of the lyrics were rewritten to incorporate a telephone-call mode, also inspired by a Wences performance, and a scene in Godard's film *Weekend*. Matthew performed a telephone-call solo to a prospective life-insurance client, recalling the insurance sales dialogues of the piece's start, although complicating them with material from Hal Hartley's film *Simple Men*. The tone of these texts in turn led to the piece's closing monologue, which combined a speech spoken by the actor Martin Donovan at the end of Hal Hartley's film *The Book of Life* with various lines extracted from the performance itself as a kind of recapitulation.

Music

The group decided to learn the hymn "My Life Flows On" in four-part harmony, with the help of a recording of Teresa Pankratz Saner's piano accompaniment. The performance of the hymn became further complicated by the overlap of the "Lost Keys" movement sequence, which the performers attempted while singing.

The Sarabande movement from Johann Christoph Pezel's *Brass Suite* had been selected to accompany portions of the dance section of Part 2. Smokey Hormel composed and performed a series of original variations on this theme. His "Sarabande of Doom" variation accompanied the construction of the image of Karen with the flame fans. His "Sara's Band" variation played below Matthew's closing speech, and continued through the dismantling of the flame fan image and the performers' bow and exit at the piece's end.

*

"Last night we learned something. We relearned something from the incessant coughing of some members of the audience that lasted through the entire performance.

1. Never underestimate how demanding this work is.
2. It is like a fine ecosystem that is balancing many things at one time.
3. And although we are performing for an audience, we cannot depend on, or draw on, their energy.
4. In fact, I feel it's just the opposite. They are drawing on you for focus—your centeredness, your concentration—and it is through this balance, your balance, and the fine balance of the piece, its rhythms, ideas, transformations, that they come into balance.
5. This is our gift of piece. This is how we contribute to a world that is constantly changing and shifting, that is now at war, at another time in its highest state of prosperity—now joyful, now ill.
6. We, with this work, offer, night after night, creative focus and balance.
7. And so as challenging as it might be, do not pick up the rhythms out there, but stay with the piece and its, and your, internal focus.
8. That's why Mark at the end when doing the Phantom Child dialogue said he was staying with it—its rhythm, not the cough rhythm. That was the right choice.
9. Those internal rhythms already run in some ways counter to the expectations of the text. That's why they can be complex and difficult. Mark's is the strictness from Michael Caine in *The Italian Job*, Karen's is from Jack Nicholson's restraint in *Marvin Gardens*, Bryan's is from Hijikata's statement about doing a good performance because he caught a cold at a public bath, Matthew's is from Martin Donovan— detached and slightly annoyed. These will keep the piece on track and not sentimental. It will be emotional, but the emotions are not for the performers to experience, but for the audience to experience separate from the piece.
10. Think of beginning your focus one hour and fifty minutes before the performance, when we begin our warm-up. That focus should continue to deepen until the performance begins."

Lin Hixson, notes to the performers on October 10, 2001.

GOAT ISLAND

Goat Island is a Chicago-based collaborative performance group: Karen Christopher, Matthew Goulish, Lin Hixson (director), Mark Jeffery, CJ Mitchell (company manager), Margaret Nelson (technical director), Bryan Saner and Litó Walkey. Members contribute to the conception, research, writing, choreography, documentation and educational demands of the work.

In their own words: "Characteristically we attempt to establish a spatial relationship with audiences, other than the usual proscenium theater situation, which may suggest a concept, such as sporting arena or parade ground, or may create a setting for which there is no everyday comparison. We perform a personal vocabulary of movement, both dance-like and pedestrian, that often makes extreme physical demands on the performers, and attention demands on the audience. We incorporate historical and contemporary issues through text and movement. We create visual/spatial images to encapsulate thematic concerns. We place our performances in nontheatrical sites when possible. We research and write collaborative lectures for public events, and often subsequently publish these, either in our own artists' books or in professional journals."

Goat Island was founded in 1987 and incorporated in 1989 as a not-for-profit organization to produce collaborative performance works developed by its members for local, national and international audiences. Eight completed works include *Soldier, Child, Tortured Man* (1987); *We Got a Date* (1989); *Can't Take Johnny to the Funeral* (1991); *It's Shifting, Hank* (1993); *How Dear to Me the Hour When Daylight Dies* (1996); *The Sea & Poison* (1998); *It's an Earthquake in My Heart* (2001) and *When will the September roses bloom? Last night was only a comedy* (2004). The company has toured the U.S., England, Scotland, Wales, Belgium, Switzerland, Croatia, Germany and Canada. 2005 sees the start of development on a new performance.

FERDINAND LEWIS teaches "Art as a Public Good" in the Public Art Studies graduate program at the University of Southern California, School of Fine Arts in Los Angeles. He has also taught methodology courses for the USC School of Policy, Planning and Development, where he is an Irvine Doctoral Fellow in Urban Planning. He served on the faculty of the California Institute of the Arts for nine years, as well in the California Community Colleges and the California State Summer School for the Arts. He consults in education, the arts and community development, and has won four APAC awards for community curricula published by Los Angeles PBS affiliate KCET. Mr. Lewis is the co-author of *Touch Graphics: The Power of Tactile Design* (Rockport Publishers, Gloucester, MA, 2001), author of *Cornerstone Community Collaboration Handbook* (Cornerstone Theater Company, Los Angeles, CA), and has written freelance arts journalism for the *Los Angeles Times, Variety, American Theatre* and other publications.